Apartments Townhouses & Condominiums

Apartments Townhouses & Condominiums

THIRD EDITION

EDITED BY
MILDRED F. SCHMERTZ, FAIA
EXECUTIVE EDITOR
ARCHITECTURAL RECORD

AN ARCHITECTURAL RECORD BOOK
McGRAW-HILL BOOK COMPANY

NEW YORK	JOHANNESBURG	PANAMA
ST. LOUIS	LONDON	PARIS
SAN FRANCISCO	MADRID	SÃO PAULO
AUCKLAND	MEXICO	SINGAPORE
BOGOTÁ	MONTREAL	TOKYO
HAMBURG	NEW DELHI	TORONTO

THE ARTICLES IN THIS BOOK
WERE WRITTEN BY THE EDITORS OF
ARCHITECTURAL RECORD.
EDITORS FOR THIS BOOK WERE
JEREMY ROBINSON AND PATRICIA MARKERT.
THE DESIGNER WAS FAYE H. ENG.
PRODUCTION SUPERVISORS WERE
ELIZABETH DINEEN AND SALLY FLIESS.
PRINTED AND BOUND BY
HALLIDAY LITHOGRAPH CORPORATION.
COPYRIGHT © 1981 BY McGRAW-HILL, INC.
ALL RIGHTS RESERVED.
PRINTED IN THE UNITED STATES OF AMERICA.
NO PART OF THIS PUBLICATION
MAY BE REPRODUCED,
STORED IN A RETRIEVAL SYSTEM, OR TRANSMITTED,
IN ANY FORM OR BY ANY MEANS,
ELECTRONIC, MECHANICAL, PHOTOCOPYING,
RECORDING, OR OTHERWISE,
WITHOUT THE PRIOR WRITTEN PERMISSION
OF THE PUBLISHER.
1234567890 HDHD 89087654321

LIBRARY OF CONGRESS
CATALOGING IN PUBLICATION DATA
MAIN ENTRY UNDER TITLE:
APARTMENTS, TOWNHOUSES, AND CONDOMINIUMS.
"AN ARCHITECTURAL RECORD BOOK."
ARTICLES BY THE EDITORS
OF ARCHITECTURAL RECORD.
EDITION OF 1975 EDITED BY E. K. THOMPSON.
INCLUDES INDEX.
1. APARTMENT HOUSES. 2. ROW HOUSES.
3. CONDOMINIUM (HOUSING)
I. SCHMERTZ, MILDRED F.
II. THOMPSON, ELISABETH KENDALL, COMP. APARTMENTS,
TOWNHOUSES, AND CONDOMINIUMS.
III. ARCHITECTURAL RECORD.
NA7860.A7 1981   728.3'1   80-18086
ISBN 0-07-002356-5

ARCHITECTURAL RECORD BOOKS

AFFORDABLE HOUSES

ARCHITECTURE 1970-1980: A DECADE OF CHANGE

THE ARCHITECTURAL RECORD BOOK
OF VACATION HOUSES, 2/E

BUILDINGS FOR COMMERCE AND INDUSTRY

BUILDINGS FOR THE ARTS

CONTEXTUAL ARCHITECTURE

ENERGY-EFFICIENT BUILDINGS

ENGINEERING FOR ARCHITECTURE

GREAT HOUSES FOR VIEW SITES, BEACH SITES,
SITES IN THE WOODS, MEADOW SITES, SMALL SITES,
SLOPING SITES, STEEP SITES AND FLAT SITES

HOSPITALS AND HEALTH CARE FACILITIES, 2/E

HOUSES ARCHITECTS DESIGN FOR THEMSELVES

HOUSES OF THE WEST

INSTITUTIONAL BUILDINGS

INTERIOR SPACES DESIGNED BY ARCHITECTS, 2/E

OFFICE BUILDING DESIGN, 2/E

PLACES FOR PEOPLE: HOTELS, MOTELS, RESTAURANTS,
BARS, CLUBS, COMMUNITY RECREATION FACILITIES, CAMPS,
PARKS, PLAZAS, PLAYGROUNDS

PUBLIC, MUNICIPAL AND COMMUNITY BUILDINGS

RELIGIOUS BUILDINGS

RECYCLING BUILDINGS: RENOVATIONS,
REMODELINGS, RESTORATIONS AND REUSE

TECHNIQUES
OF SUCCESSFUL PRACTICE, 2/E

A TREASURY OF CONTEMPORARY HOUSES

ARCHITECTURAL RECORD SERIES BOOKS

AYERS: SPECIFICATIONS FOR ARCHITECTURE,
ENGINEERING AND CONSTRUCTION

FELDMAN: BUILDING DESIGN FOR MAINTAINABILITY

HEERY: TIME, COST AND ARCHITECTURE

HEIMSATH: BEHAVIORAL ARCHITECTURE

HOPF: DESIGNER'S GUIDE TO OSHA

PORTMAN AND BARNETT: THE ARCHITECT AS DEVELOPER

Contents

PREFACE
VIII

CHAPTER ONE
COMBINED HIGH-, MEDIUM- AND LOW-RISE HOUSING
X

CHAPTER TWO
HIGH-RISE BUILDINGS
22

CHAPTER THREE
LOW-RISE URBAN AND SUBURBAN CONDOMINIUMS AND APARTMENTS
52

CHAPTER FOUR
HOUSING FOR THE ELDERLY
102

CHAPTER FIVE
HOUSING FOR SKI RESORTS
124

CHAPTER SIX
RECYCLING AND ADAPTIVE RE-USE
144

INDEX
196

Preface

What kind of urban and suburban housing environments do we want today and what are our chances of getting them in the next decade? The apartments, townhouses and condominiums in this collection were chosen because they seem not only to respond to contemporary needs but to be sensible models for the future.

For example, growing environmental concerns, coupled with the gas shortage, call for more economical use of land. All the housing developments shown in this book are relatively compact, thus using land sparingly. And because housing costs have been rising faster than personal income, the plan configurations, construction systems and choice of materials represent new ways of saving money. Within a few of the developments are extensive community facilities — shopping, laundromats, child care centers — principally to meet the demands of two groups whose numbers are rapidly increasing — working wives and the elderly.

Unfortunately, few of the dwelling units described in this book are for rent. The shortage of reasonably priced rental apartments persists. (Only slightly more than one-half million units were constructed in 1979.)

The good news, however, is to be found in the wealth of innovative ideas — in design, rehabilitation, financing or all three — that have emerged in the past decade. Among the best examples described in this book are the combined high-, medium- and low-rise mixed-income developments of architect Josep Lluis Sert in New York City, which because of their size are able to incorporate a broad range of community facilities and park and recreational areas. Other good examples are the community sponsored and financed developments in Boston by architect John Sharratt.

The recycling and adaptive re-use of older buildings is one of the best ways to help renew the housing stock. The elderly, for example, are beginning to benefit from the recycling of obsolete public schools, old wharf buildings and an outmoded tannery — all described in the last chapter.

Most of the housing in this book, however, has not been constructed for the poor, those of middle-income or the elderly. It has been built for the upper income market and as such represents the best our economy can produce at present without major subsidies. Not so surprisingly, except for the remodeled apartments in the last chapter, none of these dwellings seem luxurious. On the whole they are minimal and simple, their quality the result of good design rather than lavish outlays of space and material.

If such dwellings are indeed to become sensible models for the future, the public and private sectors must find ways to bring them within reach of people with average to modest incomes. In the postwar era through the 1960's, the U.S. economy met the housing needs of most of its growing population. The challenge of the 1980's is to find ways to do it again. **Mildred F. Schmertz**

CHAPTER ONE

COMBINED HIGH-, MEDIUM- AND LOW-RISE HOUSING

High-rise, high-density, low-to-moderate-income urban housing has been under attack for the past decade as inhumane, the cause of feelings of isolation and helplessness, and contributory to the collapse of the family, crime, juvenile delinquency, vandalism, indifference and neglect. Low-rise row or semidetached housing, on the other hand, is argued to be humane, the source of feelings of well-being, and contributory to family harmony, law abiding behavior and concern for the immediate environment — one's own garden. High-rise housing is also attacked on esthetic grounds as harsh, stark, punitive, hostile, looming, cold and oppressive — imposing a rational, industrial, managerial ethic upon the captive human spirit. Low-rise housing, on the contrary, is acclaimed as the opposite of all these bad things.

High-rise, high-density housing, however, doesn't have to be bad. If combined with medium and low-rise elements and thoughtfully designed to a program which incorporates a broad range of community facilities and well-planned recreational space, it can be very humane indeed. Josep Lluis Sert, who designed Eastwood on Roosevelt Island in New York City and Riverview in Yonkers (pages 2-9), is a leading spokesman for, and designer of, balanced, compact housing designed with an equal emphasis upon community and privacy within a range of densities. For him, balance is the key word which implies a correct relationship of all parts to the whole. At Eastwood and Riverview, he and his team attempted to achieve a balance between the number of dwellings and the supporting services and amenities available. Balance was sought between people and automobiles, buildings and open space, people and trees, passive and active recreation, and between natural and man-made amenities.

Eastwood and Riverview have many qualities which were achieved through intelligent planning rather than the expenditure of money. A variety of dwelling sizes and plan layouts have been provided to offer a range of choices to families and individuals of different needs and life styles. Most units are open to the air and good views in at least two directions permitting cross ventilation, natural light and sunlight. All tenants have access to recreational land and other land has been set aside for community garden plots. Good proportions, scale, color and texture were achieved without additional expense. These two projects were constructed in the early seventies by the New York State Urban Development Corporation under the Federal 236 rental program. Through the use of this and other funding mechanisms, it was possible to include an unusual mix of community facilities within the structures or on the sites. These include schools, day-care centers, recreational facilities for the aged, communal laundries, playgrounds, parks, open space, plazas, garages and commercial facilities.

In contrast to Eastwood and Riverview, which were built with only minor community participation, the projects in this chapter designed by John Sharratt (pages 10-21), are the result of advocacy planning. In the late sixties architect Sharratt began to volunteer his time and technical skills to the beleaguered citizens of Boston's Lower Roxbury, Mission Hill and South End. Because these lower-income communities lacked the money and skills to defend themselves and because their areas were the most deteriorated and least expensive to acquire, they became the first victims of the Boston Redevelopment Authority's efforts to find in-town sites for higher-income housing, highways, consolidated schools, hospitals and other forms of institutional expansion. Unified by crisis and aided by their churches and a few philanthropic organizations, they welcomed Sharratt's offer to keep them from being evicted and dispersed. The achievement of these communities in building well designed and constructed mixed-income housing for themselves and others has been truly remarkable.

1

From its very beginning, Roosevelt Island was conceived as a community with a balance of services and amenities tightly integrated into the residential fabric. It includes a complete school system composed of a series of mini-schools, two of which have been completed within the Eastwood complex, allowing every child to walk to school on the island. The two-story structure in the foreground of the photograph (far right) is an elementary school and daycare center. Health facilities and community meeting rooms are integrated within the residential buildings. Commercial space for local services such as groceries, drug stores, dry cleaning shops and small restaurants has been provided on the lower floors of the residential buildings which front upon the major pedestrian networks. Cars entering the island must park in a garage, designed by Kallmann & McKinnell, located near the point of motor access. From there an electric bus transports island residents and visitors to the units.

The mix of incomes on Roosevelt Island ranges from low to high—rich and poor and those in between living within a few hundred yards of each other. Eastwood consists of 1003 units of low- and moderate-income housing for approximately 4,000 people. It is located on the east side of the island facing the principal bisecting street called Main Street to the west and Queens across the river to the east.

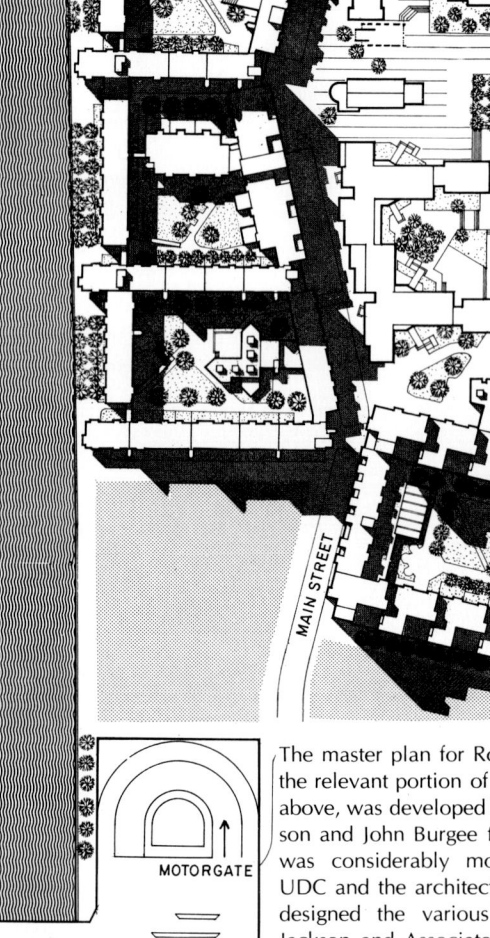

The master plan for Roosevelt Island, the relevant portion of which appears above, was developed by Philip Johnson and John Burgee for the UDC. It was considerably modified by the UDC and the architectural firms who designed the various parcels—Sert, Jackson and Associates for Eastwood and Westview, shown with cast shadows on the plan; and Rivercross and Island House designed by Johansen and Bhavnani and shown in line. Nonetheless, the basic ideas of Johnson and Burgee were maintained. Their plan called for a principal street winding down the center of the island and this has been implemented as the plan indicates. Buildings were to step down from this central spine to the water's edge and they do. Pedestrians and cyclists were to be able to move around the entire perimeter of the island unimpeded by traffic and the construction facilitates this.

© *Steve Rosenthal photos*

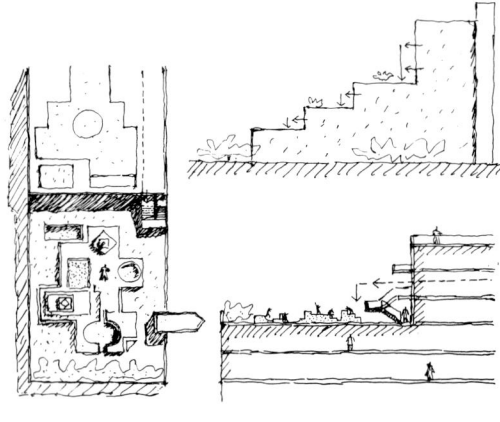

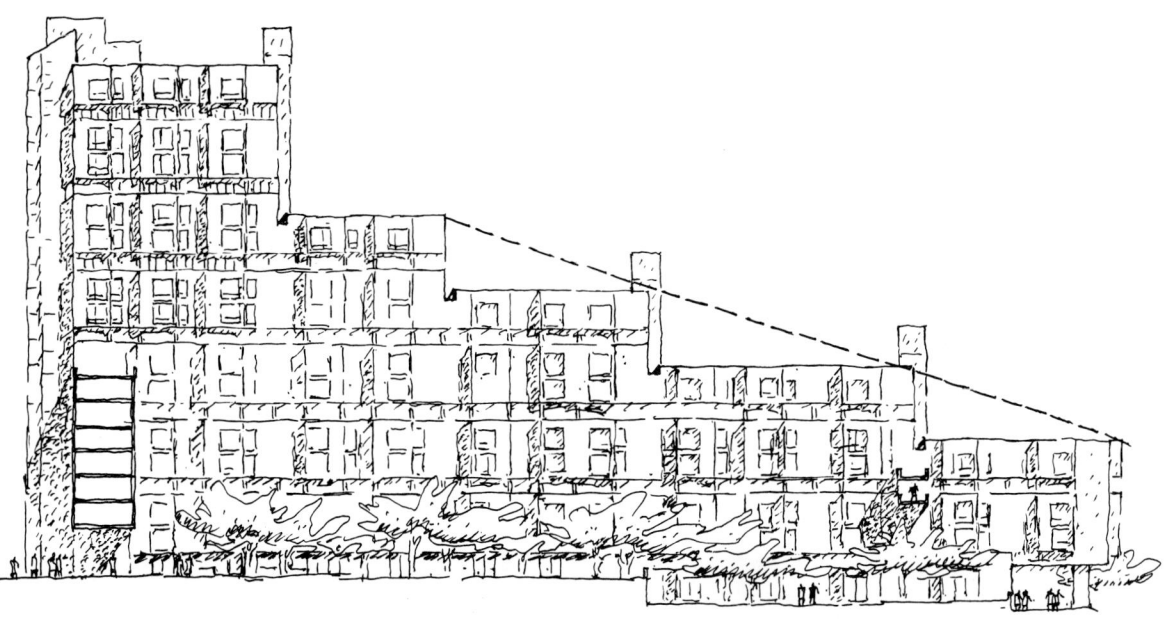

The photograph (opposite page left) taken from the entrance ramp which connects the island to a bridge from Queens, looks south toward Eastwood and Westview. The photograph above looks north toward Eastwood with an elementary school and small park in the foreground. The dotted diagonal line on the sketch at left is an over-all control line for determining the profile of the terraces. Staying within the shallow angle creates a restful contour. If Sert had prevailed over the UDC, the terraced roofs would have become play areas for children under their mother's surveillance as shown in the sketch (opposite page left). The UDC opposed this idea on the grounds that it would add considerably to costs to make the terraced roofs usable and safe, and that supervision would still be difficult.

Westview (included in the bottom photo on page 2 but not otherwise illustrated or discussed in this article) consists of 360 units of middle-income housing constructed to the west of Main Street and facing the Manhattan skyline.

The three parcels on the east side of Roosevelt Island which comprise Eastwood cover approximately six acres. The residential buildings have a density of 166 dwelling units per acre, net. They have been placed to form a series of well-defined courtyards landscaped with large existing trees, lawns and paved walks, punctuated by natural rock outcroppings. From each courtyard one can see the East River, visible through a large pass-through. These three major courtyards are defined by stepped buildings which rise from six stories up to twenty-two stories at Main Street. At regular intervals between the tall-stepped buildings are seven-story buildings which face Main Street and admit daylight to what would otherwise be a canyon. The Eastwood buildings along Main Street project over the sidewalk forming a continuous protected arcade a thousand feet long. The commercial areas in this arcade are at present renting very slowly as prospective merchants wait for the residential units to fill up. As the shops gradually open, however, Main Street will become progressively more lively. Schools, community meeting rooms and the residential elevator lobbies also enliven the arcade.

The tallest buildings at Eastwood are not by New York standards very tall at all. Isolated tower forms were deliberately avoided by the architects, largely because of the limited human amenities provided by these forms but also because such shapes would appear dwarfed by nearby Manhattan. The best views from Roosevelt Island are up and down the river, not directly east or west. The views down river are handsomely framed by the 59th Street bridge. For this reason, most units in the taller buildings look south, down river. Even though only a small percentage of the units actually face the water's edge, nearly all of the units have some visual relationship to the water.

Eastwood contains approximately 300 units especially designed for the elderly. These units are clustered into a T-shaped building in the center court. The elderly have their own lobby, a senior citizens center and will eventu-

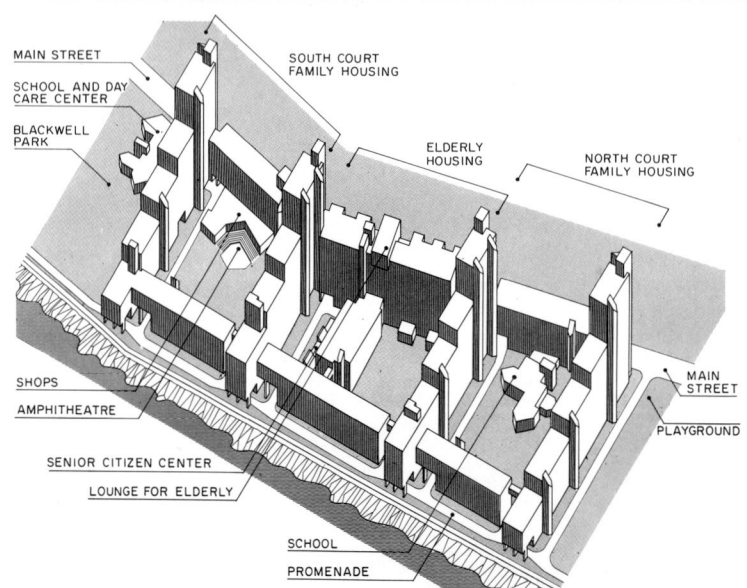

The plaza in the photo above opens off Main Street and includes a landmark church to be seen at the far left of the photograph. The glass-enclosed space is in front of one of the residential lobbies. The amphitheater in the foreground of the residential courts (opposite page top) has commercial facilities underneath. This courtyard, one of four in Eastwood, enhances the views from the buildings' corridors. The subtle bend of Main Street can be seen in the photo at right. This bend is preferable to a long unbroken vista and will discourage rapid movements of traffic until the streets are closed to cars as planned. The arcade (right) is for pedestrian use.

ally have a health care center.

The type of dwelling units developed by Sert, Jackson Associates for Eastwood (but not for Westview because UDC—but not Sert—believes that higher rent paying tenants do not want to go up or down stairs in their apartments) are organized around the elevator access system called "skip stop." The elevator stops at every third floor only and from this corridor level floor, inhabitants take a private stair up or down one flight to their apartments. A third apartment is at the corridor level. Thus a three-story stack of apartments is the basic cluster which is repeated vertically.

The basic living unit found above or below the corridor level is composed of two modules. The living module is a single through-space containing the living room, dining area and the kitchen. Adjacent is the bedroom module which has a bedroom on each side of a central bathroom. By adding another bedroom module, a four-bedroom unit is achieved, and by adding a half module, a three-bedroom unit (see plans opposite page top). All dwelling units get direct sunlight and most have two different exposures since they are floor-through apartments. Because the living module is one space subdivided by two low counter-height walls, and since all windows have operable sash, cross ventilation is possible. Only the corridor apartments are not floor-through units.

All the larger dwelling units, for families with many children, are concentrated in lower buildings and in units which are on ground level. The latter have small yards fenced in.

The structural system for all of the residential buildings consists of 8-inch concrete bearing walls and 6½-inch post-tensioned slabs. Non-bearing walls are brick cavity. Metal forms were used to cast the walls and "flying tables" for the slabs. The elevator towers and stair towers were slip-formed from metal forms. The mechanical provisions include all electric, heat and air conditioning sleeves. Tenants may install air conditioning units at their own expense if they desire, but it is probable that for many the cross ventilation will be adequate for all but the hottest days of summer. Trash disposal is by means of a vacuum system which propels trash under pressure through large pipes to a central processing plant for the island.

The total project includes 1.09 million square feet of residential space, 15 thousand square feet of commercial space, and 47 thousand square feet of schools, day care center and senior citizens center.

EASTWOOD, ROOSEVELT ISLAND, New York, N.Y. Client: *New York State Urban Development Corporation.* Architects: *Sert, Jackson and Associates, Inc.—William Lindemulder (project manager); Edward T. M. Tsoi (project architect).* Engineers: *Paul Weidlinger Associates (structural); Cosentini Associates (plumbing and mechanical); Eitingon & Schlossberg Associates (electrical).* General contractors: *Building Systems Housing Corporation and Turner Construction Corporation.*

2 BR.	4 BR.	LEVEL ABOVE CORRIDOR	3 BR.- 3BR.
1 BR.	2 BR.	CORRIDOR LEVEL	2 BR.- 1BR.
2 BR.	4 BR.	LEVEL BELOW CORRIDOR	3 BR.- 3BR.
2 BAY MODULE	3 BAY MODULE	5 BAY MODULE	

Shown above are the basic planning modules at three different levels. In the typical elevation (left), the projecting elements are living rooms. The sketch below shows the proportioning system for the facades. 'A' denotes a square, slightly tall to correct for perspective. 'B' is a double square, and 'C' is a golden section. Windows were carefully studied to arrive at an harmonious division of glass. Each projection is proportioned as a golden rectangle. Sert, a disciple of Le Corbusier, adapts the latter's Modulor dimensions wherever possible. Two views of a floor-through unit show their virtues—cross ventilation, views from the dwelling in two directions and exposure to sunlight during different times of the day.

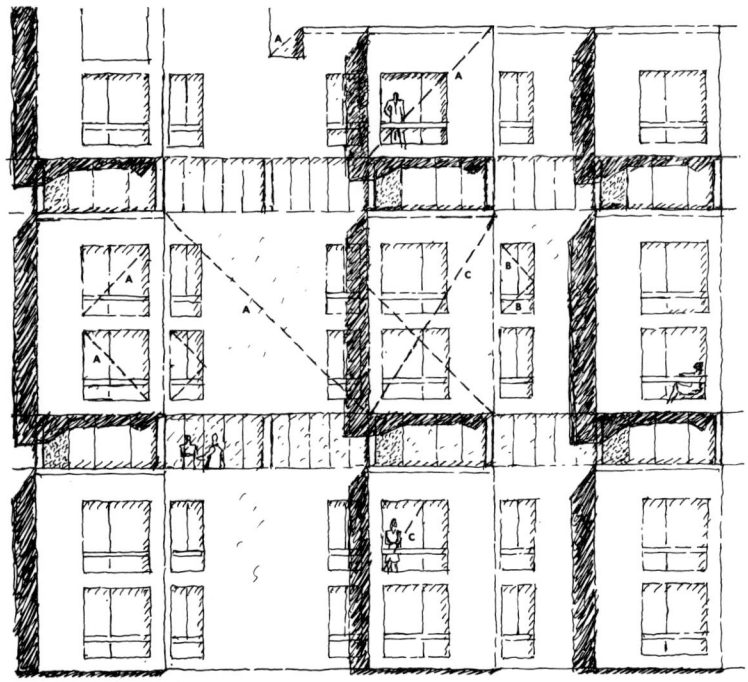

2

Sert, Jackson and Associates began design for Riverview 1 and 2 in 1970. Constructed by the UDC, it is a two-stage community of 798 moderate-income rental apartments on a 7.8 acre (six city blocks) site within an urban renewal area near the previously decaying downtown core of Yonkers, New York. Financed by the Federal 236 rental program for approximately 3200 people, it has a density of 103 dwelling units per acre net.

An elementary school already existed at the center of the site. To the south of the school is phase 1 of Riverview and to the north is phase 2. Although the site is surrounded by existing development on all sides, Riverdale Avenue is the most active edge, with a good mix of retail facilities.

In response to these site conditions, the architects designed the Riverdale Avenue edge of the new housing complex as a continuous wall along the property line (see photo opposite page bottom) to give definition to the

street. To continue the kind of mixed uses in adjoining blocks, the new development includes along this street, shops, a day care center and a community lounge. As the previously cited photo indicates, the new configuration on Riverdale Avenue is a combination of high and low buildings punctuated by the vertical stair shafts. The buildings are taller along Prospect Street, which faces a mixture of residential and commercial uses. Parking garages are located at the outer edges of the site to minimize the intrusion of cars onto the site.

As in Eastwood on Roosevelt Island, the buildings are arranged to form well-defined courtyards. These courtyards provide a sense of place for the community, are interesting to look at from the apartments and corridors which face them and provide an oasis from the noise and confusion of the adjacent streets.

RIVERVIEW HOUSING PHASES 1 AND 2, Yonkers, N.Y. Client: *New York State Urban Development Corporation.* Architects: *Sert, Jackson and Associates, Inc.*—*William Lindemulder* (project manager); *Robert Campbell* (project architect). Engineers: *Paul Weidlinger Associates* (structural); *Batlan and Oxman* (electrical and mechanical). Contractors: *Phase 1: Building Systems Housing Corporation; Phase 2: Halpern Building Corporation.*

© Steve Rosenthal photos

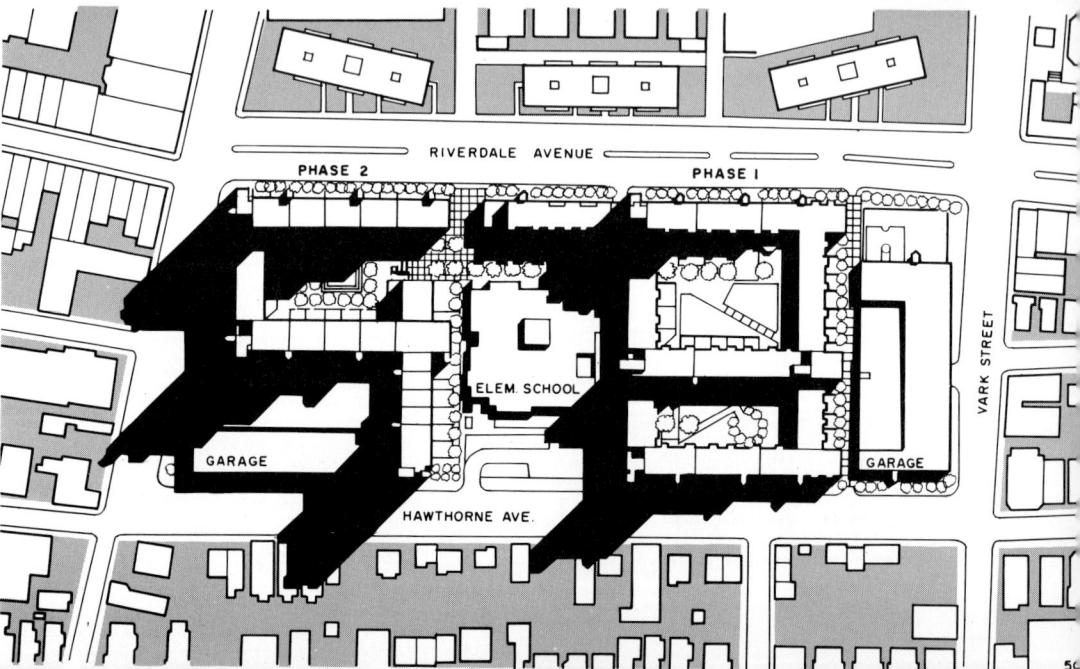

The unit plan for phase 1 of Riverview is similar to Eastwood. The unit plan used in phase 2 is a further development of the three-story skip-stop module. The fundamental difference is in the living bay. The private stair is an "L"-shape and does not take up as much area. As a result, the living room is pulled back and its window is recessed three feet behind the bedroom exterior wall. This recess permits the units on the corridor level, which are not cross-ventilated, to be compensated by having a small balcony off the living room (see sketch opposite page). These modifications bring about a significant change in the exterior expression. The photograph (left) looks south toward phase 1, but flanking the vista to the east and west are two wings of phase 2. In the phase 2 facades the bedrooms, instead of the living rooms, protrude. Shown below is a mock-up of the kitchen, dining and living area within the basic module. The cost of the total of 815 thousand square feet of residential space, parking, commercial and community facilities and landscaping was $27 million in 1976; $33.10 per square foot; or $33,750 per dwelling unit.

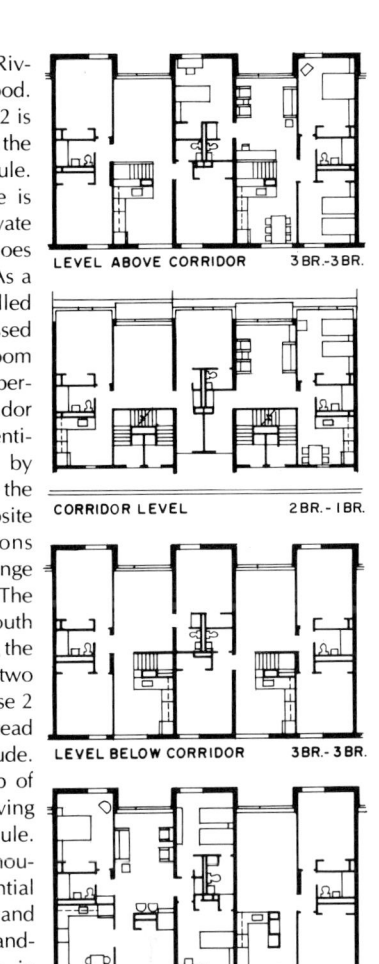

3

John Sharratt began working with the Lower Roxbury community before he had his own firm. "I was working as a regular architectural employee—first with TAC and then with Catalano and Belluschi. But I was interested in finding ways to build better housing for people of low incomes. I joined a group in Boston with similar concerns called Urban Planning Aids. They were young people starting out as transportation planners, sociologists and architects—a good group. I decided to give my evenings and weekends to the problems this group was attacking. There was no money to pay us."

UPA and Sharratt knew that Boston's poorer communities were far less able than middle-income groups to resist the destruction of their neighborhoods by large-scale projects. "In the sixties," says Sharratt, "the planners never touched the upper middle-class neighborhoods which had plenty of volunteer lawyers to defend them. They pushed their highways and their over-size schools into the poor communities, where people don't have the time or skills to defend themselves."

UPA had a request for help from a predominately black group in Lower Roxbury, 400 of whose homes were about to be demolished to make room for a 5,000-student high school. No relocation housing in the neighborhood was to have been provided—in fact, as Sharratt says: "There was no longer to be a neighborhood." The construction of two major expressways also threatened the community's future. Their situation was clear: the residents of Lower Roxbury were being robbed of everything that made for community life—their homes, neighbors and churches—without representation, participation, consent or compensation.

Sharratt and the UPA helped get the community organized and assisted them in presenting to the Renewal Authority alternatives to the proposed high school and the expressways. Says Sharratt: "We asked the city why the school needed to be that big—did it really need 56 acres? I showed them how they could put the school on 15 acres leaving 16 acres for housing—some to be renovated and some new—and additional acres for other amenities. The agency planners would do all kinds of little studies on land use with figures to prove we were wrong, so we did even more drawings and models and diagrams to prove that we were right. Finally we got the city to shrink the high school to

©Steve Rosenthal photos

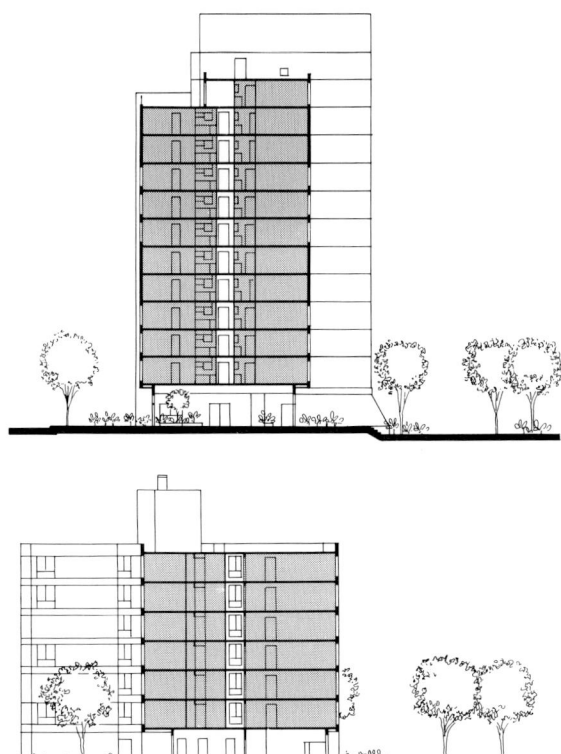

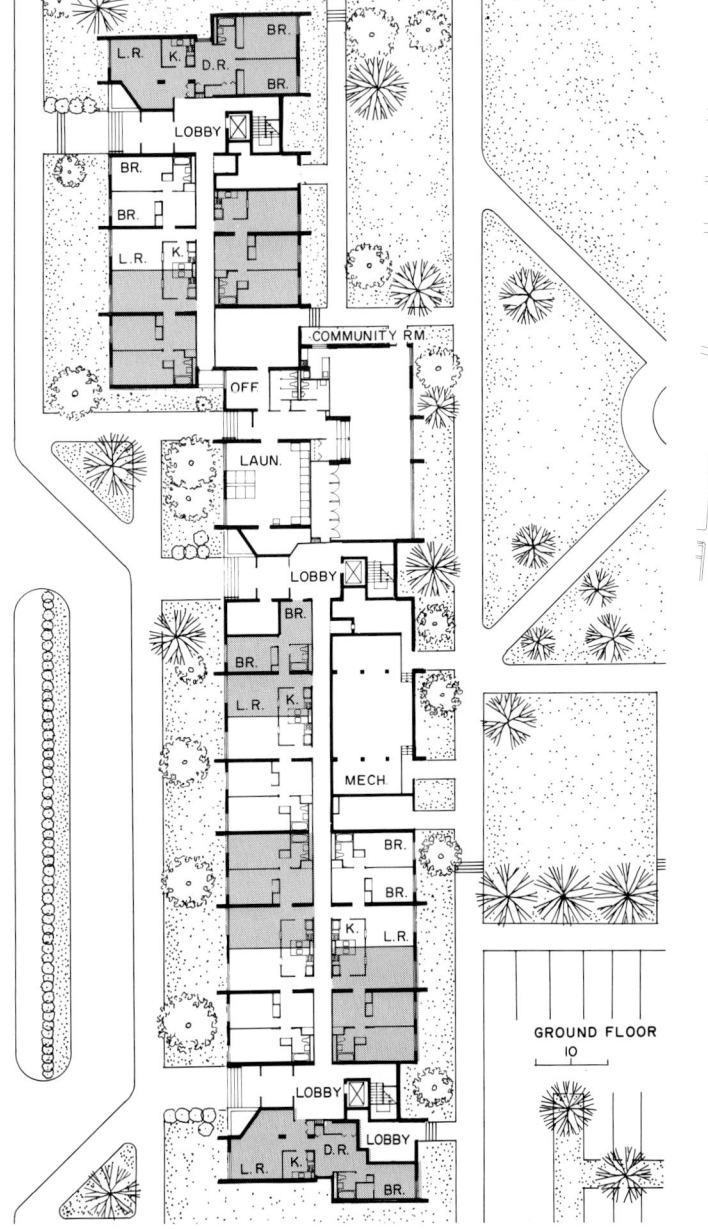

provide enough room for housing. Our victory was essentially political. The Boston politicians at last realized that this strong and vocal group of people who were against them could become an active constituency if they were treated right."

The Roxbury residents formed themselves into the Lower Roxbury Community Corporation (LRCC) and decided that they should develop and own their own housing. The BRA finally agreed and designated them developers for a 15-acre parcel contingent upon BRA approval of the development team. The LRCC overcame one further hurdle by persuading the BRA that Sharratt—who had not ingratiated himself with the agency during the years of fighting—be commissioned by the community as their architect.

HAYNES HOUSE, SMITH HOUSE, TOWNHOUSES OF MADISON PARK, Boston, Massachusetts. Owner: *Lower Roxbury Community Corporation*. Architects: *John Sharratt Associates, Inc.*—project architect: *John Sharratt*: project manager: *Liviu Brill*. Associated architects for Haynes House and Smith House: *Samuel Glaser and Partners*: for townhouses: *Glaser/ de Castro/ Vitols*. Consultants: *Brown-Rona, Inc.* (structural); *Haley and Aldrich, Inc.* (foundations); *R.G. Vanderweil Associates, Inc.* (hvac); *Harris Associates* (plumbing); *Goodall-Shapiro Associates* (electrical). General contractor for Haynes House and Smith House: *George B.H. Macomber Co., Inc.*; for townhouses: *John B. Cruz Construction Co., Inc.*

4

In the early 1960s Harvard University and other major institutions began large-scale real estate acquisition programs in a section of Boston known as Mission Hill. It was a community of moderate incomes composed of Irish Catholic, German and a smaller number of black and Spanish-speaking families.

Beginning in 1964 Harvard having bought the houses in the neighborhood began to rent to transients instead of families. Rents increased and maintenance deteriorated. Families were finding it difficult to remain. In 1968 the University announced its plans to build a new hospital complex. Harvard intended to evict the tenants of 182 apartments and tear them down by 1971.

Then came the Harvard student strike of 1969. The University's poor treatment of the Mission Hill community was one of the major issues of the strike. The students visited the neighborhood and helped the residents organize into a group which was to become the Roxbury Tenants of Harvard (RTH).

At this time John Sharratt volunteered his technical skills to the community to help them analyze their problems and to find solutions. He helped them produce a 300-page document entitled "Stop Harvard" amply illustrated with photographed evidence of poor maintenance—water dripping through light sockets, ruin and rot. The booklet also contained the community's proposed master plan, prepared by

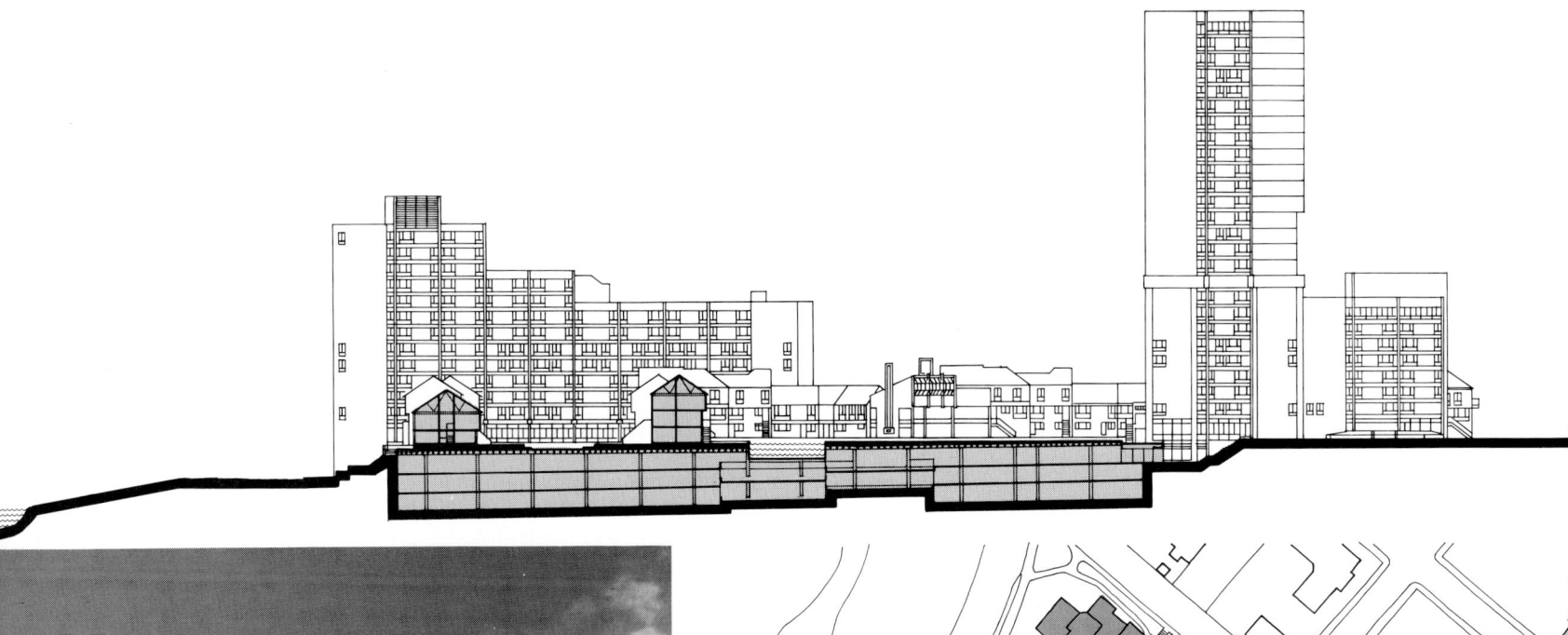

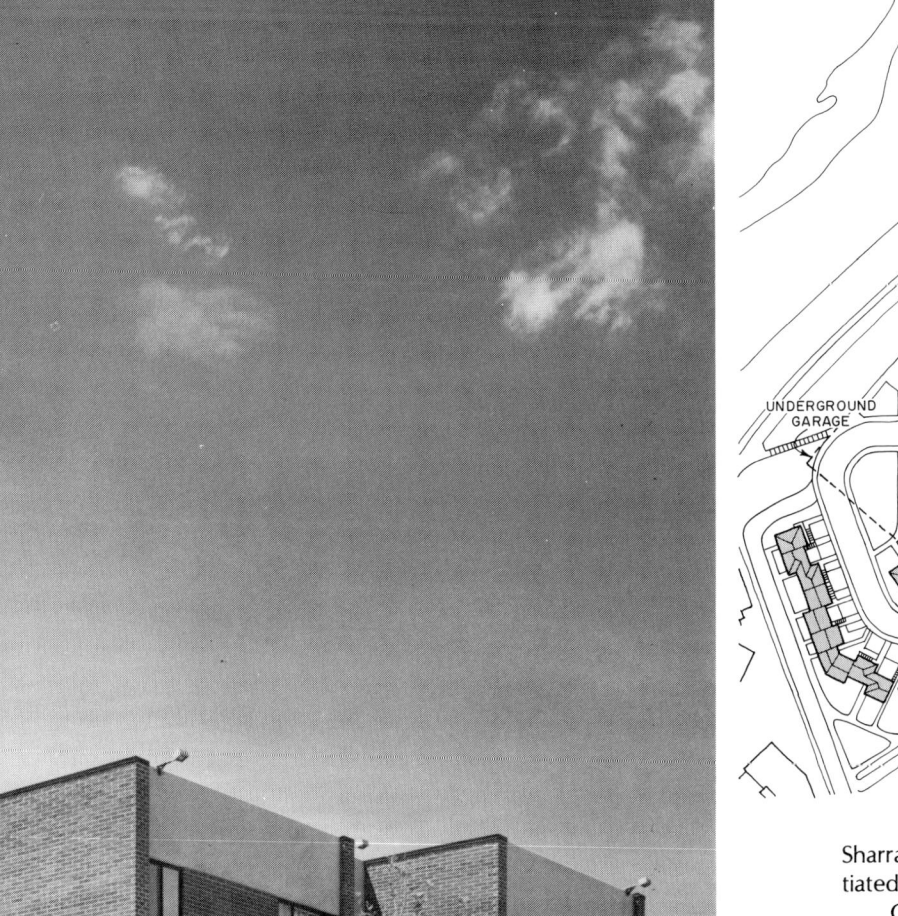

Sharratt and suggestions for negotiated terms with the University.

Only after RTH had demonstrated its ability to attract the attention of the media and its willingness to disrupt the daily business of the University, did Harvard begin to take them seriously. Negotiations with the Harvard Corporation began and by 1970 an agreement between Harvard and RTH provided that: first, the University should provide adequate repair and maintenance of the existing housing; second, a specified area within the site should remain a community residential area; third, RTH and/or their designate should sponsor and develop new housing on land currently owned by Harvard known as the Convent Site; fourth, Harvard University should assist RTH in securing the required financing and subsidization programs to guarantee rents all existing tenants can afford; fifth, Harvard should help to provide community facilities. Thus, after a year of effort, the neighborhood was not only saved but it had a future. Shown at left is the recently completed mid-rise building, with the high-rise, still under construction at the rear.

MISSION PARK, Boston, Massachusetts. Owner: *Mission Park Corporation.* Architects: *John Sharratt Associates Inc.—project architect: John Sharratt; project manager: Robert H. Egan.* Associated architects: *Glaser/deCastro/Vitols Partnership.* Consultants: *Brown-Rona Associates, Inc. and Cleverdon, Varney and Piek (structural); Goldberg Zoino, Dunnicliff and Associates (foundations); Atkinson Engineering Inc. (mechanical); Goodall Shapiro Associates (electrical); H.W. Moore Associates (site).* General contractor: *George B.H. Macomber Co.*

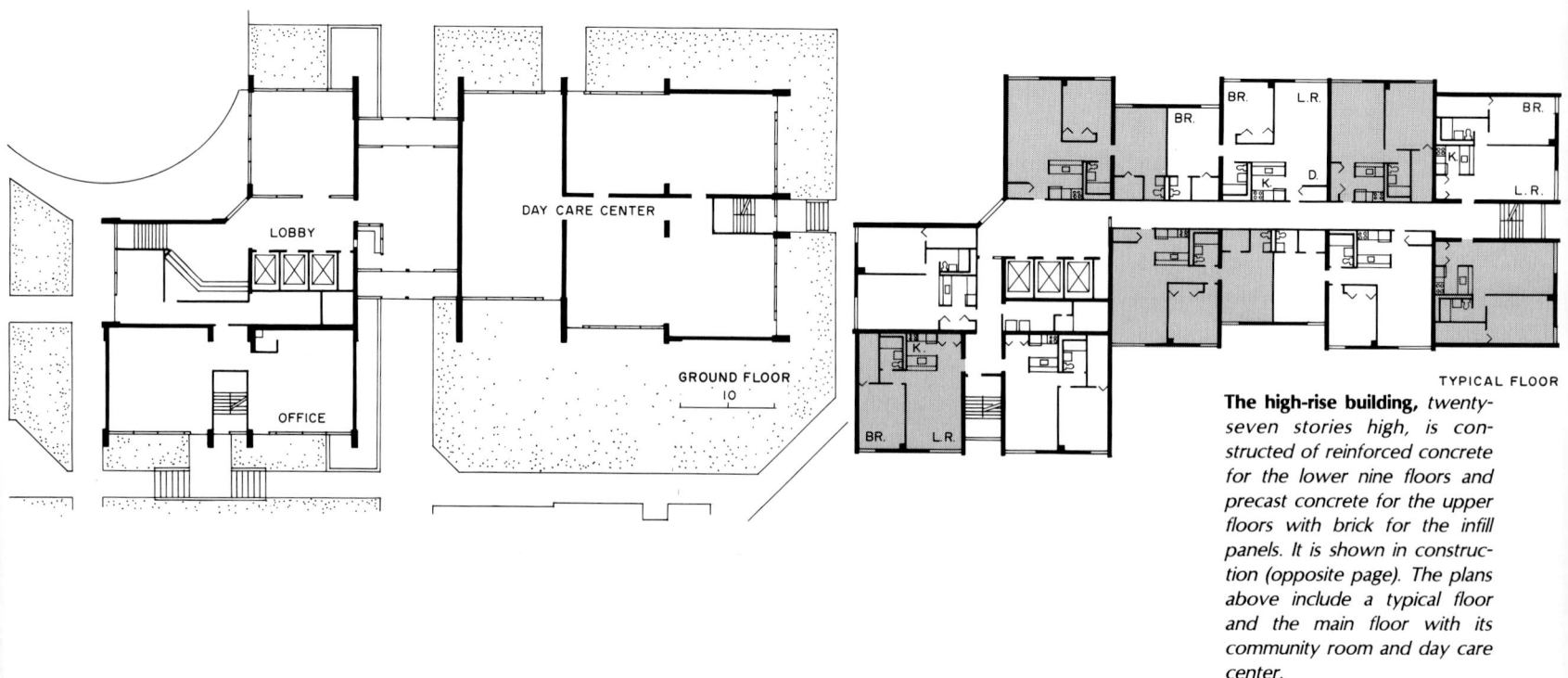

The high-rise building, twenty-seven stories high, is constructed of reinforced concrete for the lower nine floors and precast concrete for the upper floors with brick for the infill panels. It is shown in construction (opposite page). The plans above include a typical floor and the main floor with its community room and day care center.

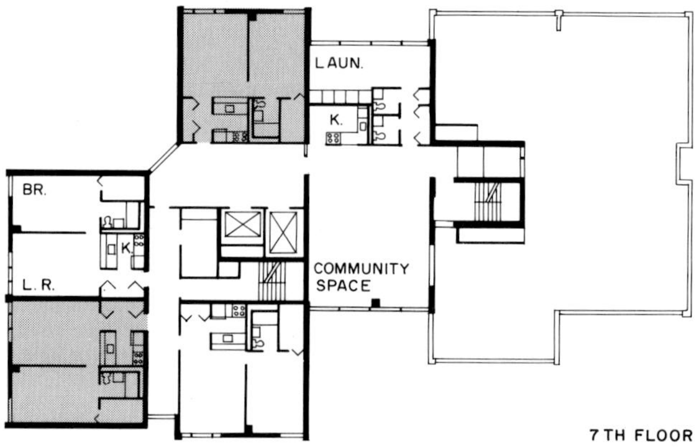

©Steve Rosenthal

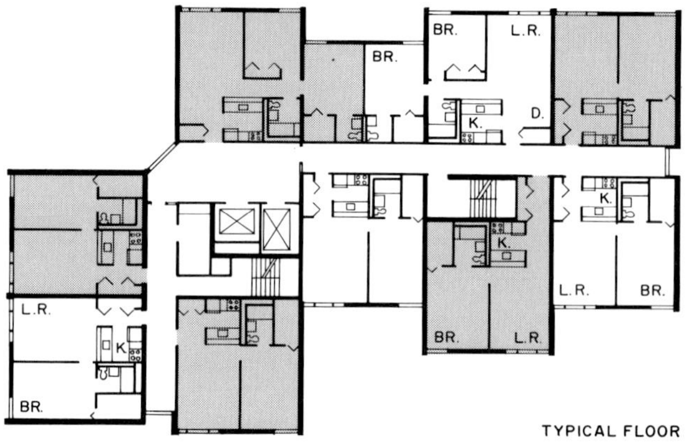

The mid-rise building steps up from four stories to thirteen. It is constructed of masonry load-bearing walls and precast concrete floors with brick as the exterior material. Shown above is a community room within the structure.

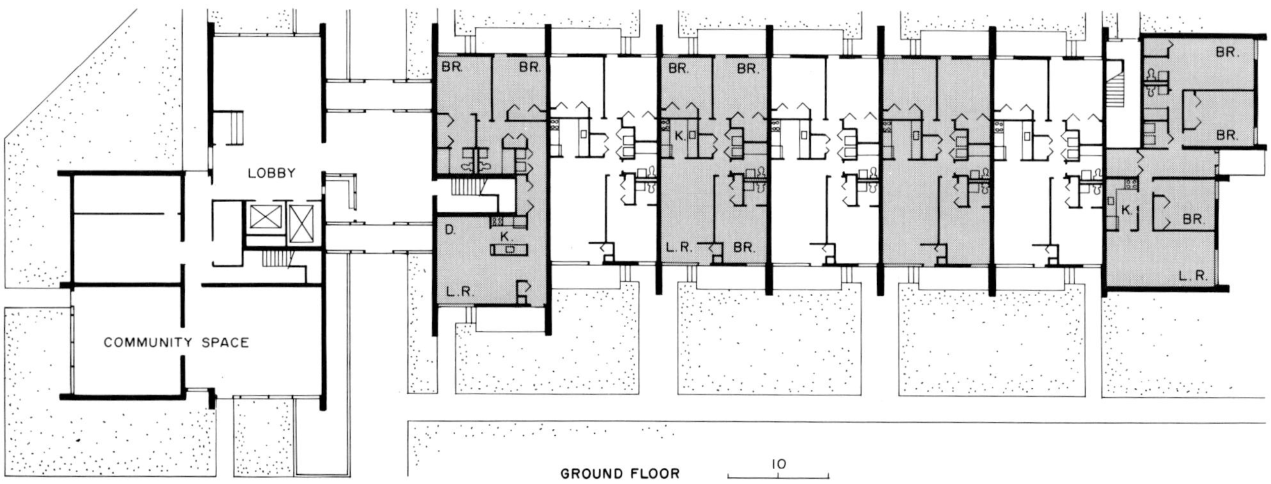

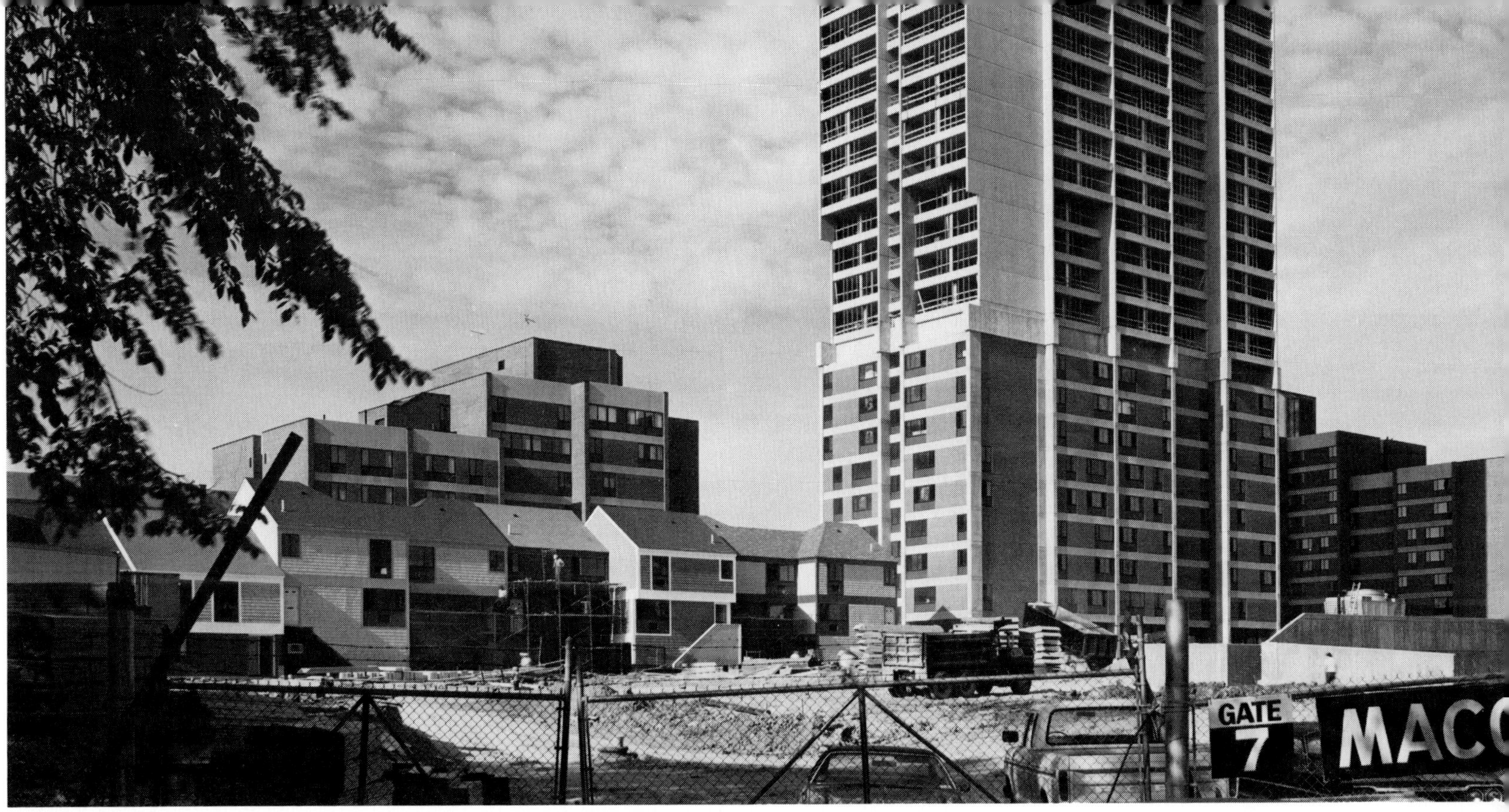

The townhouses *are wood-frame construction with brick and wood shingles as the exterior material. They are being constructed over a 1,274-car underground garage of precast concrete. Available to all the residents in the high-rise, mid-rise and townhouses are dishwashers, disposals, a swimming pool, tennis and basketball courts, six play areas for small children, a formal plaza with a fountain and extensive landscaping.*

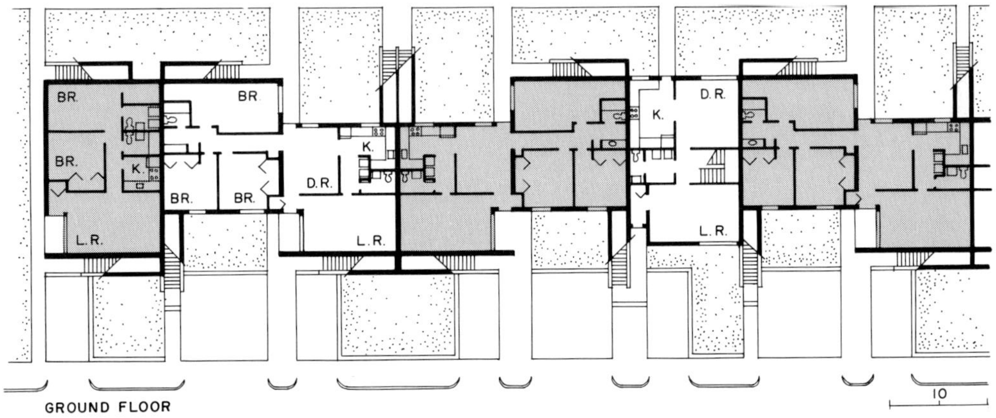

GROUND FLOOR

The community building, *(right) has not yet been constructed. It is at the heart of the project which will eventually comprise 775 units of housing, 40,000 square feet of medical office space and 6,000 square feet of neighborhood shops and recreational facilities. The construction loan for the entire project was provided by the Massachusetts Housing Finance Agency and the permanent loan by the State Street Bank and Trust Company. Thirty per cent of the units are low income, 65 per cent are for moderate incomes and 15 per cent are for market income. Subsidies are provided under HUD Section 221-4 Mortgage Insurance and HUD Section 8, Rent Subsidy. The developer is Mission Park Associates, a partnership between RTH, Citicorp of New York City, and Harvard University.*

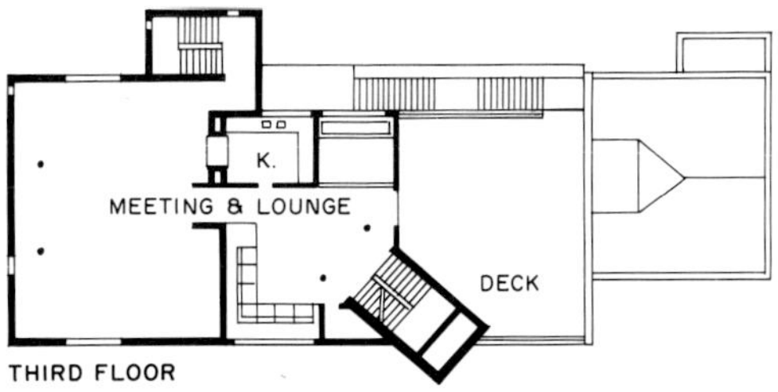

THIRD FLOOR

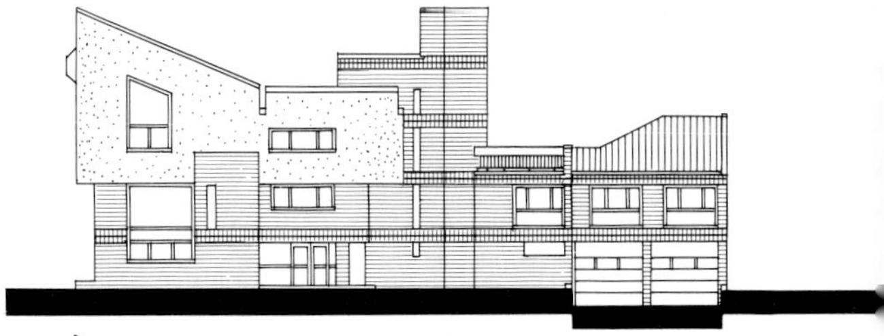

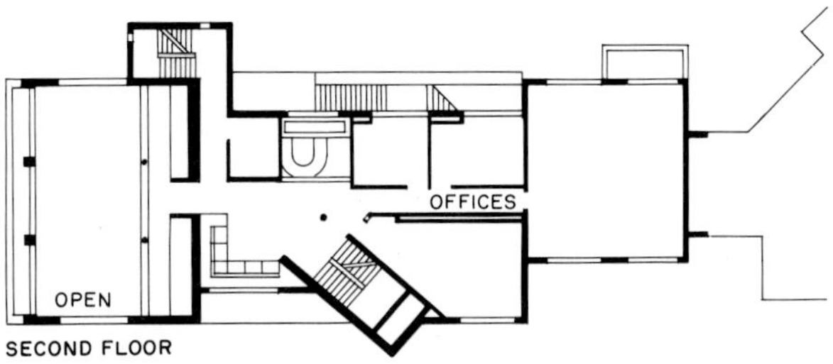

SECOND FLOOR

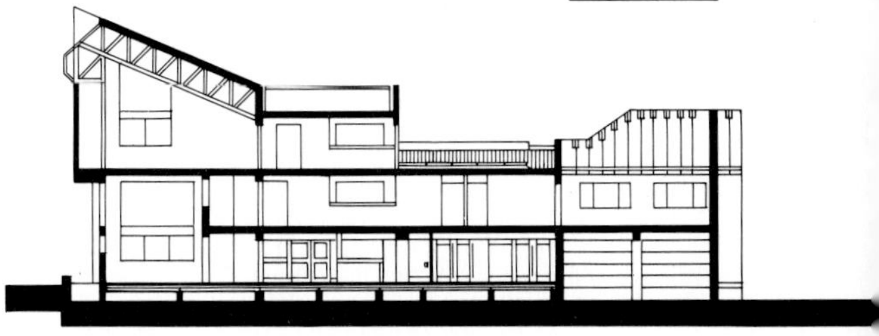

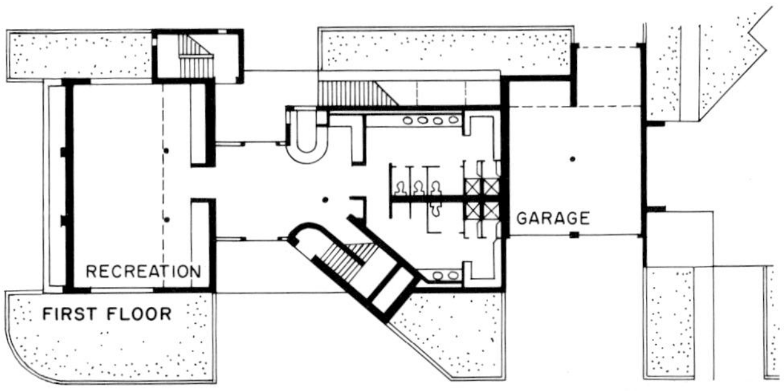

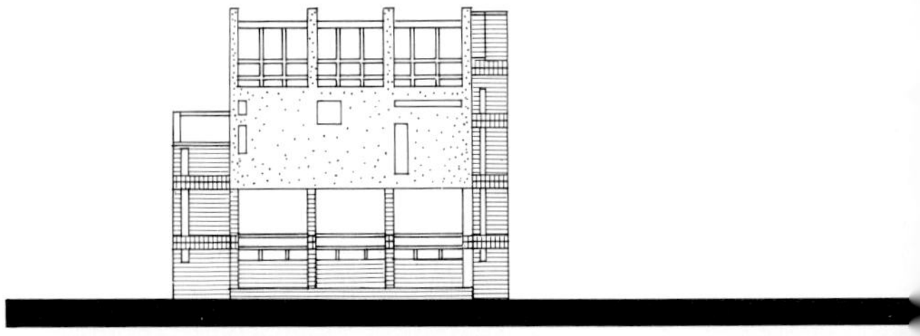

5

In 1965 the residents of a Boston neighborhood, which had been designated by HUD as the "South End Urban Renewal Area," were in great need of help. The HUD plan called for the total demolition of the area. The low-income housing and stores were to be replaced with upper-income housing and various institutional uses.

Coincidentally, at the time that this central section of the South End had been designated as an urban renewal site, there began a large migration of families from rural Puerto Rico to Boston, many of whom moved to the urban renewal area. These new Bostonians had found cheap rent, good welfare benefits, low skill jobs, a new community speaking their language, and friends and families from their villages back home.

Although the housing was cheap, services were poor. Heat was inadequate and eviction with dislocation a constant threat. A local Episcopalian minister helped organize the residents and in 1968 invited the president of the Lower Roxbury Community Corporation, which was working with John Sharratt on Madison Park, to give the South Enders the benefit of Lower Roxbury's experience. As a result of this meeting, Sharratt began to work as an advocacy planner for the South End group as well. His job was to provide the technical assistance necessary to save and rebuild the community for the existing residents.

Sharratt found the problems and solutions for this area to be similar to those of Lower Roxbury. Things were easier to accomplish, however, because of the experience that he had gained through his work with the LRCC. By this time, furthermore, the BRA had become more sensitive to the demands of community groups and more aware of the political benefits of accommodating them.

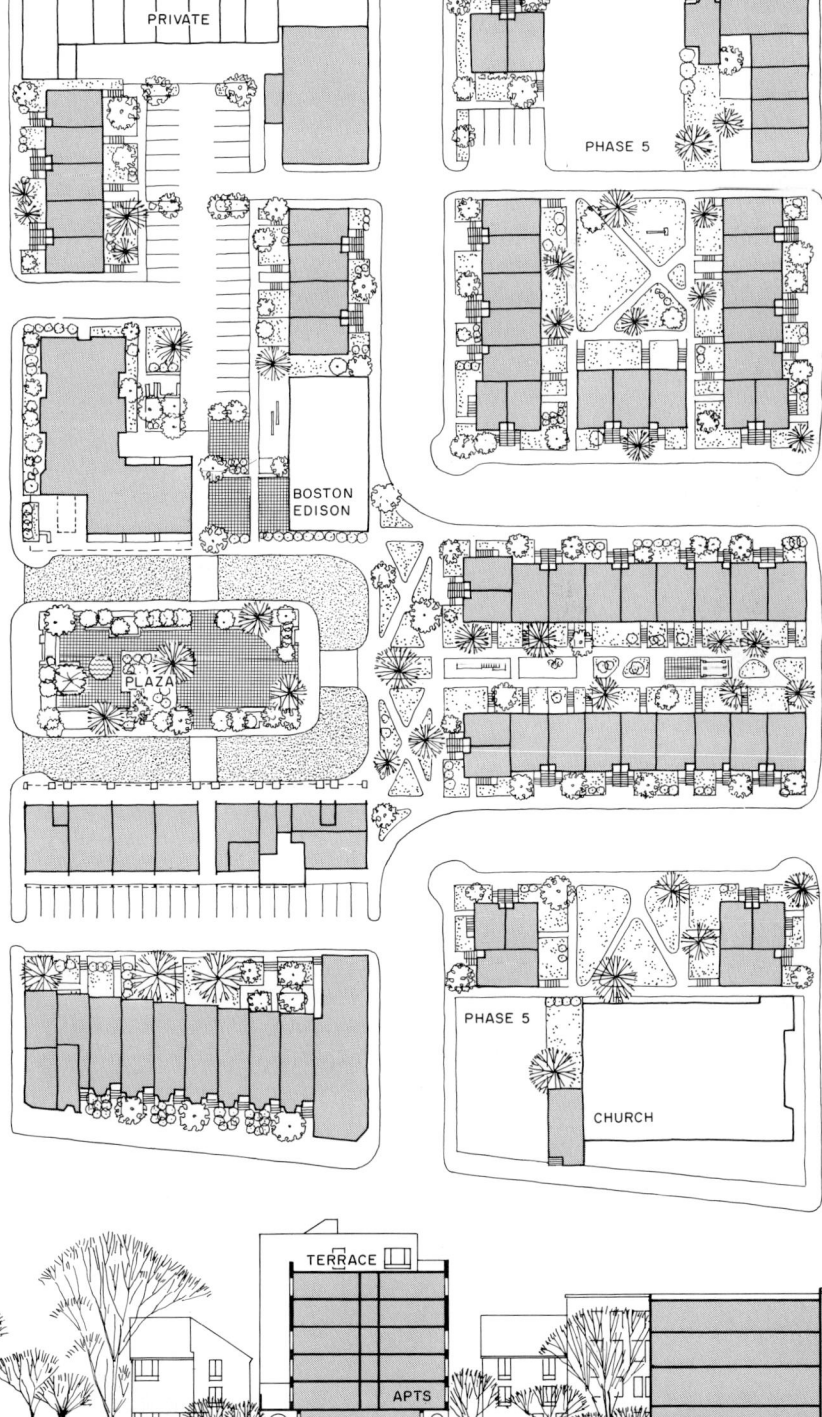

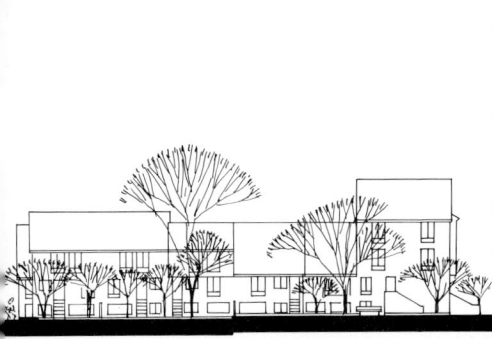

The chief obstacle to the continuing existence of the Puerto Rican community in the South End was their proximity to the downtown business area and to good public transportation. Their area was considered valuable for these reasons and highly desirable to speculators and developers.

It was evident to Sharratt upon his first review of the 1965 plan that there were many buildings scheduled for demolition that should be saved. The massive relocation problem had been ignored. He found the plan to be bad for the South End, its residents, and the City of Boston. He therefore set about to replace all the information that the Urban Renewal Authority had gathered to justify the 1965 plan. He and his team assembled and mapped the condition of individual buildings and information about land use, ownership, traffic, employment and residency with the size and location of all families.

Sharratt and the community developed a new plan for their neighborhood to which the Renewal Authority objected. Although the issues being discussed and planned centered about land use, the real issue was local control and ownership. This was a precedent which the BRA was not yet ready to accept.

The residents by this time had formed a representative group known as the Emergency Tenants Council (ETC). Sharratt produced a plan for them to which they gave formal approval. Mixed-income housing, on-site relocation and a public plaza recalling the outdoor gathering spaces of Puerto Rico were included.

The ETC then asked to be designated as the redevelopers of the entire 19-acre site, which consisted of eleven separate but contiguous redevelopment parcels. They received supporting letters from every known organization in the South End, Puerto Rican groups from Chicago and New York City, state and Federal senators and representatives, and clergy and civic leaders. After saying no many times, the BRA finally granted their request.

The South End residents started their action a year later than their neighbors in Lower Roxbury and yet received their designation a month earlier. Unfortunately Lower Roxbury paid the price for being the first to ask for the unthinkable in the urban renewal of the sixties—community control. An informal coalition was

© Steve Rosenthal photos

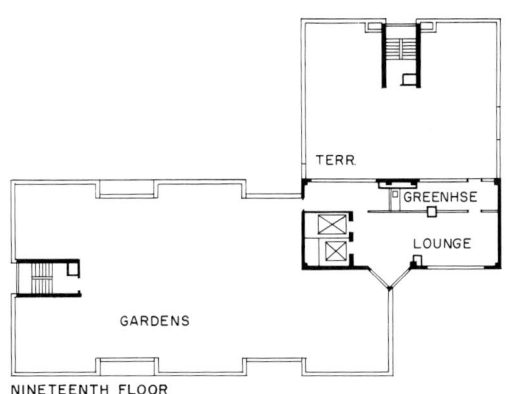
NINETEENTH FLOOR

TYPICAL FLOOR

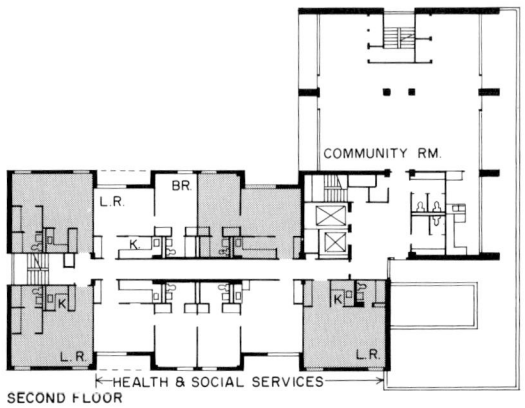
SECOND FLOOR

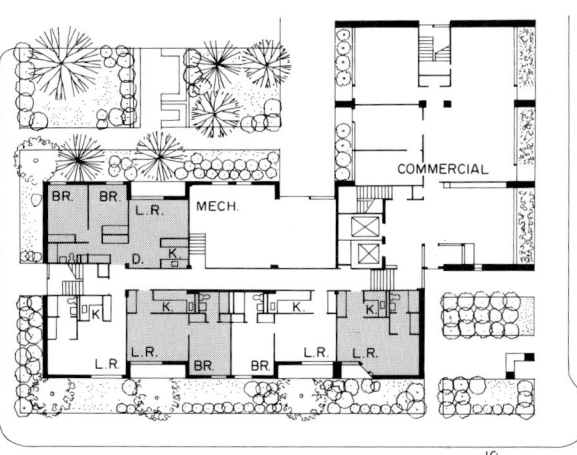
FIRST FLOOR

formed between these two neighborhoods and they continue to cooperate with each other.

Maintaining their primary objective of good mixed-income housing with on site relocation, the ETC residents have executed four phases of housing development totalling 492 homes and 26 thousand square feet of commercial space, and a six-story office building. Two hundred additional new housing units, 50,000 square feet of new commercial space, and a total renovation of a housing project nearby are in the works. They are converting an industrial building into a new church.

Phase I consisted of the construction of 71 new apartment units in a row of fine Victorian townhouses on the site (page 7). It was financed through a local bank with a HUD Section 221d3 interest subsidy. The local housing authority leases units for low-income tenants.

Phase II is "Torre Unidad" (pages 6-9). It consists of 16 floors of apartments for the elderly. The ground floor is designed for shops and the second floor is a recreational facility. It was financed through the Massachusetts Housing Finance Agency and sold to the Boston Housing Authority using the HUD Turnkey program.

Phase III is "Viviendas" (plans shown top right). Combining a mid-rise structure with townhouses, it adds 181 units of housing to Villa Victoria and over 3,000 square feet of commercial space. It was financed through the MHFA with the HUD section 236 program of interest subsidy and HUD rent supplements for low income families.

Phase IV is "Casas Borinquen." Completed in May 1977 was the renovation of nine existing brick townhouses into 36 units of housing. It was financed through MHFA with the HUD Section 8 rent subsidy program.

Three of the four projects were executed as limited partnerships, with the residents as the managing general partner. This resulted in a significant return of funds to the community to use at their discretion.

The other project was executed as a precontracted developer-owner sale by the community residents to the Boston Housing Authority for a normal, yet significant developer's fee. The entire economic approach of the ETC residents has been very sophisticated and successful.

The resident group manages

© Steve Rosenthal

all of their developments, plus 300 units owned by the Boston Housing Authority. It has contracts for the delivery of social services to the area residents. This function employs a full-time staff of over 50 residents. Since the ETC has a neighborhood priority hiring program, the developments have provided a significant number of construction jobs to the community.

VILLA VICTORIA ("TORRE UNIDAD" "CASAS BORINQUEN" "VIVIENDAS LA VICTORIA"), Boston, Massachusetts. Architects: *John Sharratt Associates, Inc.*—project manager: *Robert H. Egan.* Consultants: *Brown-Rona, Inc. (structural); Goldberg-Zoino and Associates, Inc. (foundations); Herbert G. Keating (mechanical/electrical).* Contractors: *Peabody Construction Company, Inc. ("Torre Unidad"); James P. MacFarland, Inc. ("Casas Borinquen"); Oxford Development ("Viviendas La Victoria").*

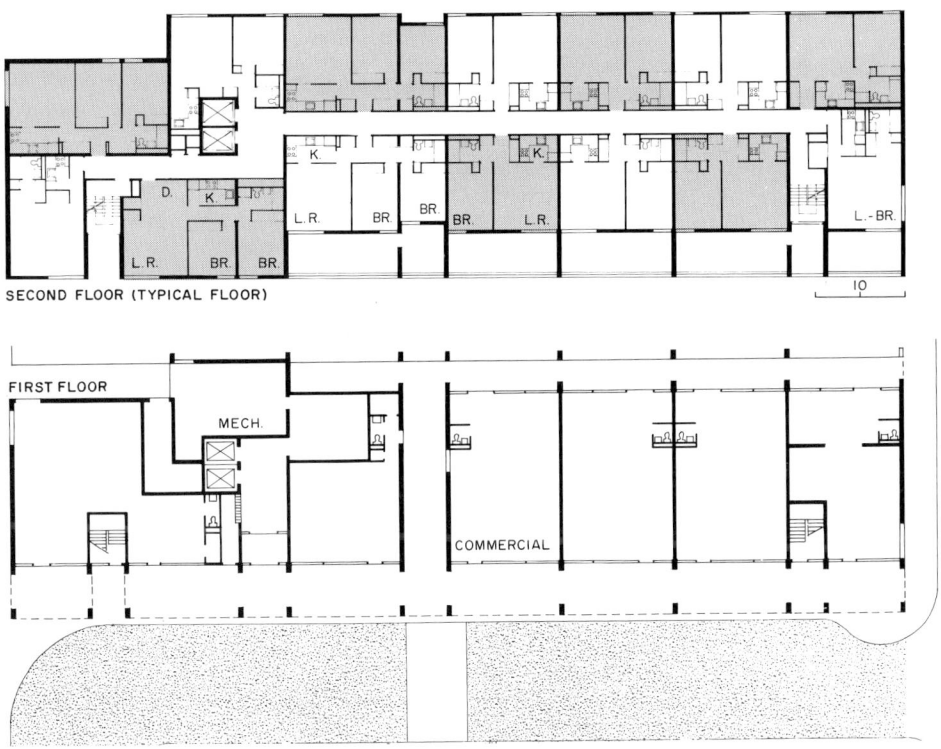

CHAPTER TWO

HIGH-RISE BUILDINGS

There is a strong, still unmet demand for high-density, high-rise apartment buildings as a result of cost and cultural forces. Today, the single family house costs more than most people, even two-paycheck families, can afford. There are reasons other than cost, however, to explain the trend toward higher density apartment dwelling.

Changes have taken place in our culture which have affected the size and formation of households, which, in turn, have influenced housing trends. There are more people living alone now than ever before. The Bureau of Census has reported that the number of adults under 35 years of age living alone has more than doubled since 1970. These statistics reflect the high divorce rate, growing career ambitions of women, a general independence of young people living separately from their parents, longer life expectancy and more older people living alone.

Further statistics substantiate the new trends by indicating that the population nationally has grown by 5 per cent since 1970, but the number of households has risen by 15 per cent. There seems also to be an increase in the number of people moving back into the center city after fleeing to the suburbs years ago to rear their families. The need to be closer to work and services, spurred by inflationary transportation costs (particularly gasoline prices), has increased the need for inner-city housing. So we will be seeing more urban high-rise apartments. Those in the chapter which follows have been selected to show a number of approaches.

Waterside (pages 24-29), designed by Davis, Brody & Associates, is the first step in a plan to expand New York City's use of its waterfront. These apartment buildings bring their residents to the East River's edge. A neighboring older community, long separated from the riverfront by a highway, has been reconnected to it by means of a new footbridge built as part of the complex. The realization of this project was not easy and the process as described in the pages which follow reveals many pointers for achieving future development on other such "found" building sites.

In the mid-seventies architect Stanley Tigerman was still at least partially under the influence of Mies van der Rohe. He designed an apartment in the Miesian manner to a program very similar to that of his fellow Chicagoan, Benjamin Weese. But Weese's building was original, not Miesian. Architect Tigerman believed at that time that Mies's esthetic still worked for apartment towers as well as for office buildings, yet could be improved upon. He tried to prove his point with Boardwalk (pages 36-37). In contrast, Lake Village East by Weese (pages 32-35) is a multi-faceted minimum perimeter tower scheme. The chapter contains their lively argument (pages 30-37) as each defends his own building and attacks the other's.

Also included is a custom tailored apartment building in Nashville, Tennessee by Barber & McMurry (pages 38-39), in which the tenants/buyers were permitted by the developer to determine the size and location of their apartments during construction of the building frame and mechanical systems. Another privately developed apartment high-rise, Gateview in the San Francisco Bay Area by Hallenbeck, Chamorro & Associates (pages 40-43), has been carefully designed to provide amenities not found in the suburbs.

Of great interest are the new mixed-use buildings which contain residential floors along with a variety of other functions such as the Galleria in New York City by David Kenneth Specter (pages 44-47), and Colony Square in Atlanta by Jova Daniels Busby (pages 48-51).

So far such apartments are strictly for the luxury market. The idea of providing dwellings in complexes which also house such functions as a hotel, convention center, office space, shops, restaurants, a skating rink, etc. is a good one for reviving downtowns and it is to be hoped that in the 1980s ways can be found to bring such housing within the means of a broader segment of the population.

1

Norman McGrath

"Waterside" is really a misnomer, because the project's 1,440 housing units, 50,000 square feet of commercial space and 900-car garage are actually built *over* the water—on 2,200 specially designed piles. The extended six-acre site is the first step in a master plan, prepared in the late 1960s by its architects, Davis, Brody & Associates, to claim a 13-block-long area (beginning lower right in aerial photo, opposite page) for an existing adjacent community and a new one along New York City's East River. The new area would occupy a recess in the shoreline currently defined by the major highway that still isolates all but the most intrepid from the greater part of the water's edge. Similar groups of buildings at both ends of the future park would provide not only badly needed housing but 24-hour activity. Whether or not the rest of the plan is ever carried through, Waterside, as it exists, provides four acres of plazas (photo above) and river-edge promenade, all linked to the older community by a pedestrian bridge. The main public plaza is surrounded by a higher level of plazas, which are the only areas reserved for strictly tenant use. Constantly programmed activities, such as concerts and exhibits, assure a large public presence.

But as salubrious as the Waterside concept may be to the city, controversy over even this phase of construction (described later) almost kept the project from being built. And a large part of that controversy involved what kind of people would live there. Waterside's tenants have a mix of limited-income levels, controlled by the nature of the project's partially public financing. The 360-unit north tower (uppermost in aerial photo) was financed by the FHA 236 program for lower-income tenants, and the apartments in this 34-story building are conformingly small in room areas. The controversy centered around the other three 40-story towers, which the private developer financed through a low-interest (approximately seven per cent) mortgage from the city and tax abatements designed to place them within reach of middle-income tenants. These units are only somewhat larger, but all are compensated by spectacular views. There are approximately 2 efficiencies for each 4 one-bedroom, 3.5 two-bedroom and 1 three-bedroom apartments. A row of "townhouses" is placed above the retail building (photo above and left in aerial view) and together the two uses provide a low-scale element and plaza buffer to the highway on the other side.

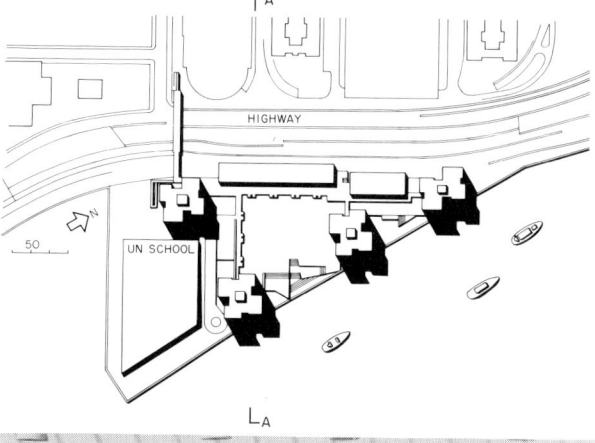

Located at one end of a U-shaped recess in the Manhattan shoreline, Waterside's site includes the United Nations School by architects Harrison & Abramovitz (low white building, opposite page). Some of the apartments were originally intended as a relocation resource to make way for planned development around the United Nations (visible in the upper left-hand corner of aerial view, across from Roosevelt Island). Waterside is immediately outboard of the Bellevue Hospital buildings. The swimming pool is located in the low glass-roofed building.

The ways in which the various levels are organized can be seen in the section, opposite. The river-edge promenade (photo, right) is intended to be continuous with planned future development to the south, and is reached from the public plaza (left in photo) by broad flights of steps. Here boats may dock, and the activity to be generated includes that of a restaurant projecting over the promenade and having spectacular views both up and down the river. Semi-private outdoor areas for the tenants (photos, opposite) connect the four towers and ring the large expanse of public plaza (opposite center), where both the public and residents are encouraged to patronize shops on the space's east side. The townhouses above the shops have their own private yards, which are one-half level above the general resident spaces. Despite the encouraged public presence, the controlled access to the project (as well as to the individual buildings) offers security through easy surveillance; and it heightens a sense of community. This sense is further encouraged by the presence of many of the needs for self-sufficiency, including office space.

Developer Richard Ravitch readily states that the separate towers were not as economical as fewer, more massive buildings would have been—but that they were necessary to avoid building a wall on the river for the buildings behind. To gain maximum views for the relatively low older buildings, to place a maximum number of the new residents near the most spectacular views and to give the towers a visual "cap," floor areas increase successively as they get higher, so that four apartments gain an extra bedroom on each of the top floors (see plans). Ravitch attributed a "minuscule" cost for the resulting cantilevered floor space.

Waterside's buildings are built with conventional poured-concrete, flat-slab construction on top of ganged piles. The sheathing of "oversized" brown brick accounted for fast placement and the ability to turn corners without special sizes. The sections of pivoting, double-glazed (because of electric heat) windows and metal curtain walls were placed first and the brick set to them. The composite piles were the major innovation, as they were driven without caissons; they are steel H sections (in the non-oxidizing layer of sludge between the river's bottom and rock) with concrete above, which could be poured at low tide.

Norman McGrath

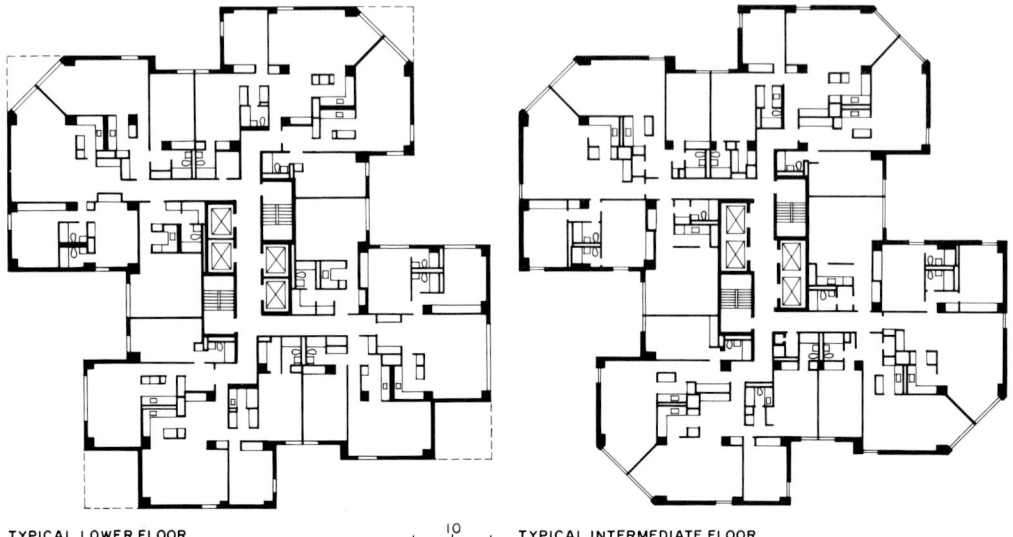

TYPICAL LOWER FLOOR   10   TYPICAL INTERMEDIATE FLOOR

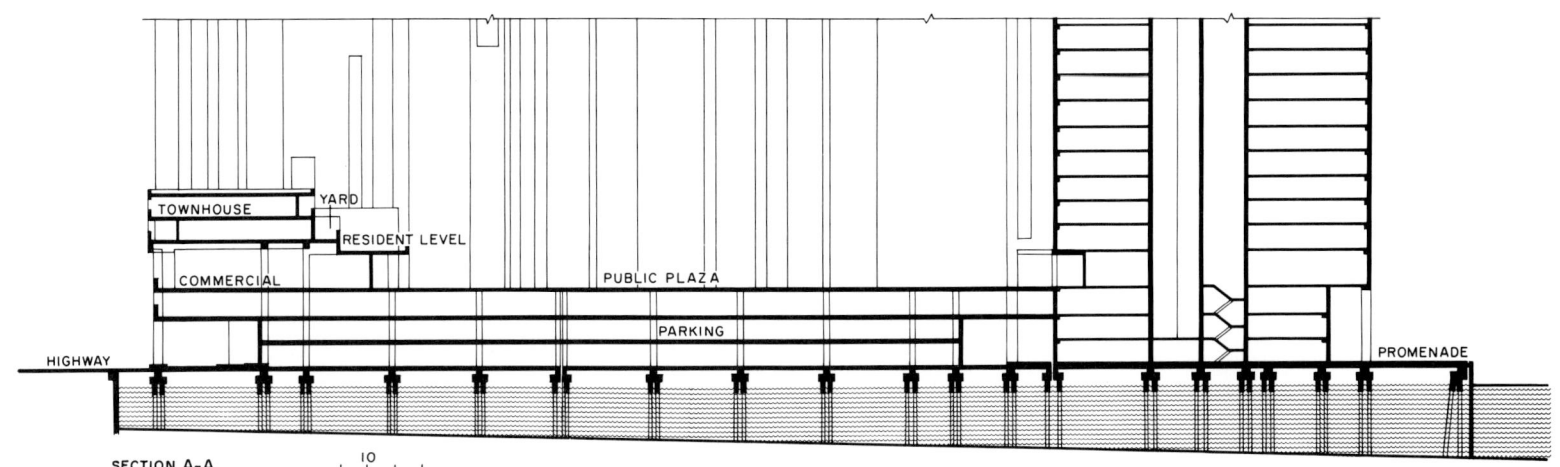

SECTION A-A

J. Alexander photos

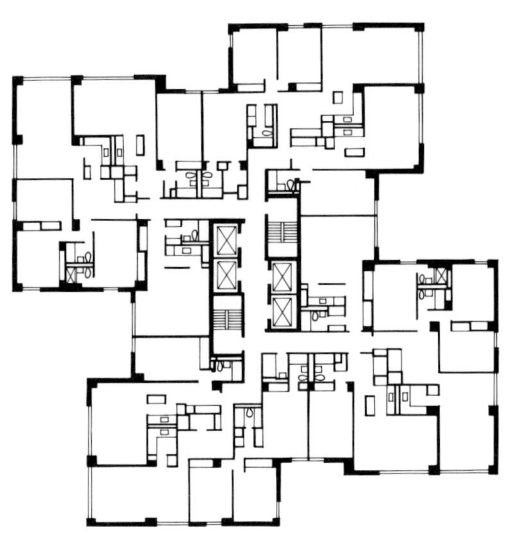

TYPICAL UPPER FLOOR

That Waterside was ever built is a tribute to the determination of both the developer and the architect, and—considering the difficult 12 years of fighting countless bureaucracies, political opposition and consequent soaring costs —it is a wonder that both parties continue to enjoy the personal friendship with which they began. Planning for the innovative project began in 1963 and stretched through several city administrations with changing attitudes. According to a *New York Times* editorial in 1967, "the local pattern for mediocrity is immutable"; given the difficulties involved here, the distinction of the project would seem heroic. Waterside was to have been built originally by purely private financing. But air rights for the "land" were to be leased from the City, which had to first wrestle control from the Department of Marine and Aviation. No bank would then finance the project, which according to a 19th-century law, could have been confiscated for interference with Federal shoreline defense. An act of Congress was required, and—due to delays—rising estimates of cost required the promise of tax abatement and limited-income financing by the City. During this period, extensive neighborhood input was encouraged to assure local interests while a group called Planners for Equal Opportunity emerged to assert that tax abatement constituted subsidy for the rich—despite the land rental income which the city would have never otherwise realized. Accordingly, the final city approval in 1967 was passed by only the personal interventions of then Mayor John Lindsay. But another three years elapsed before the city financing could be approved and the project could get started. By this time, both costs and rents had nearly doubled from the original estimates. Still, high demand has caused better than a 95-per-cent occupancy rate. And—because of solutions to many problems here, Waterside has helped pave the way for such water-front developments everywhere—which offer choice location without relocation and are still assets to inland communities.

WATERSIDE, New York City. Owner: *Waterside Redevelopment Company*. Architects: *Davis, Brody & Associates—associate: John Lebduska; project architect: Herbert Levine; project designer: Ian Ferguson; design team: Frank Frost, Jerry Lee, Edward Montano.* Engineers: *Robert Rosenwasser* (structural/soils); *Cosentini Associates* (mechanical/electrical). Consultants: *Herbert Levine, Howard Brandston* (lighting); *Chermayeff & Geismar Associates* (graphics). General contractor: *HRH Construction Corp.*

As an example of the unusual amenity here, carefully detailed brick parapet walls, separating the various levels, were estimated to cost over $300,000 more than metal railings, but were determined to be necessary to both the visual success of the plazas and privacy. Community rooms offer a constant range of activities from lectures to crafts, and the extensive facilities of the swimming pool are available to all tenants for a modest yearly fee—as are the covered parking spaces. These three photos show the stores on the main plaza's landward side and under the tenant plaza and townhouses. The top view is toward the northern tower and the swimming-pool building.

2 AND 3
INTRODUCTION

Which is better, this by Weese...

Lake Village East, a 25-story apartment tower

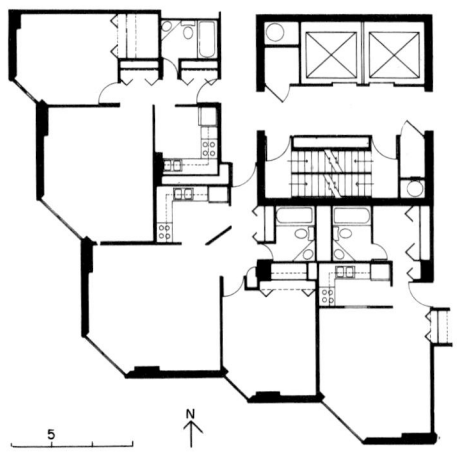

Architects Stanley Tigerman and Ben Weese of Harry Weese and Associates have each added a high-rise apartment to Chicago's skyline. Tigerman is noted as a radical and innovative designer. His fans and critics were surprised, therefore, when he elected the Miesian manner for Boardwalk, his first high-rise apartment building (right). No one was more astonished than his friend Ben Weese who lately has designed some apartment house towers which are handsome alternatives to the Mies box, including Lake Village East (left).

There is, of course, no one right way to do a building. The two under discussion were built in the same city, at the same time, at comparable costs per square foot—and yet they are remarkably different. Tigerman and Weese are in friendly disagreement about the best approach to high-rise apartment design. Both responded to our invitation to debate the issues in the RECORD offices, and their comments accompany the pictures on the following pages.

Boardwalk is massive, modular and repetitive

The Tigerman apartment house slab is a 28-story complex of reinforced concrete financed under FHA, 221-d(4). Its construction cost as bid in January 1973 and excluding land costs and fees was $8.4 million or $18,666 per dwelling unit or $15.96 per gross square foot. The project consists of 450 dwelling units made up of 128 studios, 222 one-bedrooms and 100 two-bedrooms. There are 25 typical apartment floors consisting of 18 dwelling units per floor for a typical gross floor area of 14,499 square feet.

The base accommodates a 270-car parking garage, commercial spaces, restaurant, swimming pool with bath house, tennis court and landscaped plaza deck. The total gross area including these facilities is 526,045 square feet.

The structure is reinforced concrete frame with 20-by-20-foot square bays with a peripheral intermediate column for slab stiffening. This column system produces a repetitive series of 8-by-8-ft openings which are glazed with bronze hued float glass in hard anodic coated aluminum sash. The tower is 60 by 240 feet. The building has central heating and air conditioning distributed by vertical fan coil units at the perimeter.

Lake Village East is slender, non-modular and varied

The Weese apartment house tower is a 25-story reinforced concrete structure financed under FHA 236. Its construction cost was $3.1 million or $15,500 per dwelling unit or $16.90 per gross square foot. It consists of 200 dwelling units made up of 50 studios, 75 one-

or this by Tigerman?

Boardwalk, a 28-story apartment complex

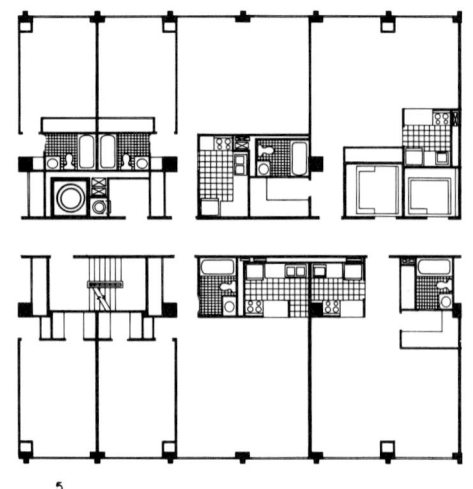

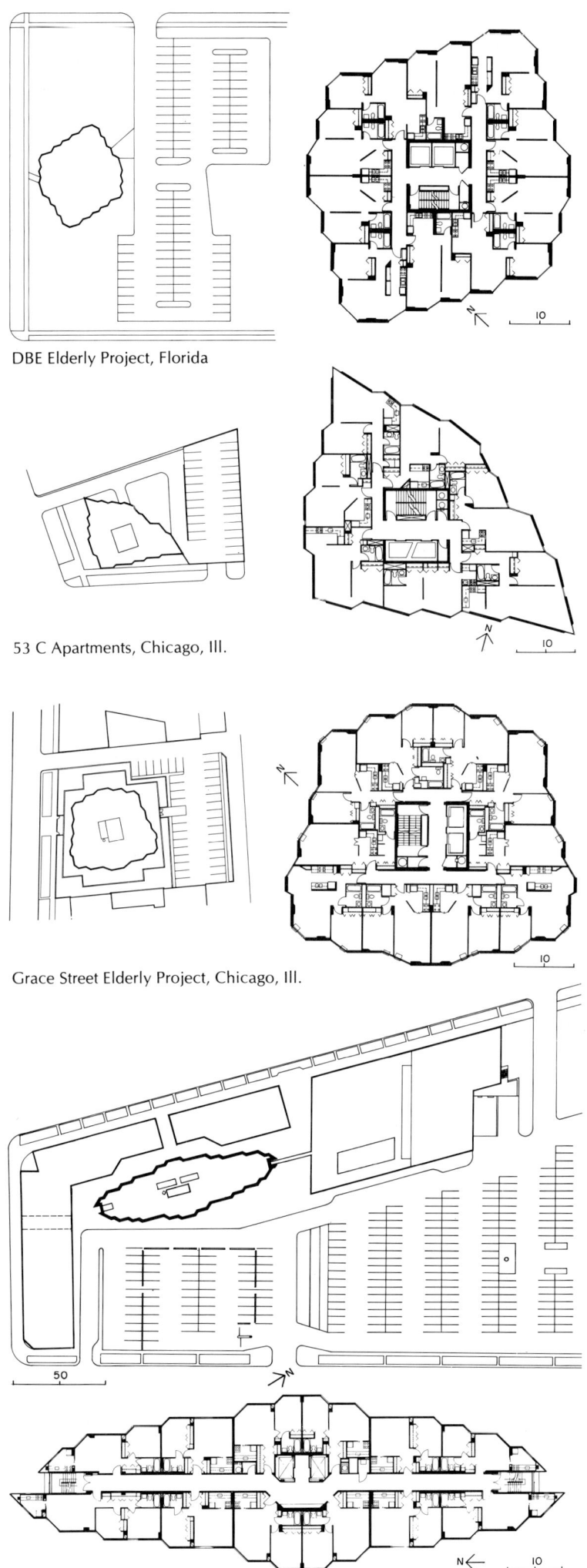

Minimum perimeter floor plans by Weese adapt to a variety of sites

DBE Elderly Project, Florida

53 C Apartments, Chicago, Ill.

Grace Street Elderly Project, Chicago, Ill.

John Knox Home Elderly Housing, Norfolk, Va.

bedrooms and 75 two-bedrooms. The 25 typical apartment floors have eight units per floor for a gross floor area of 6,255 square feet. Parking for approximately 130 cars is on grade. Its program did not call for the commercial and recreational facilities of the Tigerman project.

Lake Village East demonstrates the advantages of "minimum perimeter" floor planning. Through this approach a variety of finely tuned floor plans can be achieved. Weese has set aside rigid structural modules and predetermined plan shapes in favor of plan forms which he believes are more closely adapted to need. Permutations of these plan forms are devised to suit a variety of programs, even low-income housing. Weese has compared "equivalent area" rectangular and square floor plans. Such plan shapes, which he believes are often used arbitrarily, require sizable additional wall surface to enclose the same amount of floor area. In minimum perimeter schemes the savings in wall area can offset the extra costs stemming from the complexities of non-modular slab and reinforcing steel forming.

Weese asserts that the individual apartment units at Lake Village East are more livable than those in Boardwalk, and that the variety of unit types offered is an advantage. A minimum perimeter tower will fit well into an oddly shaped site and give a reduced sense of mass because of its receding wall planes. It may enhance views and make the most of available orientation.

Designing a building form with 38 facets

The tower, limited to 25 stories by community pressure, was planned to attract young, fairly sophisticated households who would become the nucleus of the population. Ben Weese and his team, working within the Section 236 cost limits and the tight constraints imposed by urban renewal, came forward with a complicated *parti* which departed widely from the standard rectangular form. The structure they proposed was based on developer requirements which included short corridors for efficiency and security, interesting floor plans for rentability, and structural economy. The result was a building form with 38 sides, tending toward the circular form which offers the most economical ratio of perimeter wall to floor area, while at the same time permitting standard rectangular components and rooms. The flexibility of the design allowed maximum planning efficiency, since variations dictated by floor plan considerations could be expressed in the exterior wall without cost penalties. At the same time the plan made the most of the good views toward the lakefront and downtown Chicago, while reducing glass areas to reduce heating and cooling loss.

Examining the options

Tigerman's building illustrates his belief that Miesian architectural forms and details are not only still applicable to current high-rise apartment requirements, but are endlessly perfectable in the esthetic sense. In proving his point, he has created a building which is at once more economical in cost and generous in its square foot allotments than Weese's tower. Lake Village East is of more current architectural interest, however, because it embodies genuinely new planning ideas. Its silhouette is attractive (partly because it is unfamiliar looking) and the basic concept is adaptable to many other site conditions. Neither building is really better than the other. Together they represent two of the kinds of viable, valid options we need.

**"You think you can do a brownstone in the sky,"
says Tigerman to Weese,
"but you can't"**

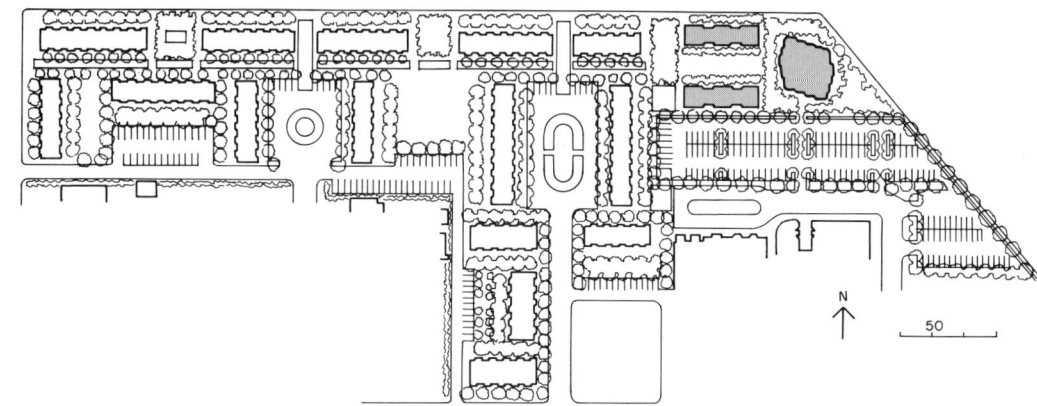

2

"True, but by trying to give apartment units bay windows and the variety of room shapes which exist in older types of dwelling places such as brownstones, it is possible to create an apartment tower silhouette of great interest and variety," counters Weese. This tower is fascinating to look at, changing shape as the viewer circles it (right). Windows are angled toward the best orientation and views, but glass area is reduced in favor of continuous vertical slabs of brick.

Weese began by developing the plan form (below) to fit the site and relate well to the two low-rise buildings included as part of his design (right). The non-modular beam and column layout came later, after the apartment units had been worked out. The additional cost of an irregular structural system is offset by the minimum perimeter skin. Tigerman, on the other hand, was limited to 20-foot-square bays to accommodate Boardwalk's basement parking garage. Money saved by adhering to this economical module was partially spent to provide the floor-to-ceiling glass for each bay.

LAKE VILLAGE EAST, Chicago, Illinois. Owner: *Lake Village Associates.* Architects: *Harry Weese & Associates—associate-in-charge: Benjamin H. Weese.* Associated architects: *Gordon-Levin Associates.* Engineers: *Cohen-Barreto-Marchertas* (structural); *Nachman, Vragel & Associates* (mechanical/electrical). Consultant: *Joe Karr & Associates* (landscape). General contractor: *McHugh Construction Co.*

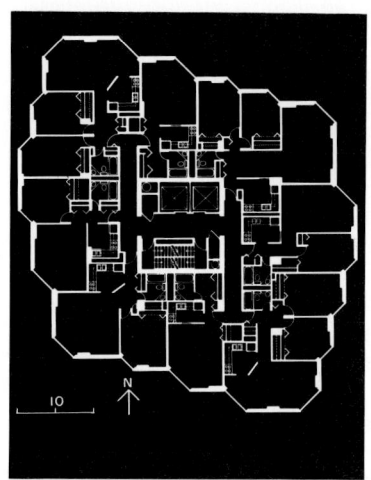

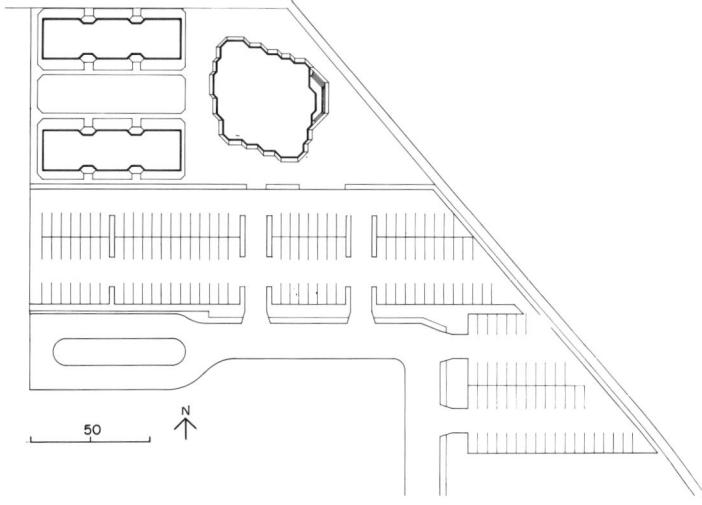

Hedrich-Blessing

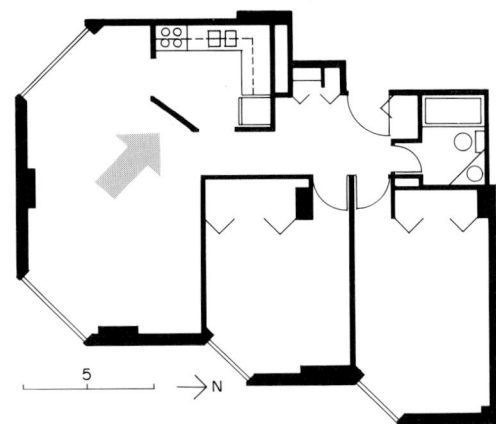

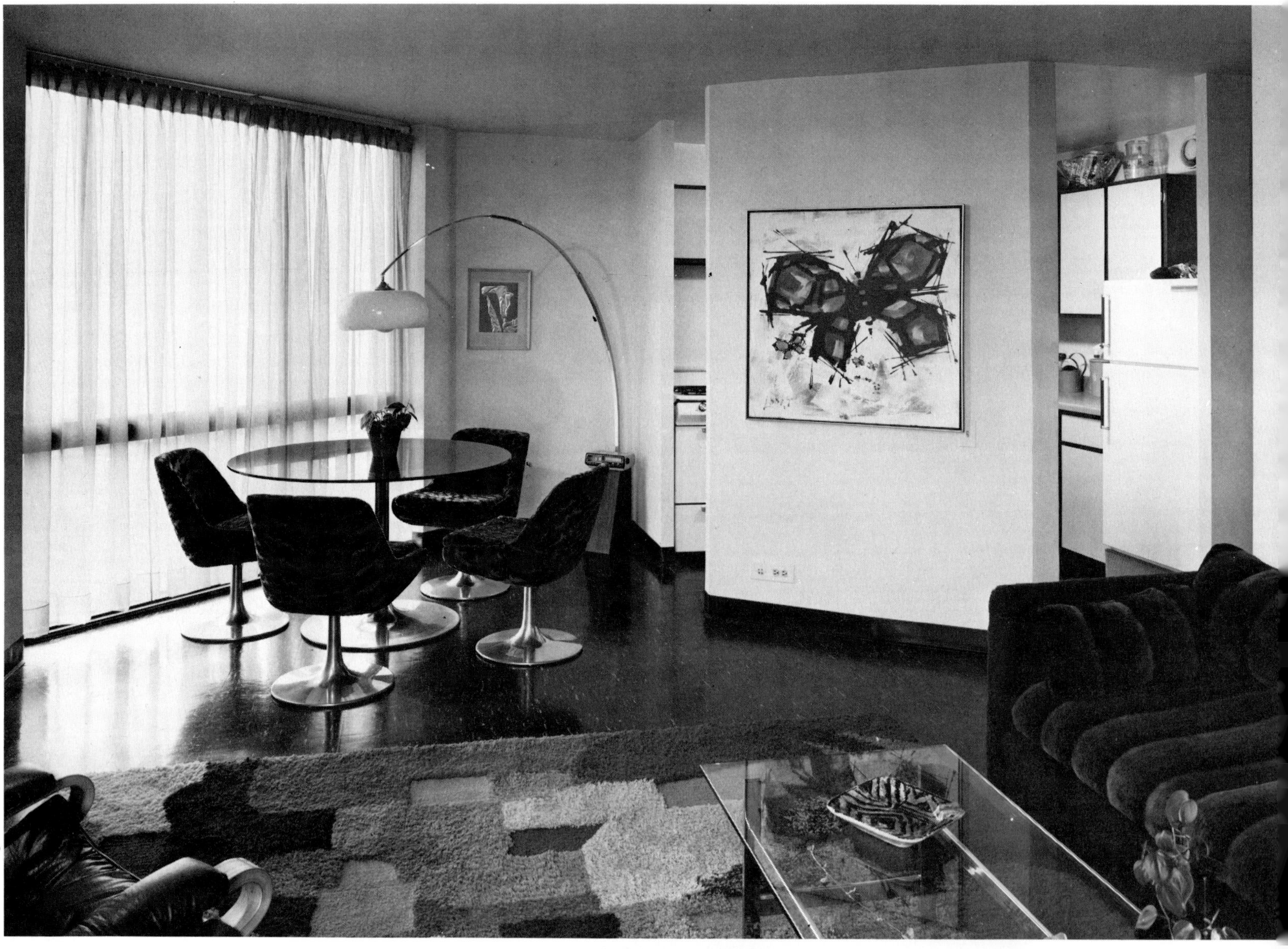

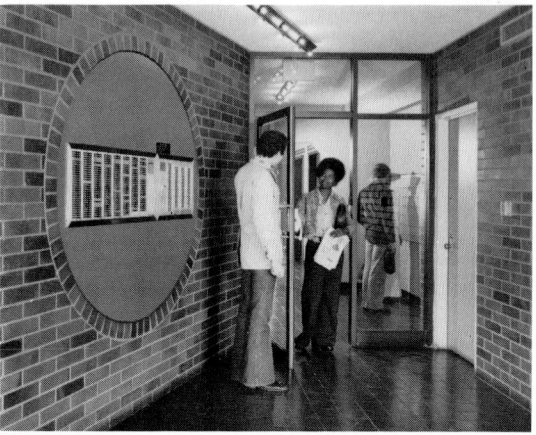

Says Weese: "Universal space is what Mies, in the name of efficiency, said people should live in. Well, I disagree. You can't furnish these spaces. Where do you put the chifforobe—against the window, as I once saw in a Mies apartment? How does a guy live with Biedermeier? We are back to that." Although the Lake Village East model apartments shown above and opposite are poorly furnished examples, Weese's apartment layouts do provide a lot of wall perimeter for chifforobes, escritoires, bibelots and other nostalgic objects to which people unaccountably cling and which are now once more in fashion.

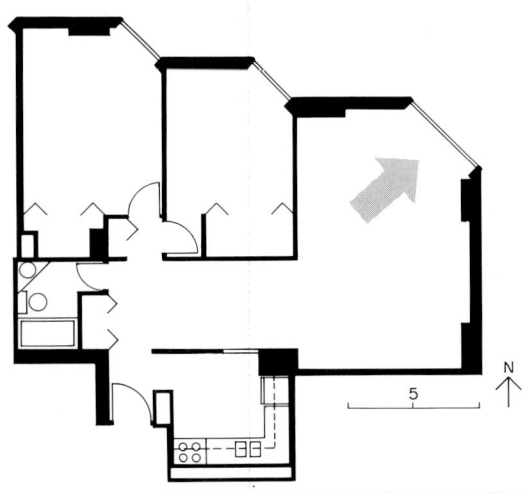

"For Boardwalk I wanted to get the biggest units and the largest area possible. I wanted a lot of glass and flexible space." Tigerman got his space. His apartment units are significantly larger than Weese's shown above and opposite. Lake Village East's studios range in net area from 434 to 486 square feet, one-bedrooms from 586 to 690 square feet and two-bedrooms from 859 to 947 square feet. These figures can be compared with those given for Boardwalk on page 30. Weese's net to gross ratio on typical floors is 87 per cent efficient as opposed to Tigerman's 89.9 per cent. Tigerman's units cost less to build.

"How many more of these can Chicago stand?" asks Weese of Tigerman

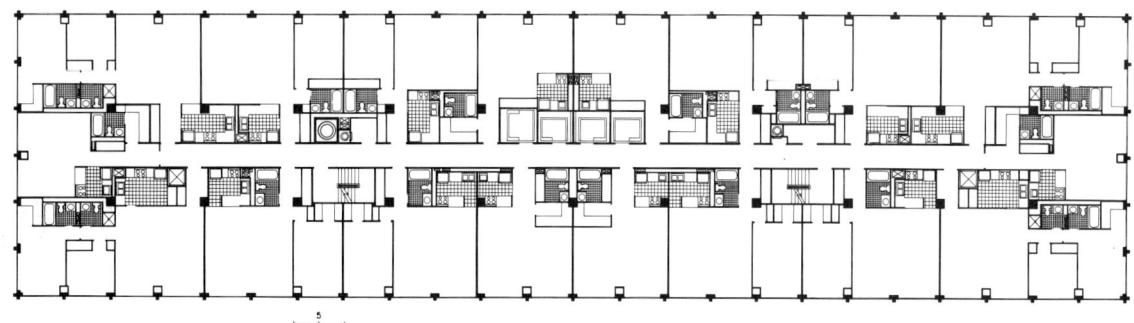

3

In Weese's view Boardwalk is simply too big. "You could have done two smaller buildings on that site, Stanley—this is brutal, austere, overpowering." Tigerman countered by emphasizing the economies of doing a "big pour" resulting in a 1973 construction cost of $15.96 per gross square foot. By confining the 450 dwelling units to a single mass a large portion of the 1.355-acre site was made available for recreation on a terrace above the parking garage. "It takes a large concentration of tenants to make such extensive recreation facilities feasible," Tigerman points out.

Says Weese: "Why do bedrooms get the corner exposure with three window bays while living rooms get only two?" Neither architect would concede that the other's room spaces were of adequate size or could be easily furnished. Tigerman's net to gross ratio on typical floors is 89.9 percent efficient, however, and the net areas of his apartment units are generous by today's standards. Studios range in net area from 481 to 570 square feet, one-bedrooms from 570 to 764 square feet and two-bedrooms from 976 to 981 square feet. These areas are significantly larger than those provided by Weese's plan.

BOARDWALK, Chicago, Illinois. Owner: *City Centrum Corporation*. Architects: *Stanley Tigerman*—associates: *Anthony Saifuku, John Haley*. Engineers: *Cohen-Barreto-Marchertas* (structural); *Wallace & Migdal* (mechanical/electrical). General contractor: *LBC, Inc.*

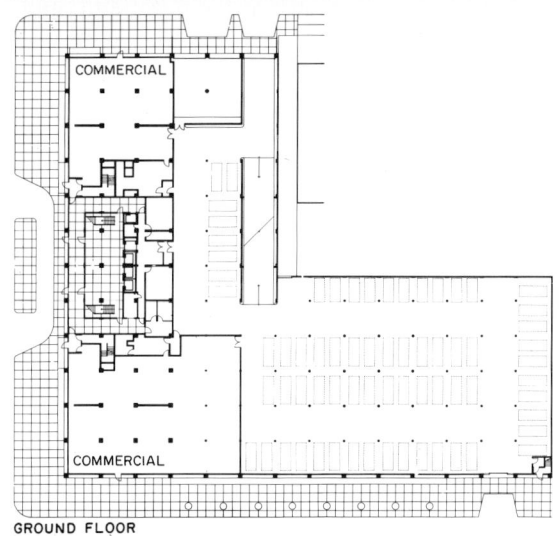

GROUND FLOOR

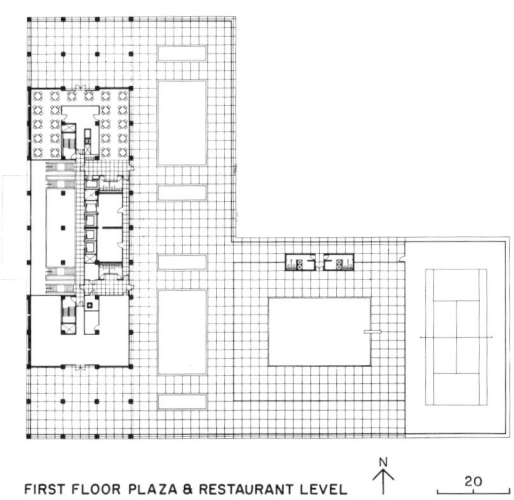

FIRST FLOOR PLAZA & RESTAURANT LEVEL

4

In an innovative approach to the design of a new high-rise apartment complex, the developer permitted the market—the tenants/buyers—to determine the size, number and location of apartments in the building during construction.

The architects devised 23 possible apartment plans from which the tenants selected what best suited their needs. Over 50 possible floor configurations, ranging from ten one- to two-bedroom suites, were studied. As buyer commitments progressed, the architects fit all the pieces together like a jigsaw puzzle.

There were, of course, some inescapable parameters that predetermined fitting the pieces together, including (most obviously) the building size and shape, plus the placement of mechanical systems for function and economy, and the fenestration detailing. The location of a series of vertical chases (containing plumbing and air circulatory equipment) was set throughout a fan-shaped building with a centralized elevator core.

The most visual and intriguing aspect of the design is the handling of the fenestration. Since the market determined the unit placement and ultimately the elevations, the window pattern reflects the various combinations of units on each floor. (In practice, certain unit designs were chosen more often; the two-story townhouse received general favor because of its spatial amenities).

This wide-open planning flexibility was attractive to the tenants, enticing middle- and upper-income-producing persons to consider high-rise living and remain in the center city, all with a degree of choice not often available in apartment houses.

ROKEBY CONDOMINIUM APARTMENTS, Nashville, Tennessee. Owner: *The Rokeby Corporation*. Architects: *Barber & McMurry Architects*. Design consultant: *Martin Holub*. Engineers: *Quickel & Bennett* (structural); *Walter L. Montgomery* (mechanical); *Vreeland Associates Engineers* (electrical). General contractor: *W. F. Holt & Sons*.

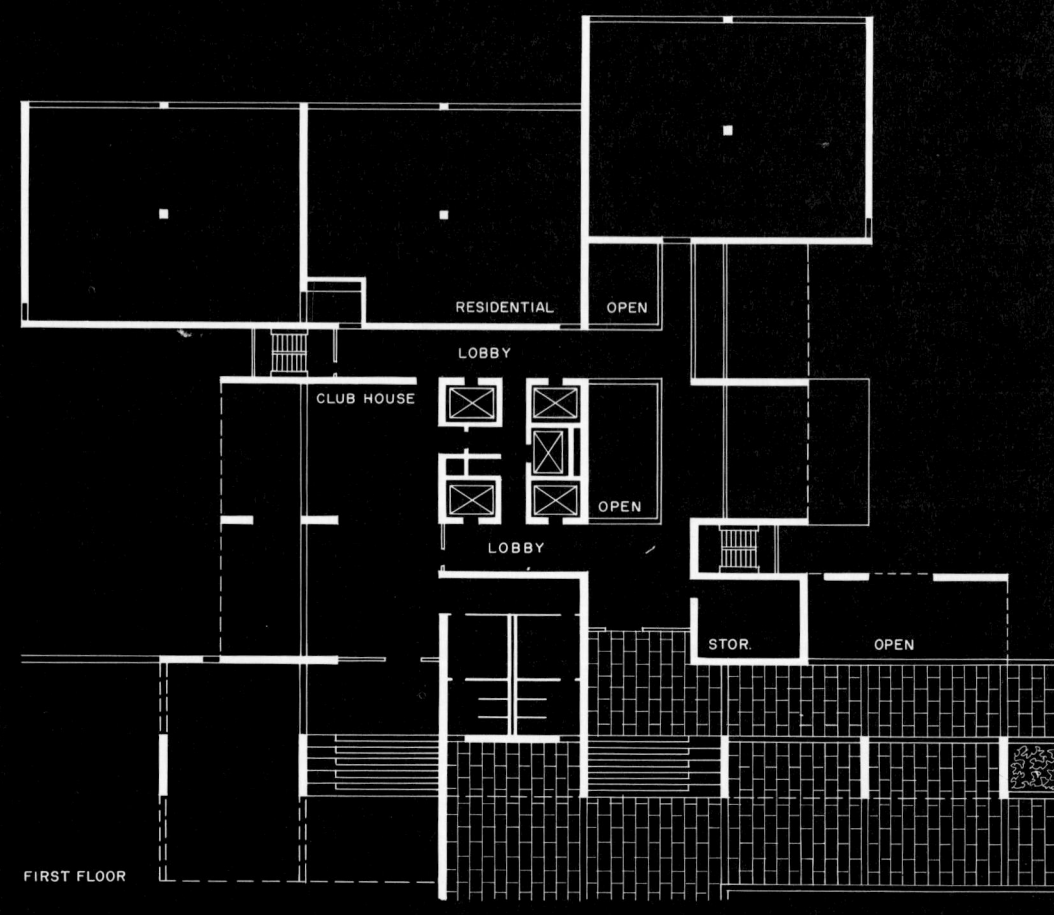

Larry Taylor photos

FIRST FLOOR

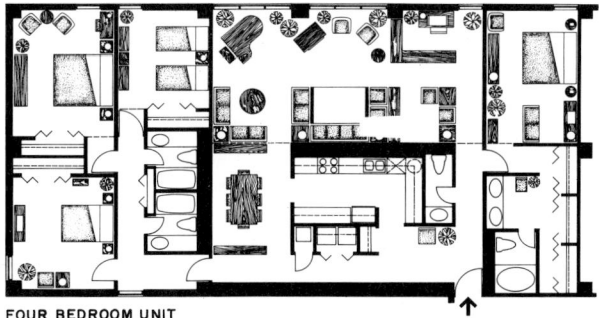
FOUR BEDROOM UNIT

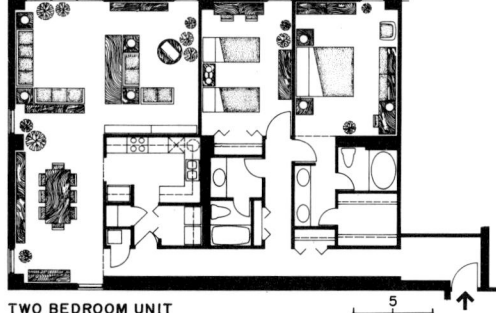
TWO BEDROOM UNIT

A variety of floor plans, from one- to four-bedroom units and townhouses, were designed in full cooperation with the tenants. All units interlock in different patterns, and there is no typical floor plan. Diverse unit combinations are noticeably reflected in the fenestration. One of Nashville's few high-rise residential structures, it is successfully competing with well-established low-rise and garden apartments. There is also a delightful, light-filled rooftop tea room (right).

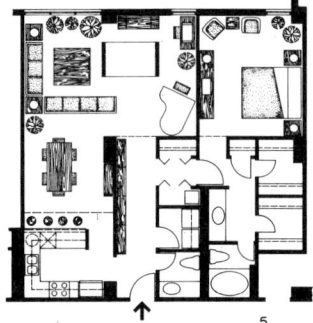
ONE BEDROOM UNIT

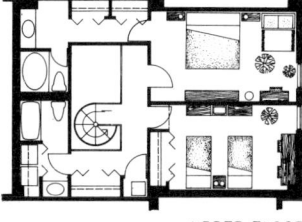
UPPER FLOOR

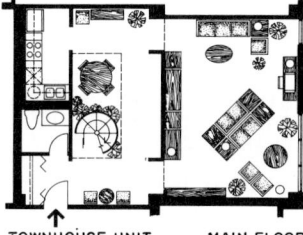
TOWNHOUSE UNIT   MAIN FLOOR

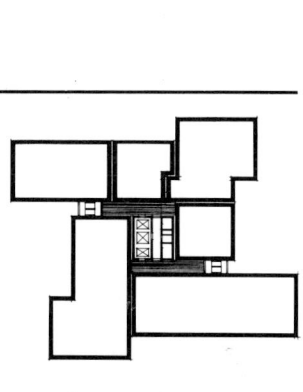

5

A new high-rise high-density apartment project in the San Francisco Bay area combines the best aspects of a true urban living experience with an unencumbered, open location, excellent for views of the Bay Area (in an area primarily surrounded by low-rise structures). The first of five phases is now complete on Gateview at Albany Hill—a fine architectural solution to problems associated with providing human-scaled high-density housing.

An unusual urban site, the project covers 36 acres, and is located near the east shore of San Francisco Bay, on the westerly face of 300-foot-high Albany Hill.

The master plan provides for all the units to be built over a 10-year period, with buildings ranging in height from 2 to 25 stories. The design objective was to develop all phases as a cohesive visual and functional whole, with each phase complete in itself.

Phase One buildings are clustered at the base of the hill, arranged diagonally to a main road and to the hillside, all atop a three-story garage. This arrangement diminishes the over-all bulk of the complex seen from the free-way, permits the best views of the waterfront from the apartments and allows diversity on the interconnecting plaza level.

Presently there are three buildings with a total of seven towers, averaging a height of 15 stories. Each building has an identifiable color (blue, green or brown). Balconies accent the complex by both color (light-colored railings contrast with darker masonry blocks) and in form, particularly noticeable when seen from across the Bay (bottom right). The over-sized top floor "scoops" denote the location of penthouses.

A mixed-use concept—recreational, commercial and community facilities—is planned. It is a self-contained "city within a city," and will be the largest privately-developed

A custom "shingle" masonry block was designed for the exterior with a large module easily perceivable from a nearby freeway. A system of building sections was conceived, each made of four to six units grouped in a way unique to that section. This is connected to one or two others until a total building plan is formed. While seemingly unnecessarily complicated, this system has assured diversity in individual apartment floor plans and differences between towers.

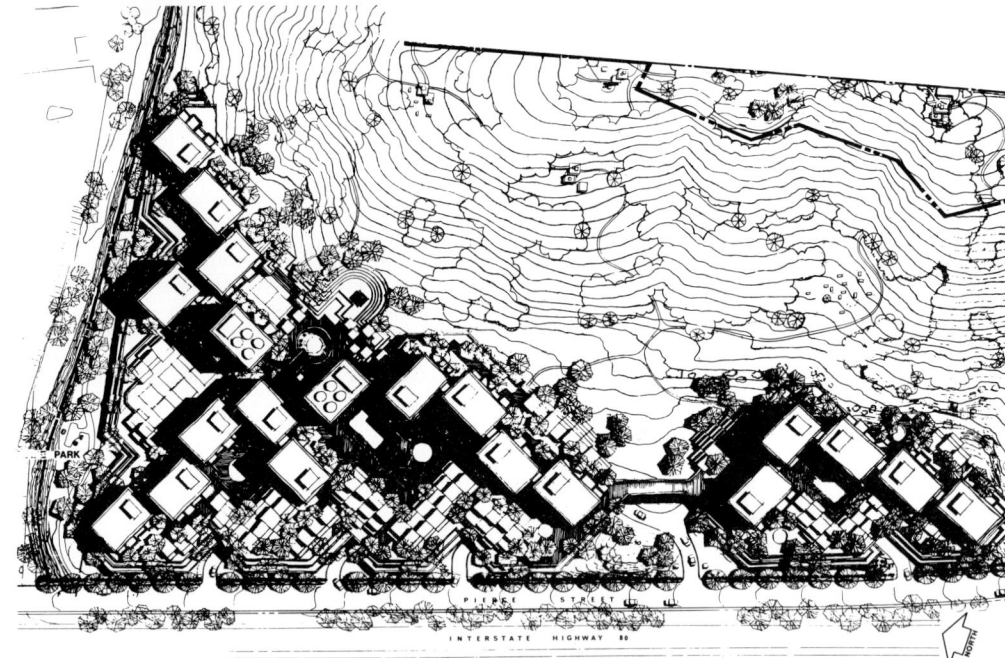

residential community in the urban Bay Area.

It is a high-density complex, and development is expected to reach 2500 units built on one-third of the 36 acre site providing approximately 200 units per acre. The remainder of the land will be preserved as permanent open space. Phase One is composed of 482 units, with a total of 478,000 square feet of living space. The buyer's market is directed to middle-income groups.

To combat the alternate lifestyle offered in the suburbs, the architects placed emphasis on aspects of the project that would provide many amenities not found in the suburbs. There are uninhibited views of the San Francisco Bay and other parts of the area to the west, and to a tree-lined hillside to the east. The proximity to transportation corridors is important, in one direction to a nearby Bay Area Rapid Transit Station (which links major cities and counties of the Bay Area) and to another, a freeway which borders the site.

Sophisticated life safety, voice communication and security systems are provided—one of the most modern in the Bay Area. A central control room monitors all these functions with special capabilities to aid emergency personnel in any kind of crisis.

GATEVIEW AT ALBANY HILL, Albany, California. Owner: *Interstate General Corp.* Architects: *Hallenbeck, Chamorro & Associates* (formerly *Goetz Hallenbeck & Goetze, Inc.*)— Harry C. Hallenbeck, partner-in-charge. Engineers: *Shapiro Okino Hom & Associates* (structural); *Cooper Clark & Associates* (soils); *G.L. Gendler & Associates* (mechanical); *Yarnell & Ron* (civil). Consultants: *Harmon O'Donnell & Henninger* (planning); *Environmental Impact Planning Corp.* (for master plan); *Bolt, Beranek & Newman Inc.* (acoustical). Interior design (apartment shown): *the Inside Story Inc.-San Francisco.* Contractor: *Williams & Burrows.*

Charles F. Holbrook

ONE BEDROOM UNIT

TWO BEDROOM UNIT

TOWER PLAN

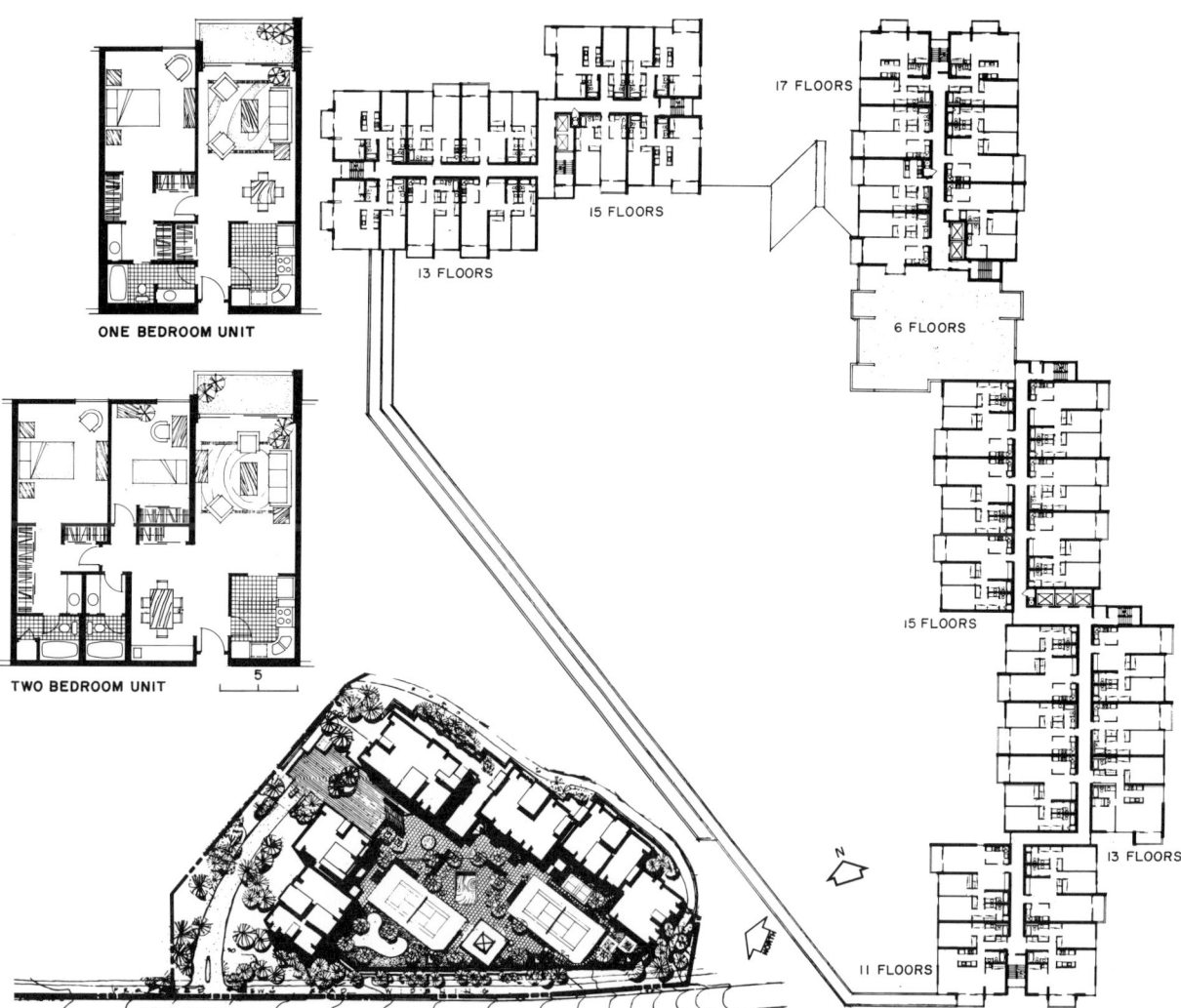

A seismic code limited the building height to a maximum of 160 feet, but the ultimate height, massing and scale of Phase One fits most appropriately with the natural setting and conforms to the slope of Albany Hill. A master plan for the complex evolved from a series of studies particularly dealing with the massing. Staggering the units—dismissing a more traditional grid-related siting system—provided a much more useful and interesting pattern to the complex while granting apartment orientation in all directions.

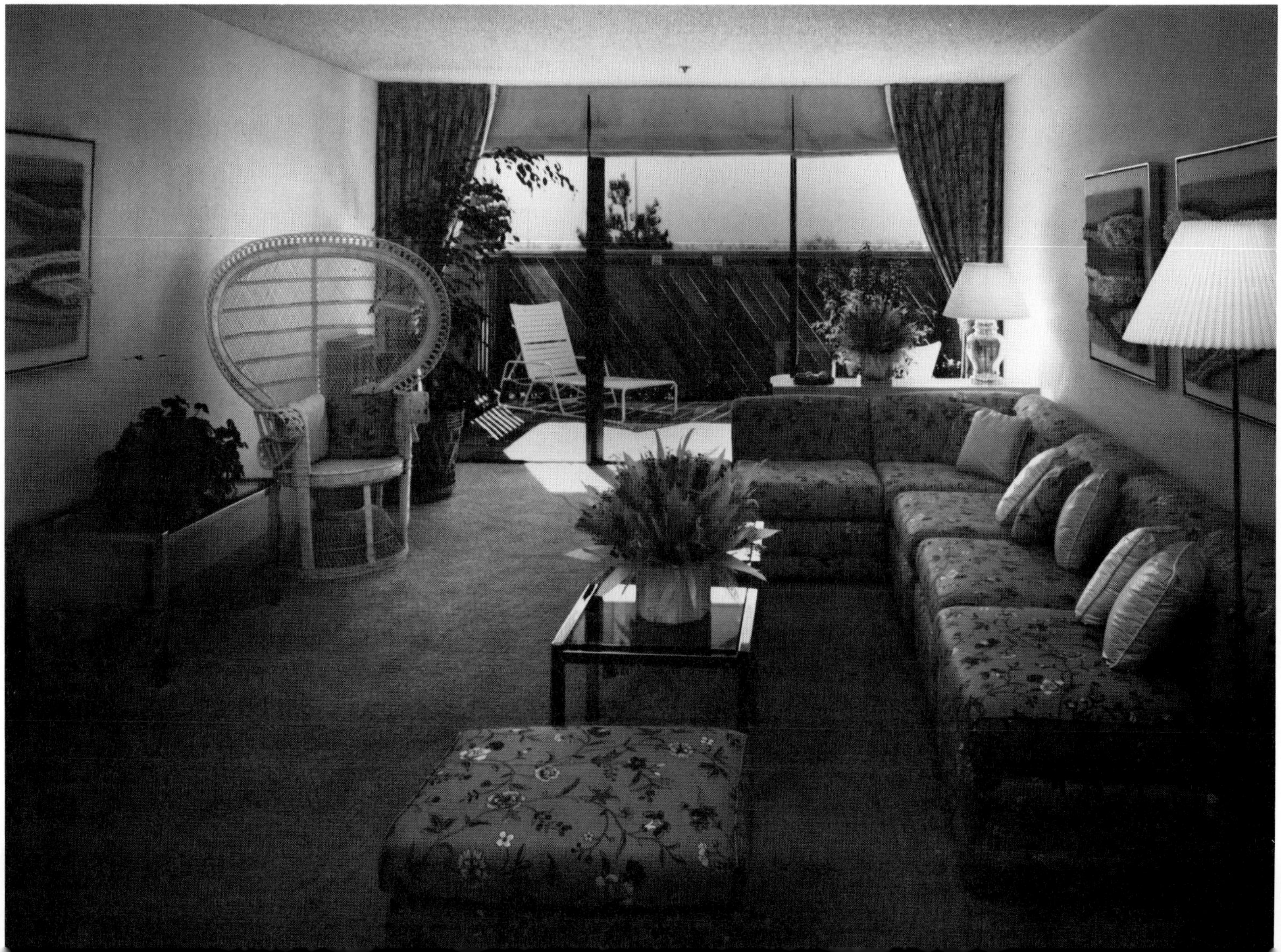

Doug Symes

6

Rising amid a cluster of high-rises on a mid-block site in the center of Manhattan, Galleria is a bold experiment in mixed use, an offspring of incentive zoning that has in its chromosomes traces of Frank Lloyd Wright's Price Tower, New York's Olympic Tower and Chicago's Hancock Building. Like these others, Galleria represents an attempt to broaden and re-structure street activity in its district by combining commercial, office and residential usages in the same structure. At street level, architect David Specter has designed a through-block shopping mall that will be lined along its offset path with shops, boutiques and a small cafe. This multi-height arcade, skylighted from the south, is richly clad in granite slabs accented by bronze-colored steel channels that serve as scale-giving devices and important visual ligaments. The linear patterns these channels trace across broad and otherwise unrelieved planes of stone enliven the whole composition and help resolve the conflicting lines of force introduced by the canted entrance element.

Above the galleria and overlooking it are six layers of offices with an unusually handsome club with dining room (photo, page 47) sandwiched between. Rising for nearly 40 stories above the offices are condominium apartments that culminate in what will be an extraordinarily lavish, multi-level penthouse for philanthropist Stewart Mott—a penthouse, visible in the photo at right, that will include enclosed greenhouses for large-scale flower and vegetable gardening.

Set back from 57th Street but rising sheer from 58th, the gently articulated tower does not seem to shoulder aside its shorter neighbors. It takes its place in the skyline easily and unaggressively.

The Galleria was designed to bring something that more nearly approaches 24-hour-a-day use to this important district and to make a productive contribution to a city that, just now—and for the immediate future—needs all the help it can get.

GALLERIA, New York City. Architects: *David Kenneth Specter—Gerald L. Jonas*, project architect; *John Davison Allen,* duplex apartment designer. Architect for apartment residences: *Office of Philip Birnbaum.* Engineers: *Erwin Cantor* (structural); *Sidney Barbanel* (consulting); Interior design of club facilities: *Ellen L. McClusky & Associates.* Construction administrator: *H.R.H. Construction.*

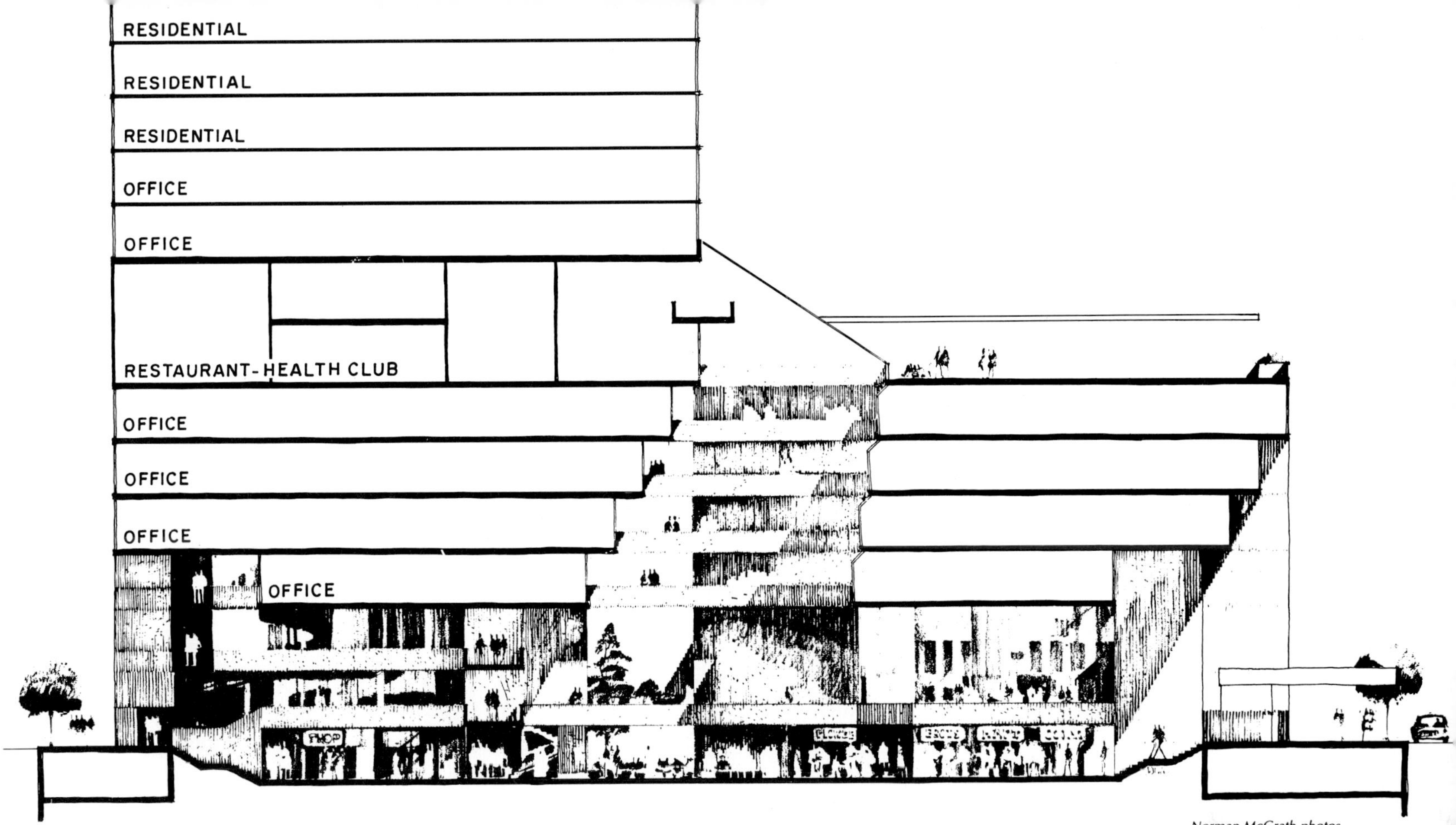

Norman McGrath photos

The elegant dining facility (photo, right) is part of a club that includes saunas and workout rooms. The sketch (below) shows the galleria space itself where shoppers and strollers mingle with diners in a spatially stimulating and nicely appointed surround. The commercial space when fully rented, may include—in addition to a cafe—a flower shop, a delicatessen, a jewelry store and various boutiques. All depend for their economic success on public support, not just patronage from within the building.

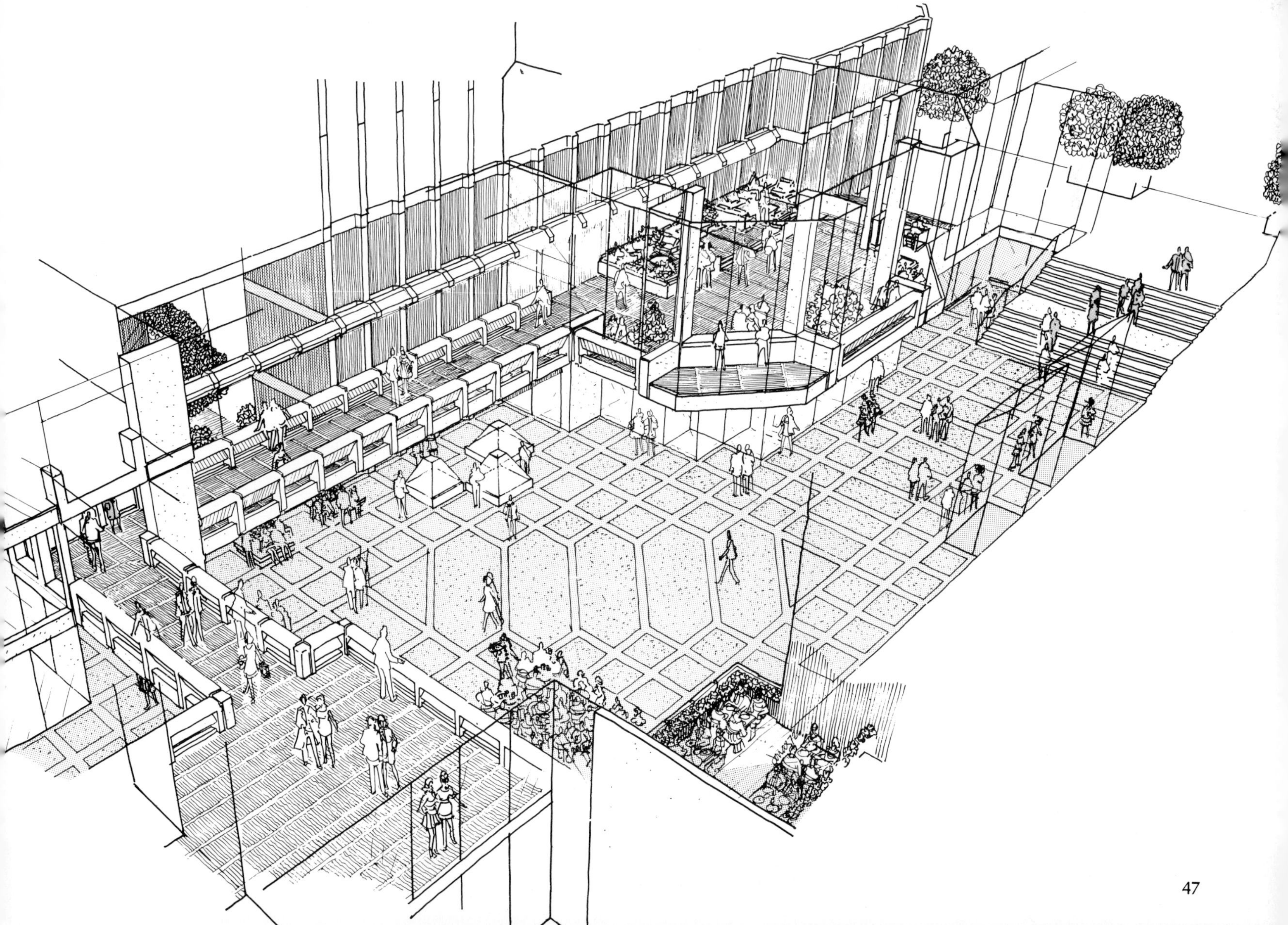

7

E. Alan McGee photos

During the seven years since planning began, Colony Square's designers have premised their work on the central theme that urban life cannot be full, varied and rewarding if certain physical criteria are not carefully met. Chief among these criteria is a generous mix of building types and, from the beginning, Colony Square has been a mixed-use project. Across its 12-acre, downtown site, the project includes townhouses and high-rise condominiums. It includes office space, a 500-room hotel, a shopping mall and landscaped plazas, a restaurant, a skating rink and three levels of below-grade parking. All these elements are sited in ways that make them share space and both the palette of materials and design vocabulary are selected with this unified theme in mind. Threading everything together is a series of landscaped courts developed with sensitivity and care—and enriched with art, through which users pass either singly or in groups without interference from automobiles or service vehicles. All parking and deliveries are confined to the levels below.

Achieving even the main points of a mixed-use credo is seldom easy. Existing zoning ordinances in Atlanta did not foresee a multi-use urban complex, so much patient dialogue with enforcement agencies was necessary before variances were issued. And the impact of the project on surrounding neighborhoods required detailed study and careful cushioning.

Colony Square, like so many current projects, has not been made exempt from the seventies. Caught in the credit squeeze, its financing has undergone revision recently and is still, at present writing, the subject of some uncertainty.

But what has happened here in Atlanta, and elsewhere, is that a group of buildings demonstrate that they can do more than meet their own individual requirements. Their overlapping functions have been made complementary and the amenities this situation creates provide one of the hallmarks of hardworking and distinguished urban space. More of the same would be welcome in cities large and small across the country.

COLONY SQUARE, Atlanta. Architects: *Jova Daniels Busby—Stanley Daniels, principal-in-charge; Brian Gracie, project coordinator; Joseph League, Jr., Robert Guinn, Kenneth Mattie, project architects.* Engineers: *Prybylowski & Gravino, Bennett & Pless* (structural); *Newcomb & Boyd* (mechanical). Contractor: *Holder Construction Company.*

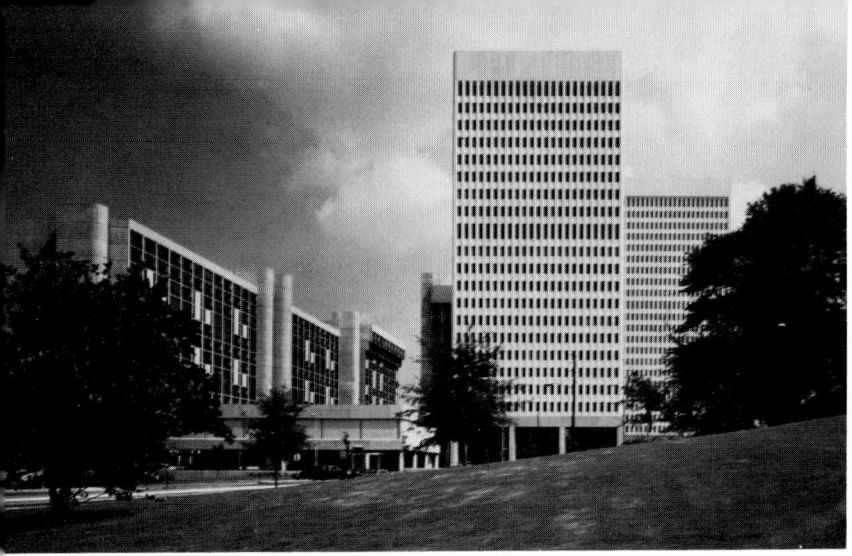

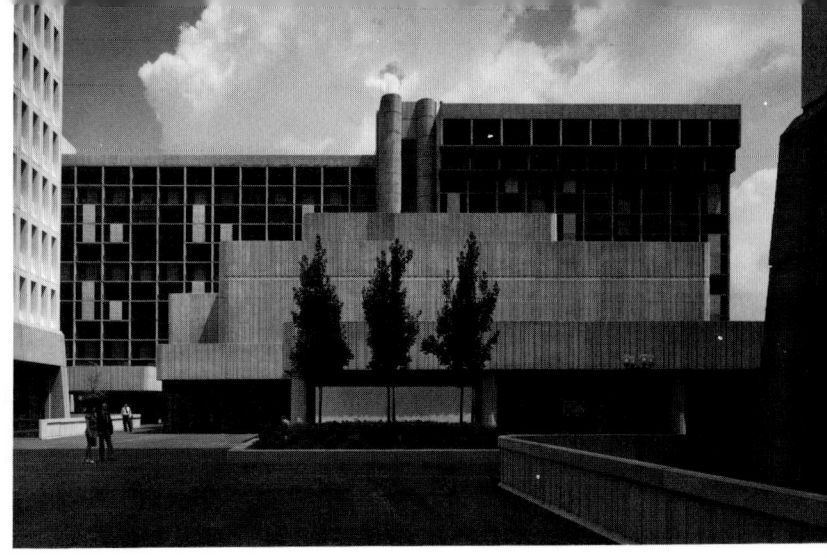

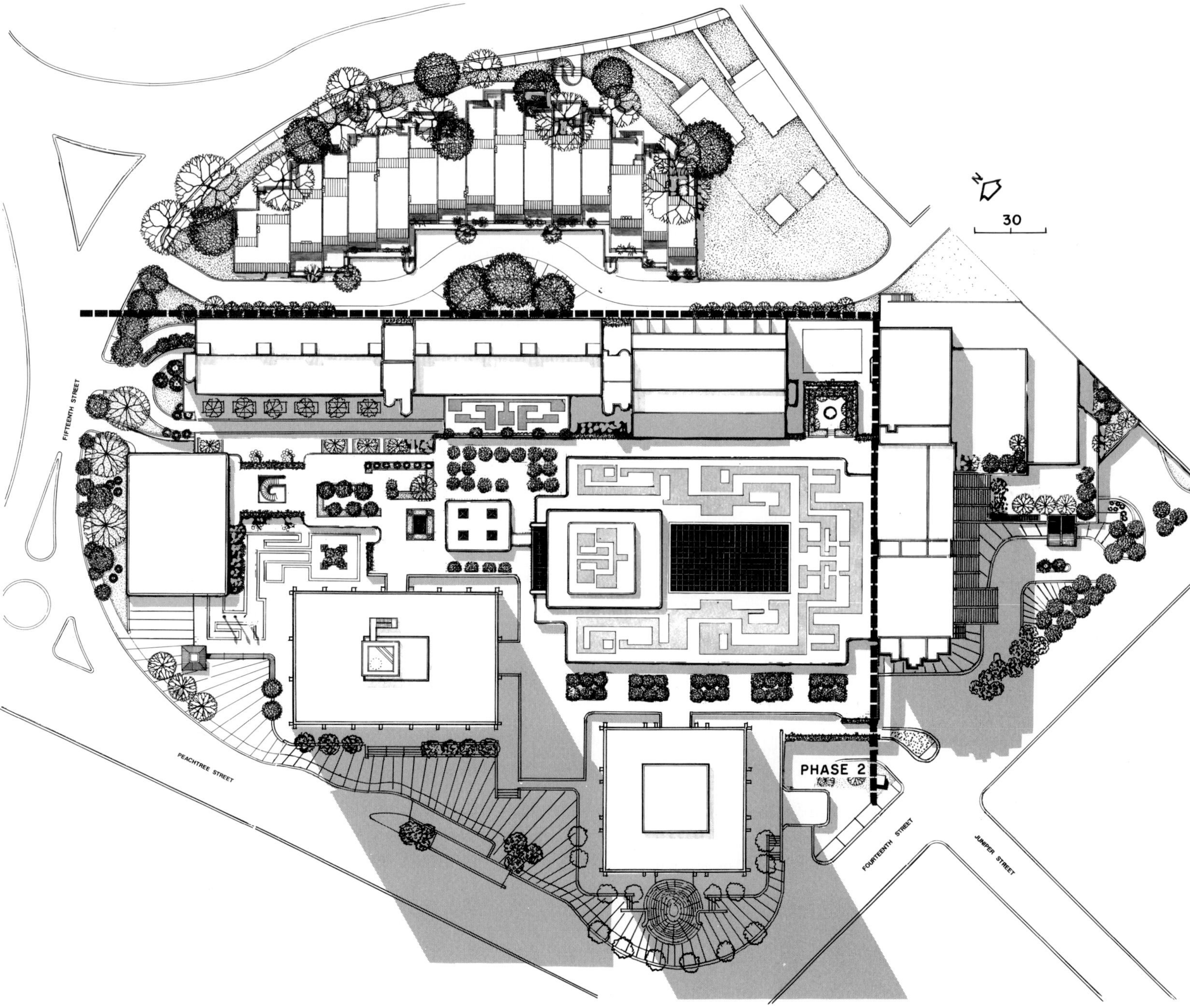
N
30
FIFTEENTH STREET
PEACHTREE STREET
PHASE 2
FOURTEENTH STREET
JUNIPER STREET

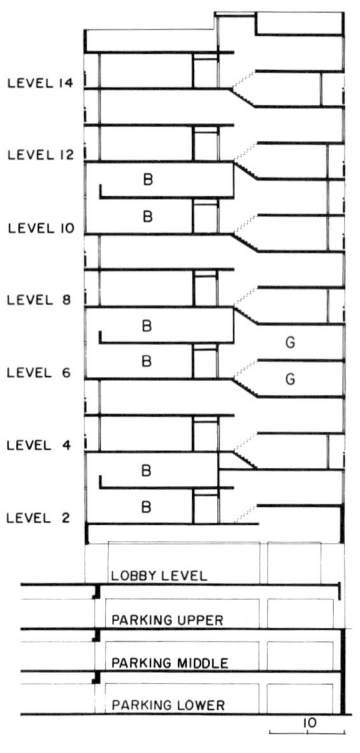

LEVEL 14	
LEVEL 12	B
LEVEL 10	B
LEVEL 8	B
LEVEL 6	B G
	B G
LEVEL 4	B
LEVEL 2	B
LOBBY LEVEL	
PARKING UPPER	
PARKING MIDDLE	
PARKING LOWER	

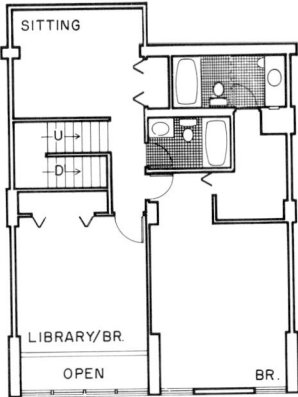
UNIT B, UPPER FLOOR

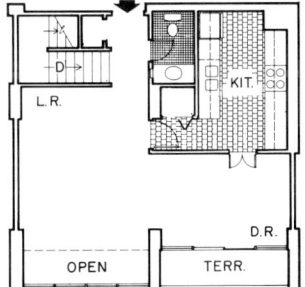
UNIT B, LOWER FLOOR

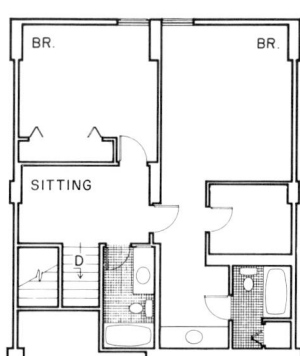
UNIT G, UPPER FLOOR

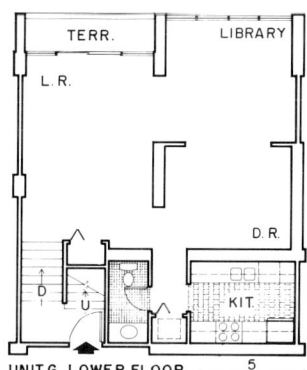
UNIT G, LOWER FLOOR

The section (opposite, left) is taken through Colony house, the project's 14-story apartment tower. Because of its unusual skip floor design, a wide variety of duplex plans are available, each with easy access from a double-height elevator lobby. Typical apartment plans (type B and G) shown (above), are located on the structure's sixth floor.

Chapter Three

LOW-RISE URBAN AND SUBURBAN CONDOMINIUMS AND APARTMENTS

Good low-rise urban and suburban clustered housing is as hard or harder to design than a good custom built single family house. As RECORD pointed out in a study of clustered housing (October 1978), the individuals whose needs and aspirations should be given built form are unknown, and so the task becomes to provide an empty but flexible stage for them rather than a complete setting — a fact, incidentally, that some architects find hard to accept. Another difficulty is that the collective social purposes which a group of houses tend to express are, in the case of cluster developments, designed in one swoop by one designer, so they are not collective at all — or, if the designer is a good one, they are only collective by proxy. Perhaps here, too, the task is to provide an empty stage, but one attractive enough to invite embellishment.

Related to this dilemma is the question of image. Should housing do what Louis Sauer Associates' skillfully does and modulate itself to the Philadelphia landmarks around it (pages 90-91)? Or should it look "modern" as the four speculative townhouses of Burdette Keeland's do (pages 58-59)? Or should it look "traditional" as Callister Payne and Bischoff's does (pages 92-93)? The first is as sensible and modest as the second is exciting and the third comforting and there seem to be no clear winners.

Another vexing problem — perhaps the least easily resolved of all — is that of the automobile. People feel ambivalent about it anyway. It is a friend and a necessity when we want it, a foe and an eyesore when we don't. In a single-family house, the car with its contradictory meanings can be successfully hidden away in the garage. In the densities to be found in cluster housing, however, the number of cars and the parking spaces and roadways that go with them require special attention on the part of the designer. Unfortunately architects who think of cars as a convenience put them close to the units. If they think of them as eyesores they banish them to the edge of the site. A good solution in the collection on the following pages is Moshe Safdie's (pages 86-89), which puts the car near but well out of sight beneath a pedestrian mall.

Not only is cluster housing often more difficult to design than the custom built house but it is more difficult to accomplish in practical terms. It requires a more elaborate political, social and economic process and a skillful negotiation of all the practical obstacles is essential. But it is important to remember that housing, like houses, is not just about finance, or about government, or about technology, or even about architectural "art," but it is about people and their simultaneously individual and social selves.

Karl Riek photos

great majority of whom are bound to react negatively. But before dismissing the project out of hand it is worth asking not if this is a bad idea but, if it really is, why? Curiously, there do not seem to be any really ready answers to all of the usual objections. Do these imitations violate the spirit of the originals? Yes, but so did Jefferson's Rotunda violate the spirit of the Pantheon without being a bad building. Is it wrong to use one form (a single house) as the stylistic trapping of another? Maybe, but people have been doing it for centuries. Is it "modern"? Anything built in the 1970s is by definition "modern." Conversely, even faithful imitations of Georgian houses built in the 1930s now look 1930s. Is it well done? Well, that's harder, and is also probably the crux, and one worth pondering in the historicism racket: the final question is not so much *that* you do it as it is how well, and that can be anybody's guess.

Victoria Mews walls itself around its site to enclose a central, private courtyard from which all of the apartments are entered. It is designed to contain 87 different units, all with the full battery of modern conveniences and in the luxury-price category.

VICTORIA MEWS, San Francisco, California. Architects: *Barovetto, Ruscitto and Barovetto*. Engineers: *Cole, Yee, and Schubert* (structural); *James Buscitto* (mechanical/electrical). General contractor: *Ralph Larson & Son, Inc.*

2

The architect and developer of these four speculative townhouses in Houston found himself with a small, in-town lot, and he wanted to capture something of the spirit of European and American urban—as opposed to suburban—houses by using nearly all of the land for the houses themselves, their cars, and related services. Accordingly, parking is on grade directly beneath the houses, with some of the living spaces on a ground floor behind (photographs below right). On the roof, two floors above, are spaces for washer and dryer rooms, wet bars, sauna tubs, storage—and for gardening. The middle floors are for sleeping and other living spaces (at the level of the windows and glass blocks on the facades in the photograph on the left).

There are two units with three bedrooms and two and a half baths, and two units, which are smaller, with only two bedrooms and two and a half baths. The houses are built of eight-inch concrete block stacked dry without mortar, then coated with fiberglass epoxy. A sheet of white fiber paper is used as a membrane in the glass block to soften the light and also to give better insulation on the south (street side) elevation. Paint grip sheet metal, left natural, is used for all gutters and flashing.

FOUR SPECULATIVE TOWNHOUSES, Houston, Texas. Architects: *Burdette Keeland and Associates*—project architect: *Donald C. Reese.* Engineer: *R. George Cunningham* (structural and mechanical). General contractor: *Keeland Associates, Inc.*

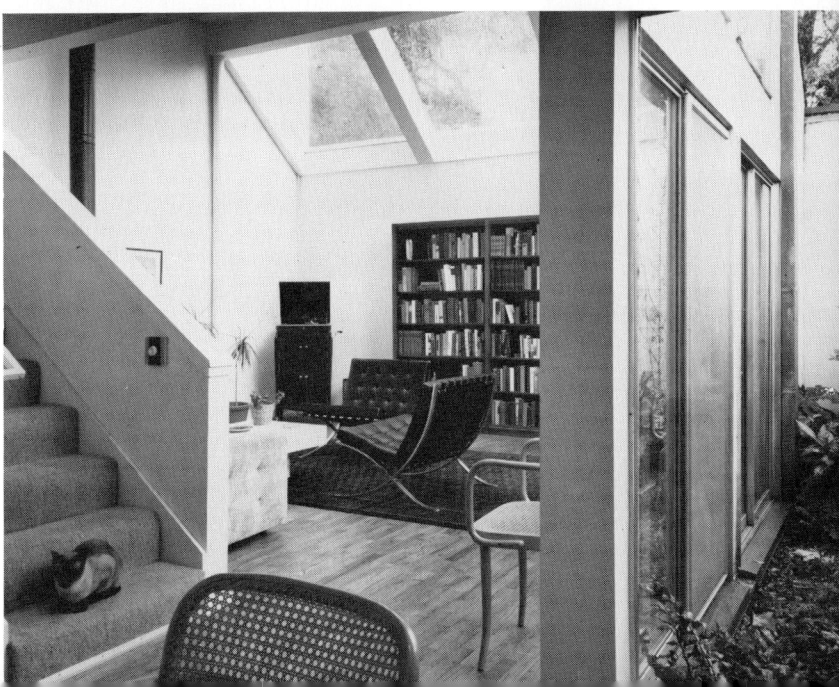

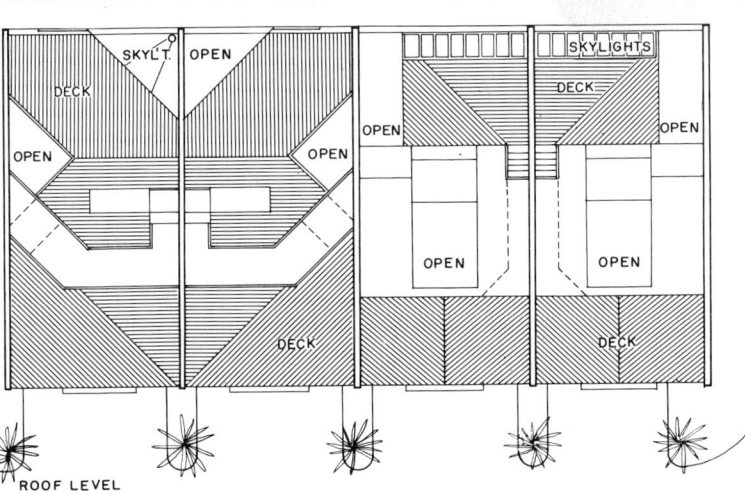

3

Like the townhouses shown on the previous two pages, these houses are the results of their architect's deciding to become a developer and put his architect-designed wares out on the shelf. Like those houses, these have also done well in Houston's bustling real-estate market. Here the program called for five different floor plans, ranging from one to three bedrooms, with different combinations of dens and libraries and other ancillary spaces. All of the units nonetheless have the same over-all shape: a tall, thin (24 feet wide), four-story triangle with a view from the top of the Houston skyline in the distance. (see section below).

Inside, there are a kitchen, dining area, and guest room on the ground floor; the living room is on the second level, overlooking the dining area (photos below). It is reached by a flight of stairs that lead from the entrance gate up to the second level. Some plans also include a library or den at this level. Above it is normally the master bedroom. The roof deck can be reached from it by a cedar stair, which is also connected to all the other floors in order to function doubly as the fire stair. Walls are textured stucco over concrete block

FIVE SPECULATIVE TOWNHOUSES, Houston, Texas. Architects: *Burdette Keeland and Associates*—project architect: *Donald C. Reese*. Engineer: *R. George Cunningham* (structural/mechanical). General contractor: *Keeland Associates, Inc.*

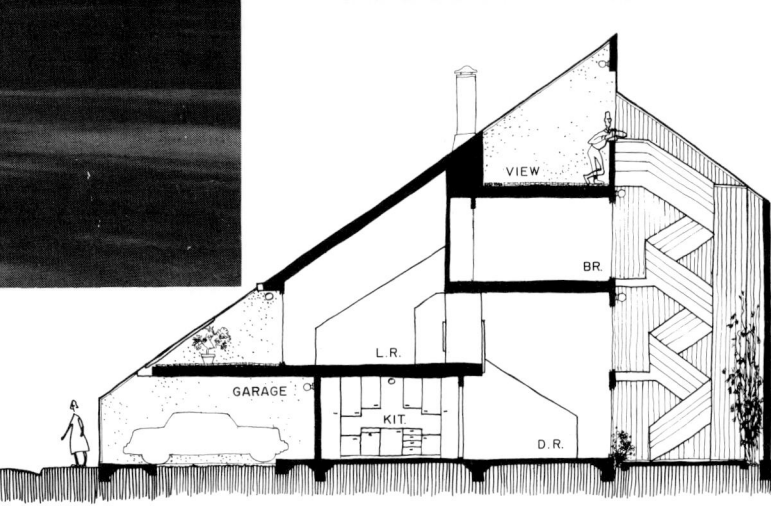

Simon Scott photos

The area known as False Creek is being developed by the city of Vancouver to provide housing for 2,800 people in 850 to 900 units. The planning concept breaks the area down into eight irregularly shaped enclaves, one of which is shown in the aerial photograph below. These enclaves are in turn being developed by a variety of sponsors for non-profit cooperative housing, for limited-dividend senior-citizen housing, for free-market housing, and by a number of other institutions.

Working with a cooperative afforded the architects much greater user input than in most housing projects, where the users are anonymous, and a large number of proposed unit types were in fact rejected because of users' preferences. Four types of townhouses were developed, all on a module of fourteen feet; a 24-suite apartment was also designed, in the same vocabulary as the townhouses. For the most part, living spaces face out from the enclaves towards park areas, public squares, and the waterfront beyond.

FALSE CREEK CO-OP HOUSING, Vancouver, British Columbia. Architects: *Henriquez Architects Urban Designers.* Engineers: *C.Y. Loh Associates Engineering Ltd.* (structural); *Keen Engineering Ltd.* (mechanical); *Nemetz Engineering Ltd.* (electrical). Consultant: *Jeffrey Phillips* (landscape). Contractor Project Manager: *Frank Stanzl Construction Ltd.*

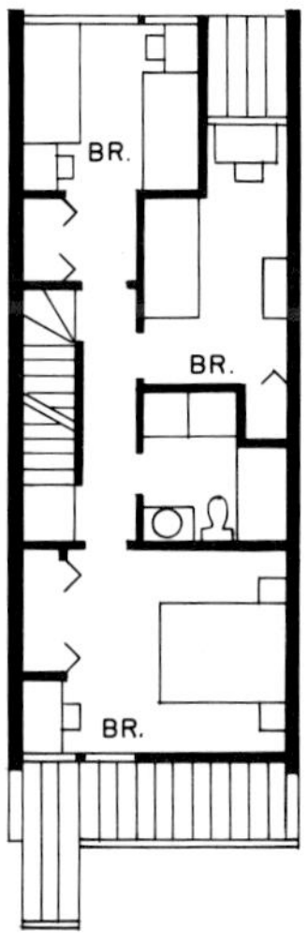

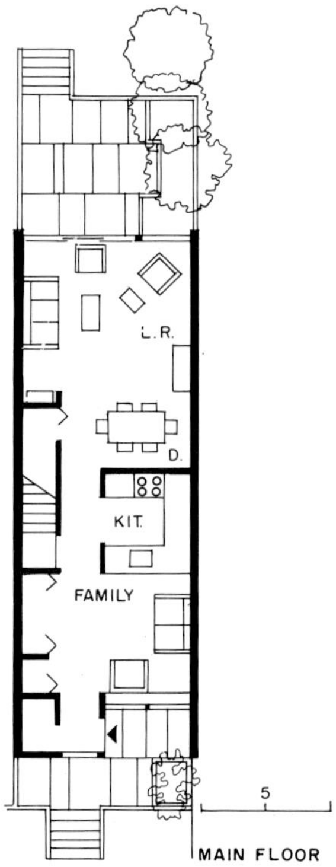

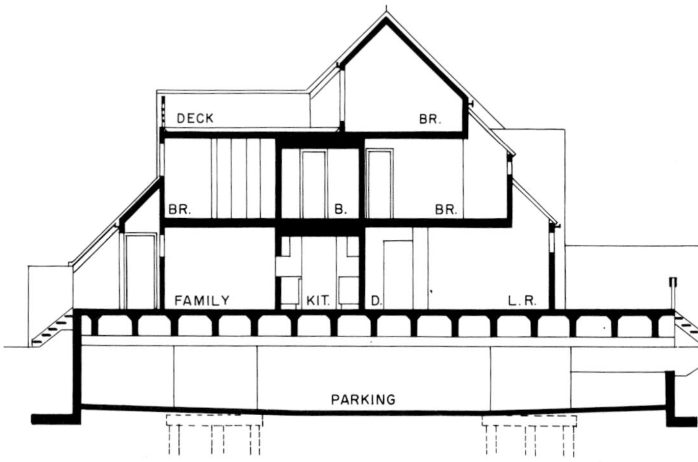

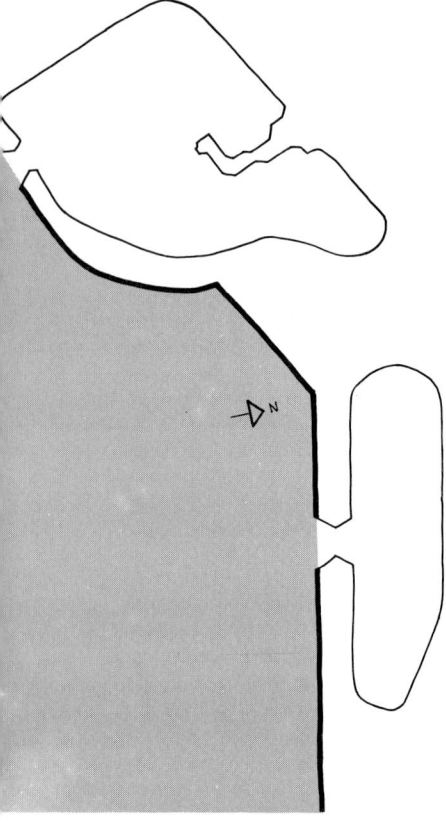

5

Located on two islands in a large, man-made lagoon near the southern tip of San Francisco Bay, this condominium development provides a fascinating geometrical configuration in which all apartments have a view to the water. Excellent site planning and design amenities in individual units create one of the most pleasant new housing developments in the area.

All condominiums are organized into six-unit, rectangular buildings—each with four flats and two townhouses. The ground level consists of two flats facing the water, and either an eight- or 12-car garage, always facing the street; the upper level consists of two, two-story townhouses in the center, flanked by two, one-story flats.

On the small island (bottom left) the buildings are positioned around the perimeter, with a circulation spine in the center, serving both pedestrian and automobile traffic. To obtain views to the water for each apartment and provide visual interest from across the lagoon, the buildings were staggered. The clubhouse—as focal point of the development—is located in the middle of the island near the entrance.

As an intentional contrast to other housing in the area, the project was painted white, and accented with yellow awnings, cedar wood details, and blue ceramic tile on roofs and as trim on windows and stair rails. Extensive landscaping, especially along streets, includes trees between garage doors.

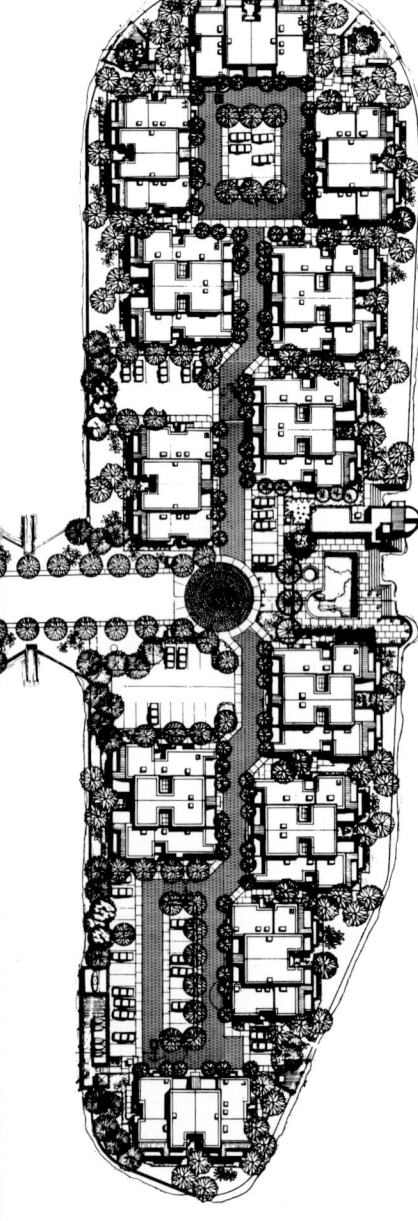

THE ISLANDS
Architects: Fisher-Friedman Associates
—A. Robert Fisher, Rodney Friedman, Robert J. Geering
242 California Street
San Francisco, California
Project name: The Islands
Location: Foster City, California
Owner: Vintage Properties
Engineers: L. F. Robinson & Associates (structural)
Burlogar, Long & Associates (soils)
Galloway & Associates (civil)
Landscape architects: Anthony M. Guzzardo & Associates
Contractor: Herman Christensen & Son
Photographer: Joshua Freiwald

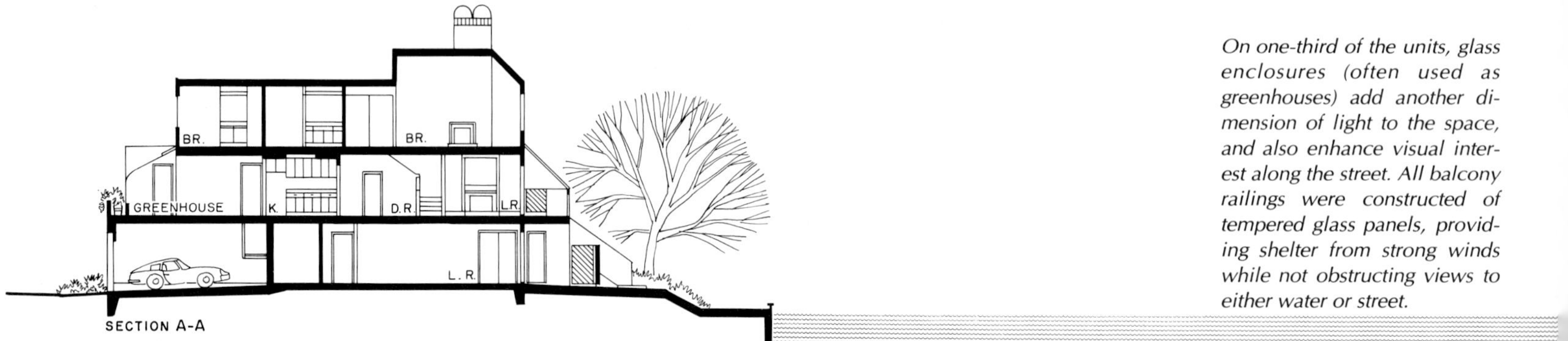

SECTION A-A

On one-third of the units, glass enclosures (often used as greenhouses) add another dimension of light to the space, and also enhance visual interest along the street. All balcony railings were constructed of tempered glass panels, providing shelter from strong winds while not obstructing views to either water or street.

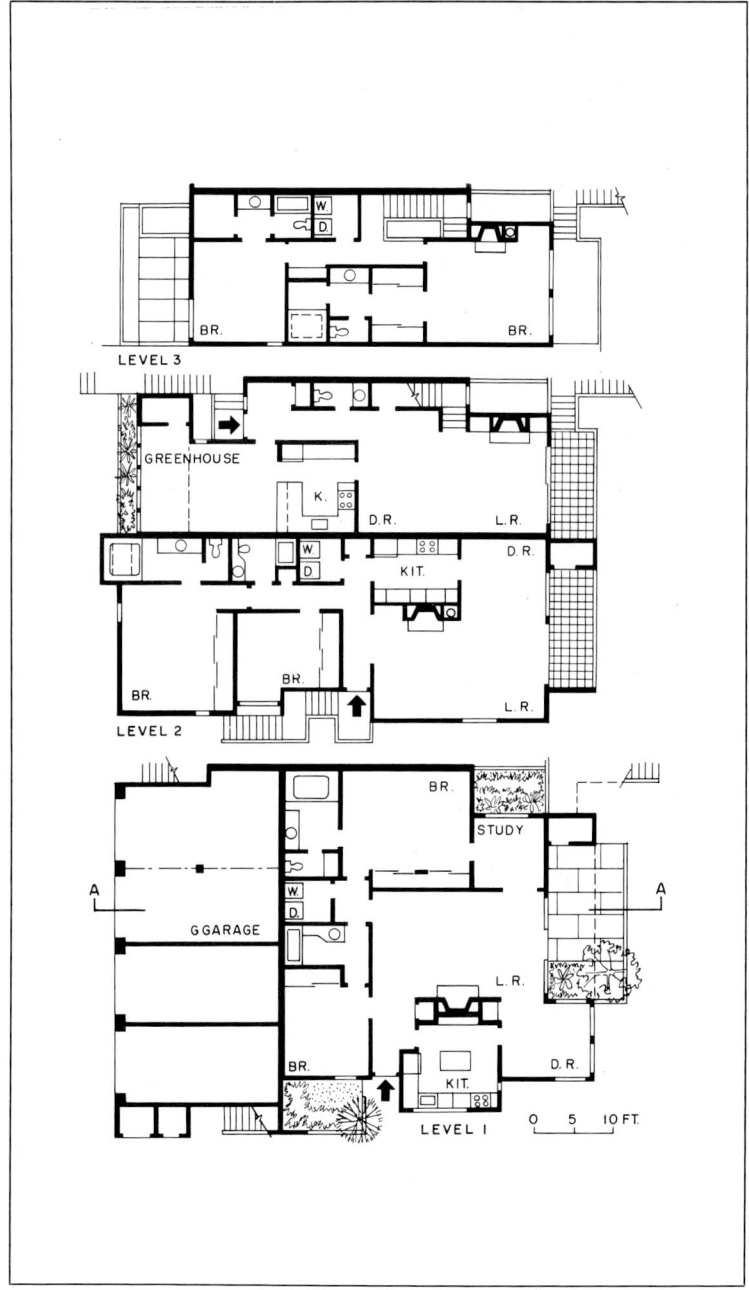

6

On the banks of Yaquina Bay in the small coastal town of Newport, Oregon, a new condominium complex has been partially completed as a marina-resort. A large complex, it will upon completion consist of 185 living units, recreation center, restaurant, convention center, commercial and maintenance building and rental boat moorings. To date, 103 units have been completed.

Designed to emphasize the salient feature of the site—its proximity to the water—the condominiums conform to the slope of the bank with the majority of the complex constructed on a bench of land near the shoreline. An angled roof line for all housing not only permits the maximum amount of sun to penetrate each unit, while not hindering views from housing on the upper slope, but visually reduces the bulk of the complex. Units are clustered together in the tradition of a fishing village. Timber construction and the prominent use of cedar shingles on the exterior allow the new structures to harmonize with the surrounding forested area.

Used mostly on a seasonal basis, only one- and two-bedroom apartments were designed, with a variety of floor plans; the largest townhouse is 1200 square feet. Each unit has a separate entrance on the inland side, connected to a system of boardwalks joining the complex with the marina and nearby beaches.

The partner-in-charge of the project is also a vice president and a director of the development firm. "In this position," Rand says, "we have been able to have more input in the decision-making process, bringing our professional talents to bear on the problems."

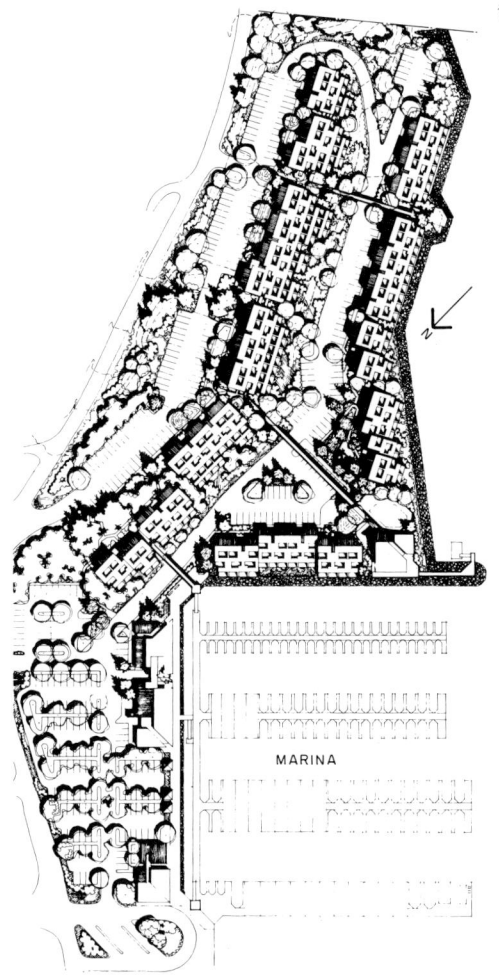

EMBARCADERO CONDOMINIUMS
Architects: Campbell-Yost-Grube
  2040 S.W. Jefferson Street
  Portland, Oregon
  Barry A. Rand, partner-in-charge
  Richard A. Campbell, design partner
  David M. M. Shelton, project architect
Developer: Yaquina Development Corp.
Engineers:
  Harlan Luck (structural)
  Dames & Moore (soils)
  Mc-An Engineering (mechanical)
  Langton-Mehlig & Associates (electrical)
Acoustical consultant: Daly Engineering Co.
Interior design: Kahl's Interiors
Contractor: Todd Building Co.
Photographer: C. Bruce Forster

Given the site's topography, the living units were positioned so the ones on the lower slope (above) have the water and boat mooring slips at their "front door," while the higher units have a panoramic view of the bay.

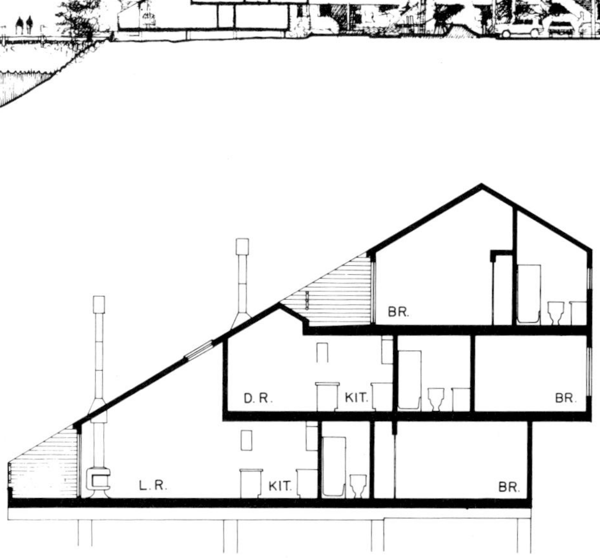

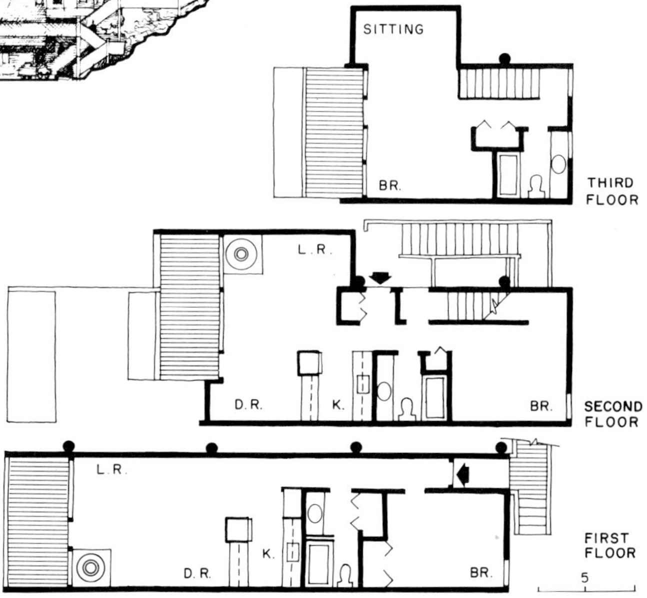

7

The site is 24 acres of orchard land bounded by a commuter rail line to the north, a major highway to the East and a group of single-family houses to the south. The Township, with its proud Revolutionary associations, was sensitive to the potential impact of this 220-unit cluster on the community. Huygens and Tappé therefore worked especially closely with the Township to accommodate their wishes in matters of siting and development.

Paved and built-upon areas were arranged to preserve the existing landscape wherever possible. Finish materials and building forms were designed to respond to the region's historical character. Two entrances have been provided to reduce on-site vehicular traffic and apartment units form cul-de-sac clusters off the main loop road. The original farmhouse was retained to give the new community a firm historical centerpiece.

The orientation of the apartments is away from the railroad and the main highway and toward a brook that runs through the site.

Fences and other external enclosures are stained, rough-sawn plywood with battens. The living units are of conventional wood construction, clad in narrow clapboards with corner boards and wood trim—all designed to evoke the traditional village image of New England but provide for these owners many of the amenities of contemporary life. Two features stand out: the saltbox profiles and the unambiguous, no-nonsense relationship of building to site. Both are old New England virtues.

CONCORD GREENE APARTMENTS
Architects: Huygens and Tappé, Inc.
  462 Boylston Street
  Boston, Massachusetts
Owner:
  Concord Junction Realty Trust
Engineers:
  Steco Engineering (structural)
  Comfort Air Systems (mechanical)
  R.D. Nelson (site)
Landscape consultant:
  Gerald F. McNeil
Contractor: E.A. Comeau, Inc.
Photographer: Steve Rosenthal

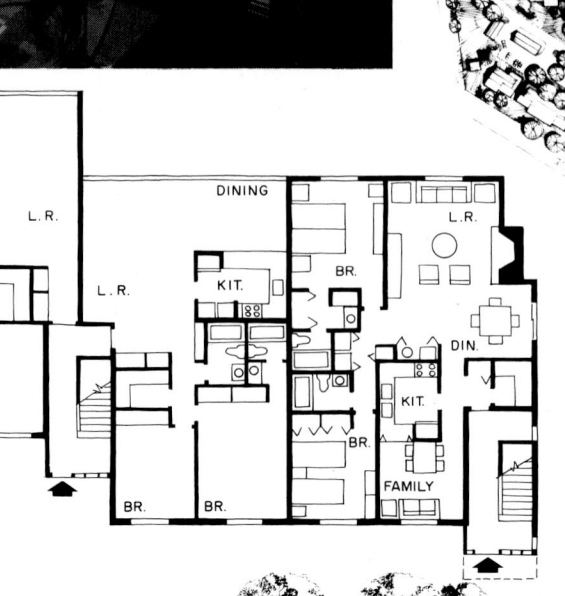

8

The brightly-painted and scalloped elevations of this 58-unit complex tend to belie the impressive amount of sober thought that went into its planning and design. Located on a 2-acre site in a Vancouver suburb, the buildings are carefully view-oriented to a golf course and park lands on three sides, and access to the surrounding grounds is easy.

All units are either split-level, two-story townhouses or corner "bungalows." Each type is designed to provide an unusual degree of amenity. Automobiles are accommodated on a parking deck that gives directly to the split-level units. The townhouses are entered from a third-floor pedestrian street that is paved, enclosed from the weather, and landscaped with hanging plants and potted shrubs (see photos next pages). It is a remarkably pleasant access space. The breakfast spaces of each townhouse project into this corridor and are skylighted.

In this way, each space borrows light from the corridor skylights above. Another thoughtful planning feature: the townhouse units are zoned vertically with main living spaces on the entry level and sleeping spaces below. This device provides a sound buffer and reduces unwelcome noise between units. The (lower) bedroom levels are reached by interior stairs from the living level above or can be entered directly from a semi-private corridor below, thus providing a second means of egress. Most of the townhouses have a small loft space above the living areas; others have roof decks as an option to the lofts. The planning throughout is tight and efficient.

The lively elevations grow out of the desire to articulate each apartment in the mass, giving each an identity as well as a clear relationship with the others. The site organization permits the surrounding parkland to be drawn into the plan at the center to create a landscaped green shared by all.

THE FAIRWAYS
Architects: R.E. Hulbert & Partners
   215 14th Street
   West Vancouver, British Columbia
   Eugene V. Radvenis—design
   John C.H. Porter—technical coordination
Owner: H.A. Roberts Group, Ltd.
Engineers:
   David Nairne & Associates (structural)
   Cook, Pickering, Doyle (foundations)
   Perelco Design Ltd. (mechanical)
Interiors: public spaces by architect;
   unit interiors by Peter Garret
Landscape architects:
   John Lantzius & Associates
Contractor: Bidwell Construction Ltd.
Photographer: Simon Scott

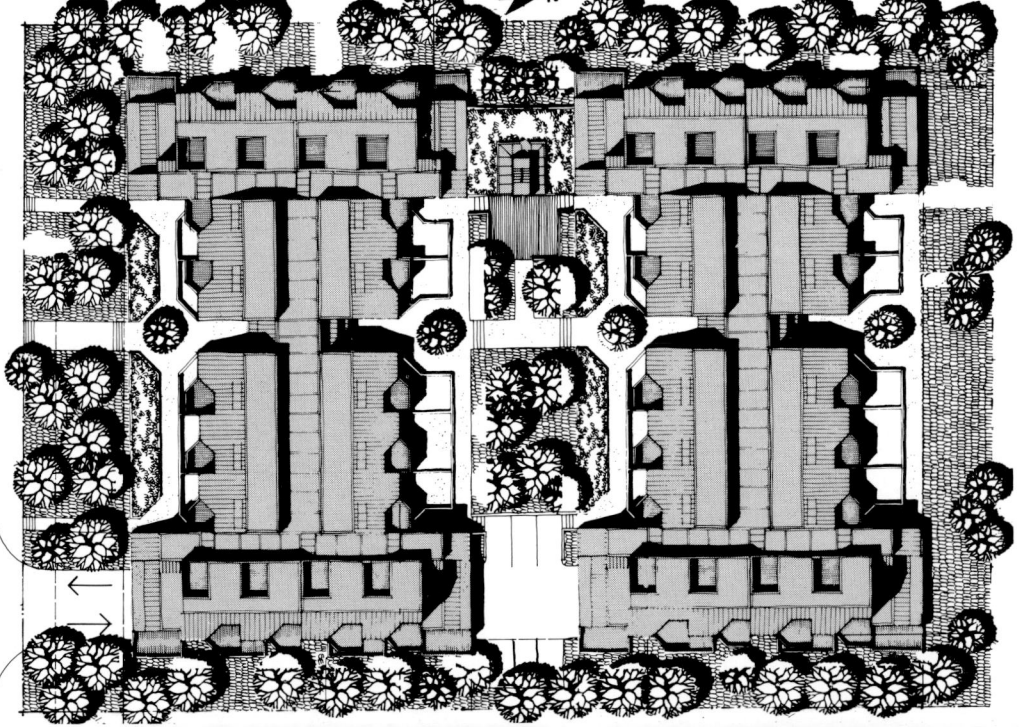

The structure is a three-story wood frame over a concrete foundation and parking deck. Cedar siding, placed horizontally and diagonally, is the principal exterior finish. Chimney flues are baked enamel over stainless; roof finish is metal sheet with standing seams.

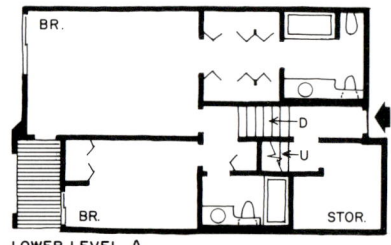

LOWER LEVEL A

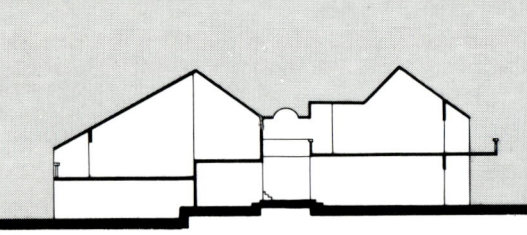

9

On a gently-contoured, wooded site outside Houston, a site that had formerly been a campsite for Boy Scouts and a site that deserved sensitive development, the architects have completed Phases One and Two of a projected 800-townhouse planned unit development. The 146 units in the first two phases are aimed at a particular market group: "empty nesters" whose children have grown up and moved away. In spite of this, the units are comparatively large and generously proportioned. All are either two-, three-, or four-bedroom designs of 2,300 to 3,200 square feet. To furnish maximum light and openness, all are planned with a double height atrium space between the living areas and the bedrooms. By this device, daylight is admitted through clerestories deep into the interiors.

Openness, in fact, was a prime concern of architects and site planners from the start. The units are clustered in a relaxed pattern and linked by sinuous, informal trails and walkways all enriched by landscaping and augmented with attractive benches. The "pull" along these pathways, the invitation to stroll, to pause, to linger, to stroll some more is almost irresistible.

The houses are massed with shed roofs facing the street so that their apparent bulk is visually diminished. The architect describes the vocabulary of brick veneer, wood boards and shingle as "a blend of California contemporary design with traditional forms that evolves into something both new and old, but not regional or specifically derivative of any familiar style."

HUDSON ON MEMORIAL
Architects: Kaplan/McLaughlin/Diaz
  222 Vallejo Street
  San Francisco, California
  Peter Gordon, designer
Associate architects:
  Langwith, Wilson, King and House
Developers: Christiana Southwest
Engineers: Al Epps (structural)
  Conditioned Air (mechanical)
  Stacey (electrical)
Graphics: Kuest Corporation
Contractor: Christiana Southwest
Photographer: Joshua Freiwald

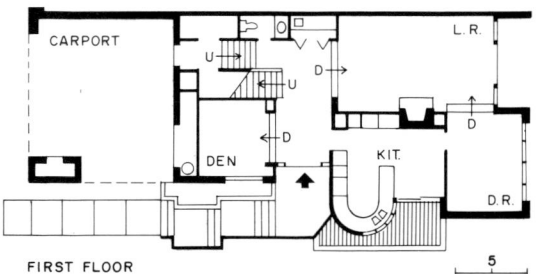
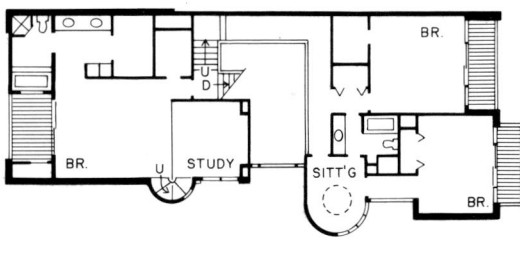

FIRST FLOOR

SECOND FLOOR

Physical security was a significant factor in the design of this townhouse complex. Access to the units in each development phase is through a single checkpoint that has direct communications with each unit as well as with the security control center.

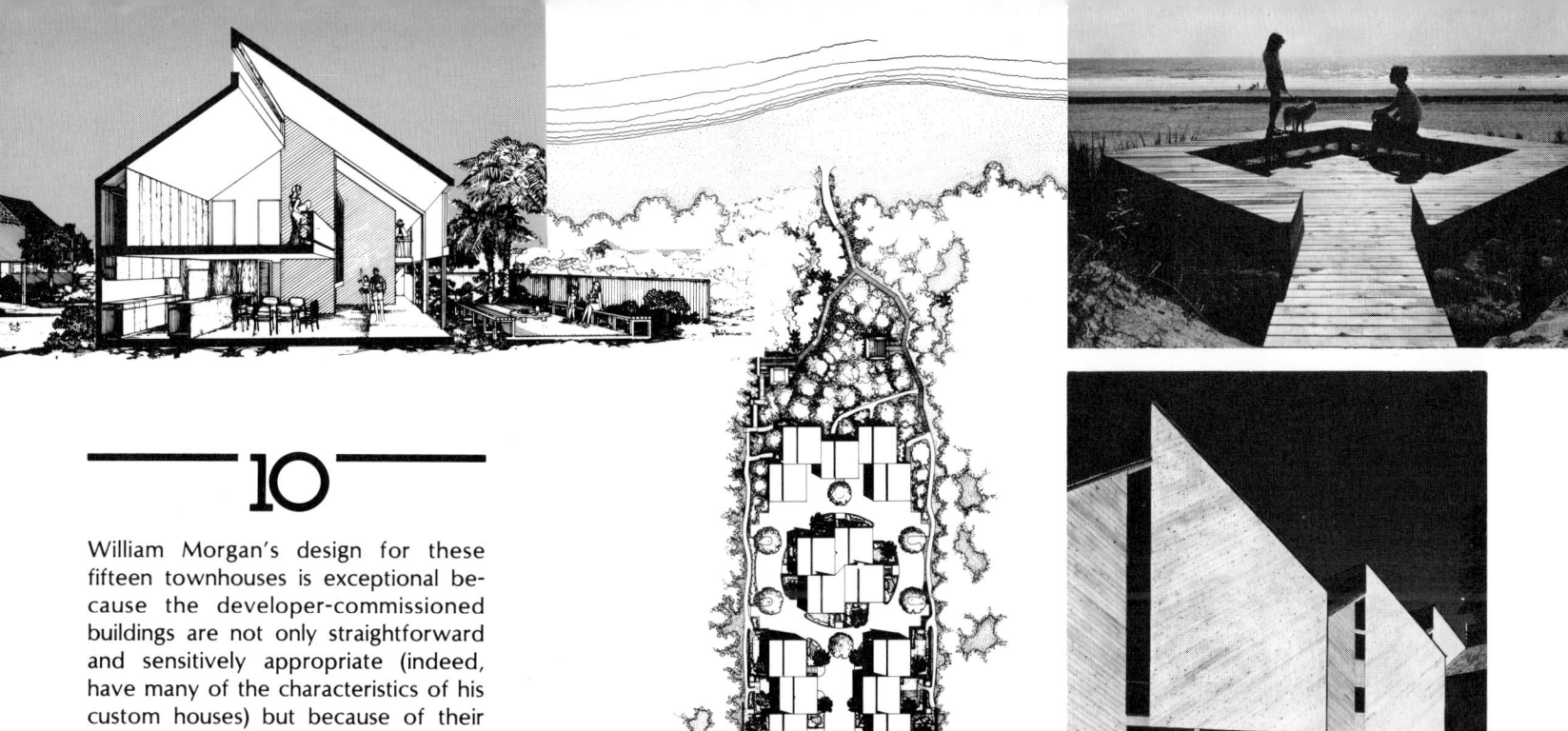

10

William Morgan's design for these fifteen townhouses is exceptional because the developer-commissioned buildings are not only straightforward and sensitively appropriate (indeed, have many of the characteristics of his custom houses) but because of their unusually sympathetic and innovative site planning. In a market that has not always placed much emphasis on design quality, these units are boldly sculptural and at the same time blend with the undisturbed natural setting.

Typically, there are three bedrooms in each 1500 square-foot unit. The second-floor bedroom overlooks the living room, separated only by a balcony railing. The third bedroom occupies a crow's nest position in a third-level loft.

To keep construction costs down, the wood-frame structures are repetitive, although the square plans have been turned and flopped to provide variety. Accordingly, units are either arranged in a staggered line or in pinwheel fashion, and the units nearest the beach are raised for views.

But the greatest interest is generated by Morgan's sensitive site plan. Despite the formal, almost urban massing, the plan preserves much of the site's original character—including major trees and most importantly the dune separating the buildings from the ocean beach. Resisting the unfortunate common practice of leveling these dunes to provide views, Morgan instead chose to accentuate the contained-in-a-forest quality of the site and to provide common access for all units over the dune. And by such use of the beach frontage, Morgan has opened the way to a future expansion of equally desirable units across the main road.

SEA GARDENS
Architects: William Morgan Architects
  220 East Forsyth Street
  Jacksonville, Florida
Structural engineers:
  Haley Keister Associates, Inc.
Mechanical and electrical:
  Roy Turknett Engineers
Contractor: Demetree Industries, Inc.
Photographer: Otto Baitz

11

On Grand Island, near Niagara Falls, the Landings is Phase One of a projected 2400 unit planned unit development called River Oaks. The first 26 units, in six blocks, border a golf course and are skewed at 45 degrees to the axis of the fairway and at 90 degrees to adjacent blocks. The triangular areas created by this siting were lowered some two feet to create a semi-private buffer area against the fairway—a design device intended to minimize encroachment by golfers in search of errant balls. Another grade change occurs closer to the buildings and defines each unit's private outdoor space. On the side away from the fairway, each unit also has its own arrival court, defined on two sides by structure and on the third by an earth berm that provides a sense of partial enclosure.

The units were planned so that they attached at the point of narrowest dimension. The party wall thus created became a fire wall as well and all nonhabitable spaces—stairs, baths, kitchens—were backed up to this wall. Plumbing and electrical chases were also incorporated and the furring they required provided added sound insulation between units.

In other aspects the plans include the amenities usually offered to a market heavily composed of "empty-nesters"—retirement-aged couples whose children no longer live at home. As many owners of this type are trading down from larger homes they no longer need, the architects have striven to retain certain of the features most closely associated with single-family houses. These include an unusual degree of privacy (no owner overlooks his neighbor's private outdoor areas), attached garage, and a material selection that includes stained cedar clapboard siding and brick pavers in the entry courts.

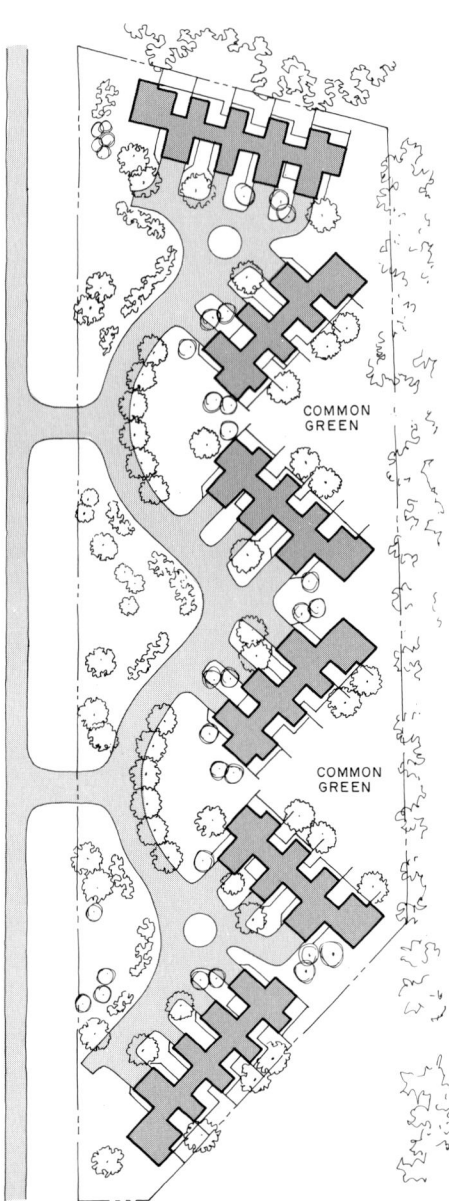

THE LANDINGS
Architects: Morse & Harvey
  350 Madison Avenue
  New York City
Owners: W.R. Development, Inc.
Engineers:
  Antony Vairamides (structural)
  Kravchenko & Assoc. (foundation)
  Goldman Sokolow (mechanical)
Landscape architect:
  Vreeland & Guerriero
Contractor: L.R.F. Construction
Photographer: Jonathan Morse

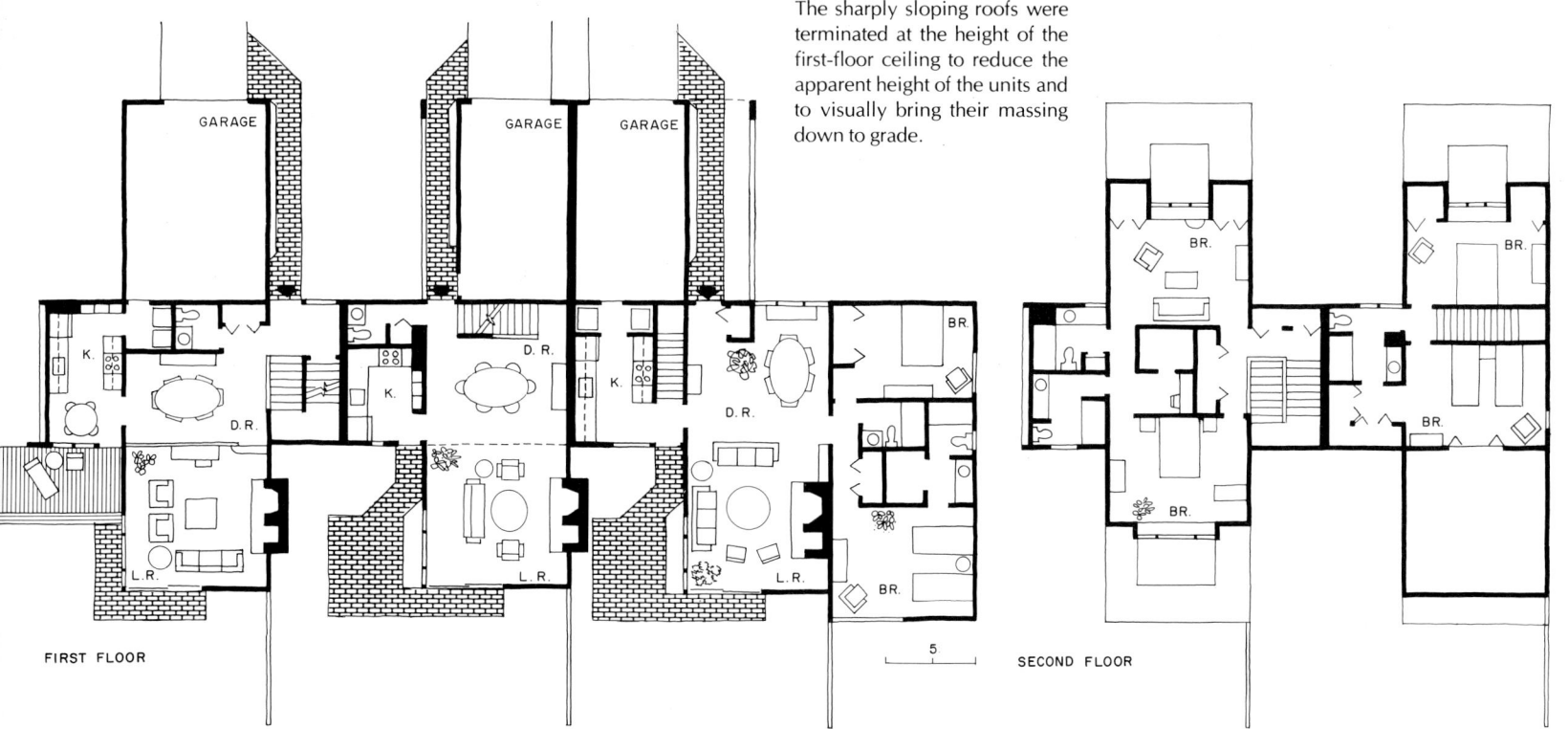

The sharply sloping roofs were terminated at the height of the first-floor ceiling to reduce the apparent height of the units and to visually bring their massing down to grade.

FIRST FLOOR

SECOND FLOOR

81

12

Ethan's Glen is a townhouse development on a site in the memorial area of Houston, 18 minutes drive from downtown. The site is part of a pine forest through which a fairly deep natural gully ran—a problem and a challenge to the developers and to the architects. Instead of retaining it as a gully and bridging it to connect both sides, the architects proposed an earthfill dam at one end to create a lake on which the development could focus. The dam proved doubly useful: its top made an excellent bed for the loop road which had to be built to serve the development. All the townhouses are grouped in clusters of eight around the lake, and the club building of the recreation center, prominently placed at one end of the lake, actually sits on piles in it. The clusters of units, set among the trees, have a long-established look, thanks to the trees—large and small—which were carefully preserved. An ingenious solution to provision of covered parking, however, was the key means of saving the trees: parking (1.5 to 1) for each cluster is provided under half of the cluster by raising the living units half a level, and excavating half a level below grade.

Each two-story townhouse unit is part of an eight-unit building, and each has private outdoor space, screened by fin walls and fences, and shared green open space between the units and along the lake. All units have unusual and interesting volumes, even flat ceilings having a height of nine feet. Exteriors are cedar plank, or shingles left to weather.

The recreation center—a club building, swimming pool and lounge deck which projects over the water—is at the end of the lake farthest from the entrance to Ethan's Glen. The club building is a small but spectacular landmark whose transparency comes from glass walls enclosing a skeletal structure. Like the townhouses, the exterior is cedar siding, but inside, the ceiling is resawn redwood. The roof is blue metal.

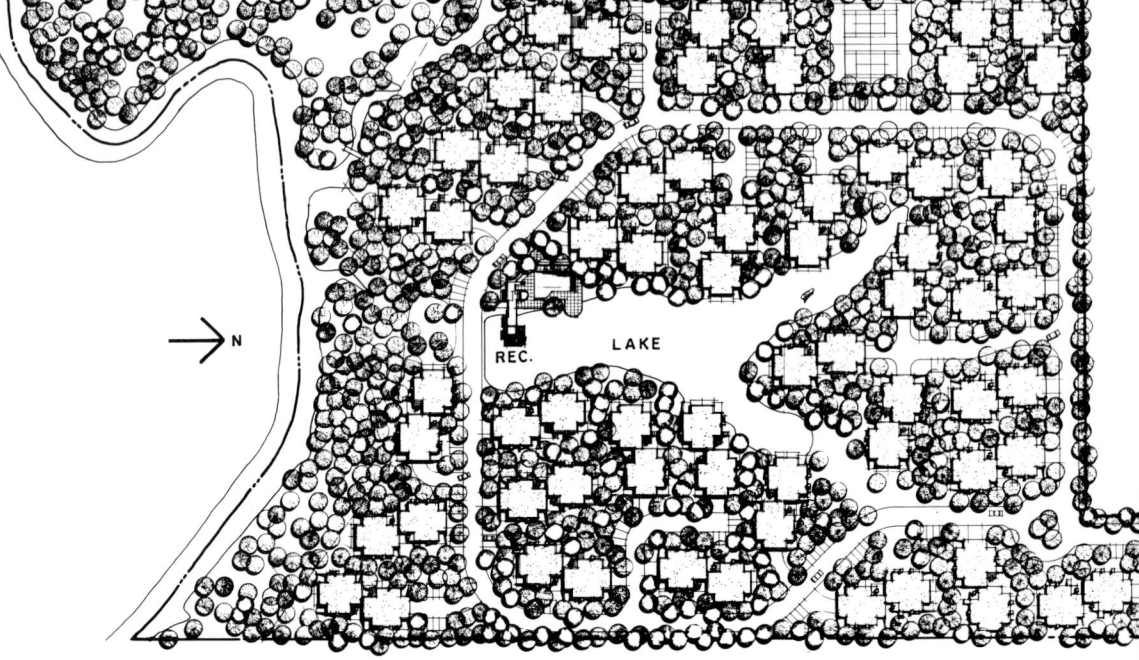

ETHAN'S GLEN
  Architects: Fisher-Friedman Associates
  242 California Street
  San Francisco, California
 Owner/developer: Green Mark, Inc.
 Project name: Ethan's Glen
 Location: Ethan's Glen, Houston, Texas
 Landscape architects:
  Sasaki, Walker Associates
 Builder: Green Mark, Inc.
 Photographer: Joshua Freiwald

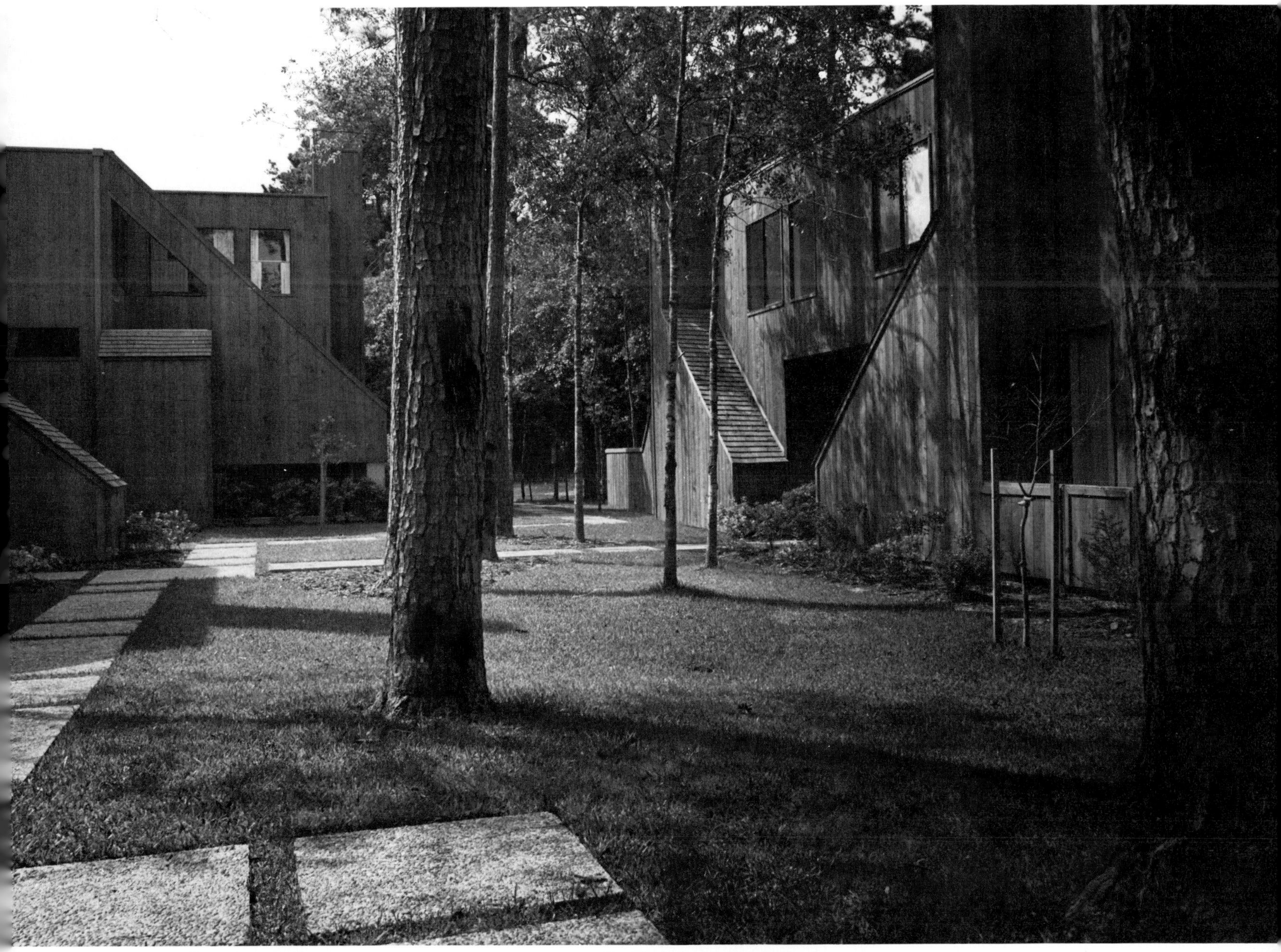

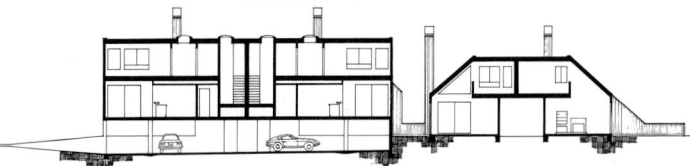

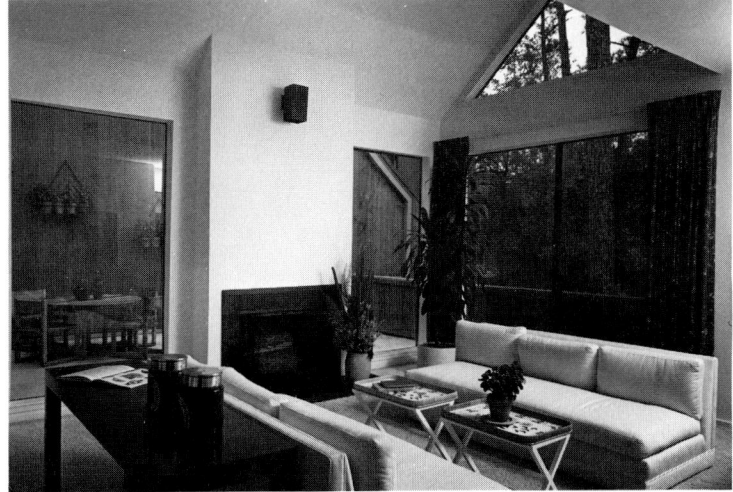

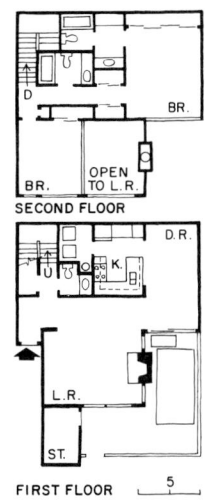

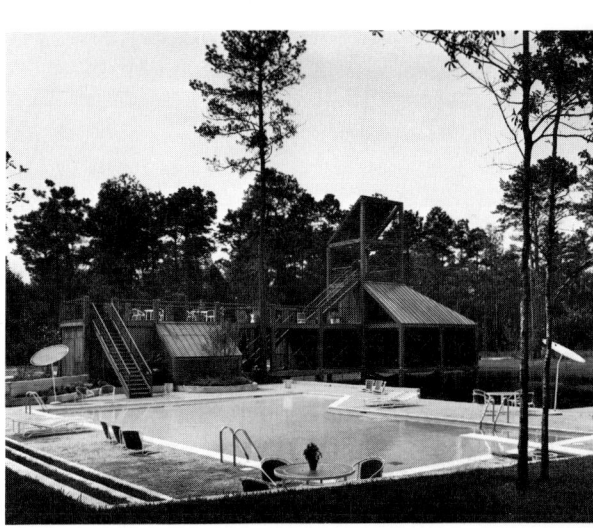

The lake is the focus for the development, all the dwelling units clustered around it, and the recreation center (below right) built on piles in the water. The straight tree trunks offset the angular forms.

D
BR.
BR.
OPEN TO L.R.
SECOND FLOOR
D.R.
K.
L.R.
ST.
FIRST FLOOR
5

13

For a densely forested site near the beach of Hilton Head Island, architects Stoller/Glasser and Marquis Associates developed an extraordinarily inventive scheme that puts 308 units on 20.6 acres—while leaving intact the forest atmosphere. Seemingly complex, the basic plan is quite simple: In each building, two units are stacked.

Placement of the units was done with extreme care. Field locations were made in the field after accurate tree surveys were made. The units were then staked and taped to determine exact locations and first-floor slab elevations. Final site plans were prepared after this field process. Even then, the contractor was given an unusual degree of individual judgment.

The elevated walkway (shown in site plan and section)—which gives so much to the character of Treetops—provides easy access to lower- and upper-level units alike; in turn it is reached by stairs and hydraulic elevators (it averages 13 feet above grade) where it reaches out to the perimeter parking area.

Design and construction combine to assure good acoustical privacy—so often lacking in such dense projects. First, upper-level units are turned "upside-down"; with bedrooms on level 3 and living rooms on level 4. Floors are 6-inch concrete slabs (4 inches of poured concrete over 2-inch precast slabs). Eight-inch block bearing walls between all units serve as fire walls and acoustic separations. Since all units are air-conditioned, windows and sliding doors can be shut against any outside noise. Finally, all units are designed with stairs and bathrooms to the walkway side for separation of major rooms from the walkway—and thus all bedrooms and living rooms open generously to the extraordinary forest views.

From the project, an easement leads to the nearby beach.

Architects: Stoller/Glasser and Marquis Associates—David Evan Glasser, partner-in-charge

Owner: Treetops Associates
Project name: The Treetops
Location: Hilton Head, South Carolina
Engineers: Berkenfeld-Getz (structural)
Interior design: Phyllis Martin-Vegue of Marquis Associates
Landscape architect: Balsley Balsley Kuhl
Lighting consultants: Jules Fisher and Paul Marantz, Inc.
Graphic design: Harper and George Inc.
Contractor: Nello L. Teer
Photographer: Alexandre Georges

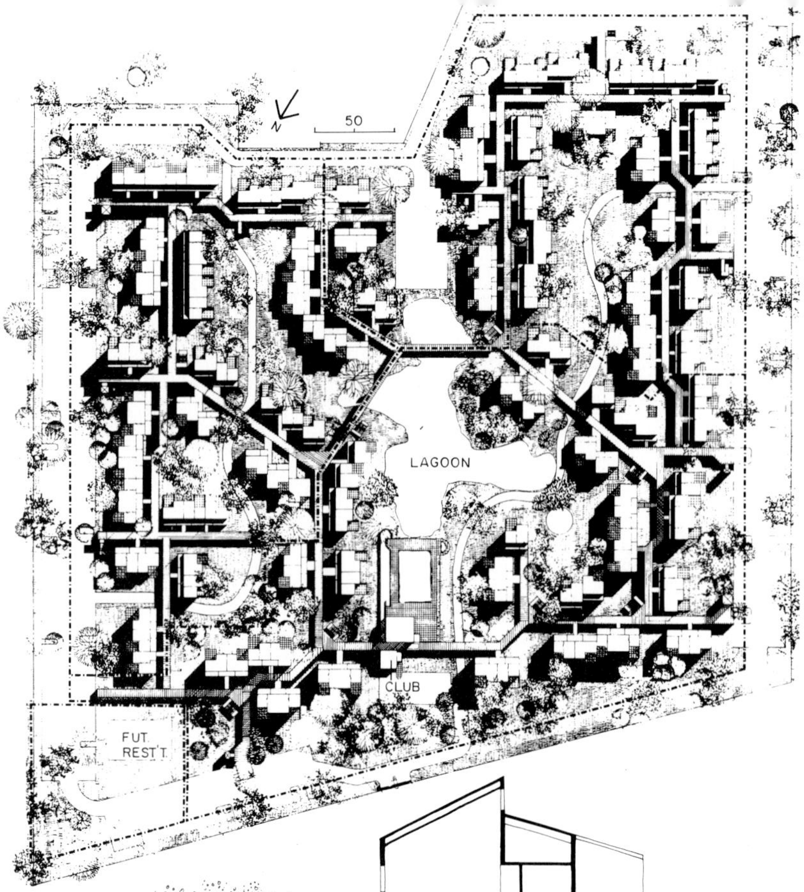

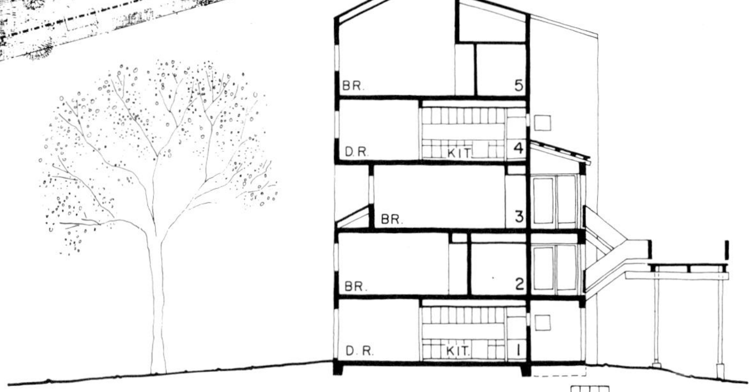

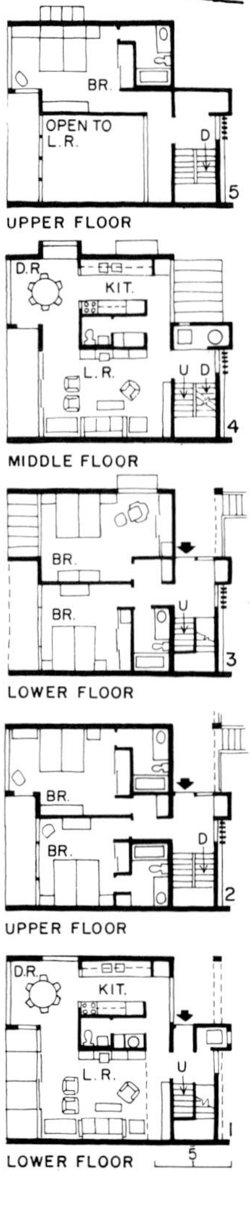

All lower units are two-story, two-bedroom units opening to patios at grade level (see levels 1 and 2 on plan and section, left). Above this base, depending on market needs as the project proceeds, can be placed story-and-a-half one-bedroom units, other two-story, two-bedroom units, or (as in the plan and section) a three-story, three-bedroom unit. This mix in upper level units creates the variety design interest apparent in these photos of the first 78-unit section. Finishes are ¾-inch stucco with fine oyster shell finish, bronze-finish aluminum, rough-sawn cypress.

14

Coldspring is designed to be a 370-acre community within the city of Baltimore and will eventually house 12,400 people in 3,780 units. Its first phase has recently been completed. It consists of 124 units which the architects, Moshe Safdie & Associates, call "deckhouses." These were intended to provide the qualities of a townhouse in an over-all density of about twice that of conventional townhouse developments. To do this without covering the entire site with parking, a pedestrian deck was designed that winds through the buildings at various levels, connected by ramps and stairs and bridges. The deck provides play spaces and also the pedestrian entrances to the houses. Furthermore it covers the parking below. About half of the units are conventional townhouses, and the other half are maisonnettes and duplexes stacked vertically. The lower of these units have direct access from the deck and from the parking area, and also they have gardens. The upper have access one flight above the deck by stairs and have gardens on the roofs of the units below. Another remarkable feature of these housing units is their low price, made possible because, even though the development is privately built, the city of Baltimore, in an effort to stem the flight to the suburbs, has become the construction lender and mortgage holder, aided by Federal development funds.

COLDSPRING, Baltimore, Maryland. Architects: *Moshe Safdie & Associates*. Landscape architects: *Lawrence Halprin and Associates*. Engineers: *Con-*

rad Associates (structural); *Brar/Beauchamp Associates* (mechanical/electrical); *Dewberry, Nealon & Davis* (civil); *Law Engineering Testing Company* (soils/foundations). Consultants: *DeLeuw, Cather & Associates* (transportation); *Gladstone Associates* (economic); *Robert Hughes and Associates* (costs).

The drawing below shows how the basic format of the new housing at Coldspring works. Maisonnettes and complexes are stacked on top of each other in the range of buildings on the left, while more conventional two-story townhouses are across the pedestrian mall on the right. Beneath the mall is the parking area, which receives natural light and ventilation through the open spaces between the edge of the mall and the faces of the buildings; these voids also offer a degree of privacy to the windows facing the mall.

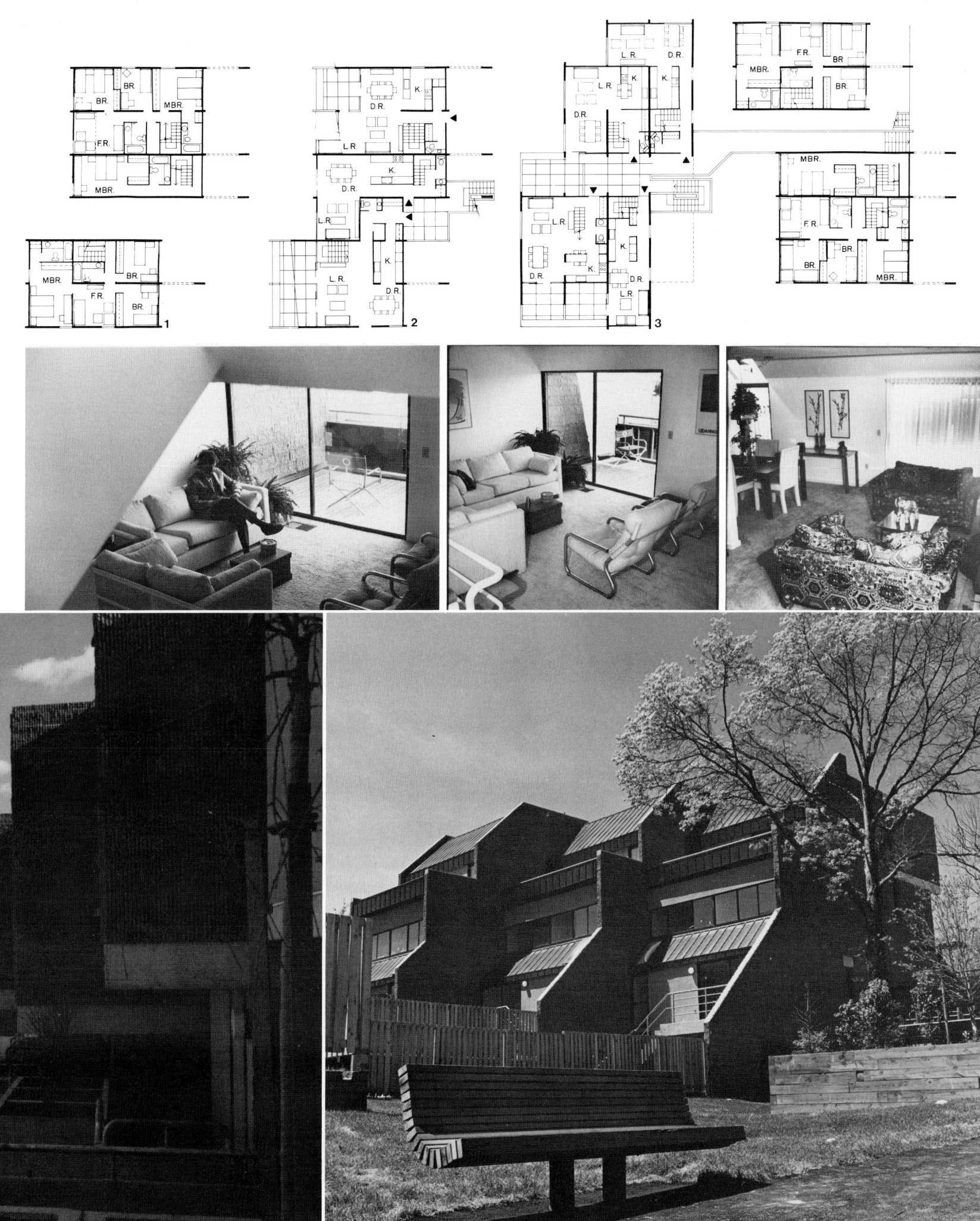

15

This low-rise development consists of eight luxury townhouses on 1.8 acre of cleared land extending the length of one block of Second Street in the Society Hill area of Philadelphia. Second Street connects the restored Head House Market and I.M. Pei's Society Hill Towers, and across the street from the new townhouses are a group of older buildings that have also been restored. Thus the new townhouses were conceived as infill connecting the old with the new while at the same time providing a foil for the historic buildings across the street, and their facades—in the manner of row houses from the past—are related as much to the street as to the individual units, making a single urban thing as well as collection of things. The rear facades are treated less formally, their planes interrupted by balconies.

SECOND STREET TOWNHOUSES, Philadelphia, Pennsylvania. Architects: *Louis Sauer Associates*. Engineers: *Joseph Hoffman and Associates* (structural). General contractor: *Joseph Haas*.

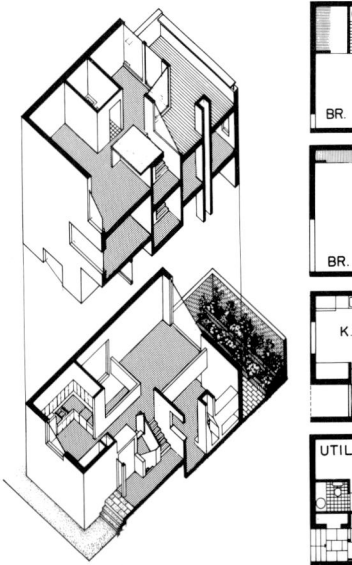
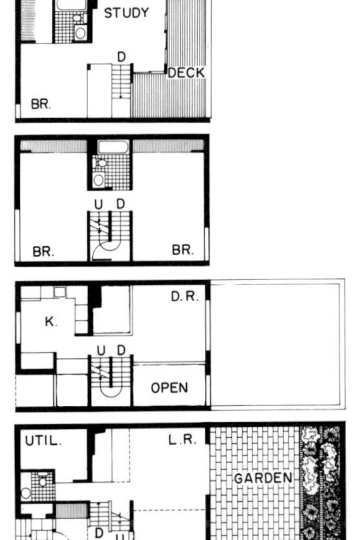

David Hirsch photos

16

The search, seen in the design of the townhouses on the previous two pages, for an architecture that is evidently emulative of the context around it is carried at least two steps further in this 92-house project in Virginia. Here the context is a relatively natural and rural one near Williamsburg. The site is long and narrow, with open fields on one side and a golf course on the other. The houses are arranged in a loose serpentine pattern, then grouped into small neighborhoods. Each neighborhood has some special identifying feature—ivy banks and sunken gardens, or larger amenities like a swimming pool, a crafts workshop, meeting houses, and a greenhouse. Five basic houses were designed, but their appearances can be varied considerably by the placement of optional latticed gazebos and attached greenhouses, plus what the architects call their "country kitchens." These are buildings that stand separate from the houses, connected to them by old-fashioned pantryways that lead to the dining rooms. Ten-foot-high ceilings allow the luxuries of tall double-hung windows and window seats. Cars enter the site and and are distributed in a fingerlike pattern into discrete automobile courts screened as much as possible from the rest of the site by berms. The central circulation system is a pedestrian one.

LITTLETOWN QUARTER AT KINGSMILL, Kingsmill, Virginia. Architects: *Callister Payne and Bischoff—project architects: Paul Bradley, Alfred Morrisette, and John Pryor.* Engineer: *Glenn Nelson.* General contractor: *Bush Properties.*

C.W. Callister, Jr. photos

17

On a hillside facing south and overlooking the Pacific Ocean at Malibu, architect Murray Milne and eight friends pooled their resources to establish the kind of living accommodations that none could have afforded without the others. "The eight friends," says Milne, "filed as a California real estate limited partnership with the architect and attorney as general partners. Each of the six limited partners contributed $10,000 and each partner agreed to buy and live in one of the eight units. With this initial capital, they purchased the land, paid architectural fees, legal fees and building permit fees. Because the project was completely presold, the bank's appraisal was very generous and the construction loan was more than adequate. When the project was completed eight individual mortgages were taken out, the construction loan was paid off, and the partnership was dissolved."

The happy outcome of this unusual arrangement is a pair of narrow structures, each containing four 3000-square-foot units, parking for 16 cars, and a community-owned swimming pool.

The precipitous slope was ideal for a stepped section, giving each unit privacy as well as a panoramic view. To solve the problem of vertical transportation (where nine flights of steps separate the lowest from the highest level) Milne cantilevered a funicular system on the outside of the building at the second-story. Powered by a standard traction motor, the path of the funicular just clears the front door to each unit and can be summoned by a call button. The cab carries four passengers on what the architect describes as "one of the most exciting rides west of Disneyland."

To reduce solar heat gain and glare, the large glazed areas are protected by a generous overhang. Each unit is insulated: 6 inches in the ceilings, 3½ inches in the exterior walls. The result of careful sun control and insulation is that, even on this southern California site, no air-conditioning is required.

COASTLINE CONDOMINIUMS
Architect: Murray Milne in association with
 Kamnitzer, Marks, Cotton and Vreeland
 18057 Coastline Drive
 Malibu, California
Engineer:
 David Taubman and Associates
Contractor: Frank Ashley Construction
Photographer: Jason Niiya

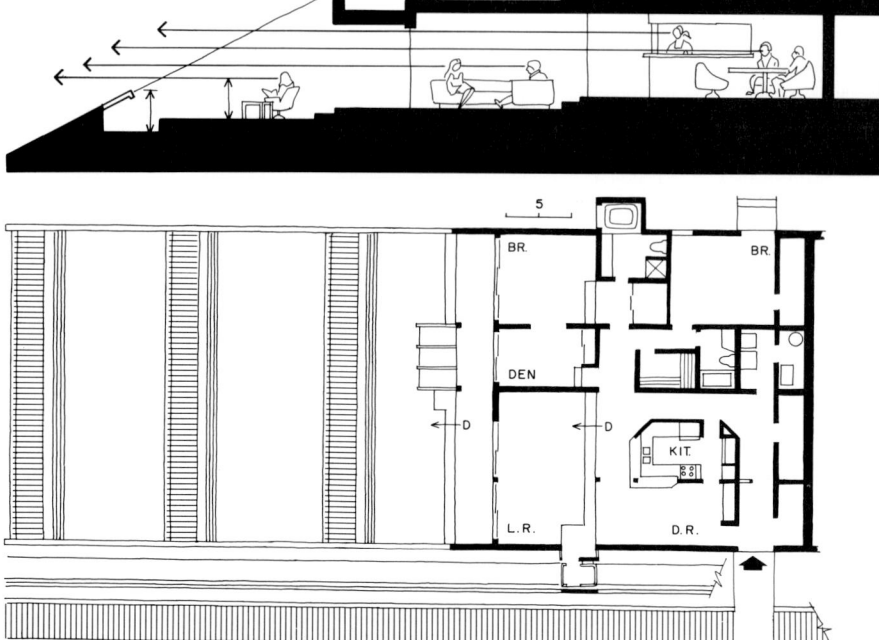

18

From almost any point of view, Promontory Point is a conspicuous and spectacular rental community. The site is a bluff overlooking Newport Harbor, Balboa and Santa Catalina Island. Beyond, the Pacific arches serenely over the horizon. But architects Fisher-Friedman Associates and site planners Sasaki-Walker Associates began with a site that was less than idyllic. It was long and narrow, treeless and steeply contoured. Parts of the bluff, particularly near the crest, had been savaged by earlier development.

The designers started with "stacking" studies that determined the main massing configuration. None of the units exceeds the 3-story local limit for wood frame construction, but all the apartments have views and those at the base of the bluff are—for all practical purposes—waterfront properties. Intermediate parking levels serve individual clusters and no one climbs more than one level from parking to apartment.

The building vernacular is textured white stucco with red tile roof, designed to blend harmoniously with existing regional architecture. Paved walks, bridges, trellises, window boxes and a small park provide additional richness.

The 520 units at Promontory Point are arranged in five, 72-unit, U-shaped elements set securely at the crest of the bluff with 160 additional units stepped down the slope toward the ocean. The apartments range from one to three bedrooms in a mix of twenty-six possible variations. The result is a community of striking visual impact—a community that expresses high density effectively, and uses simple repetitive forms to create rhythms that are subtle and interesting but never overly insistent.

PROMONTORY POINT
Architects: Fisher-Friedman Associates
  242 California Street
  San Francisco, California
Owners: The Irvine Company
Project name: Promontory Point
Location: Newport Beach, California
Landscape architects: Sasaki Walker
  Associates
Engineers: L. F. Robinson & Associates
  (structural);
  Raub, Bein, Frost & Associates (civil)
General contractor: The Irvine Company
Photographer: Joshua Freiwald

Promontory Point is more externally oriented than most developments of this size. In order to secure community approval, for instance, owners and designers provided easements for cars to use the main entrance and parking lot overlooking the bluff. Visitors may also have access to various vistas throughout the long, narrow property.

19

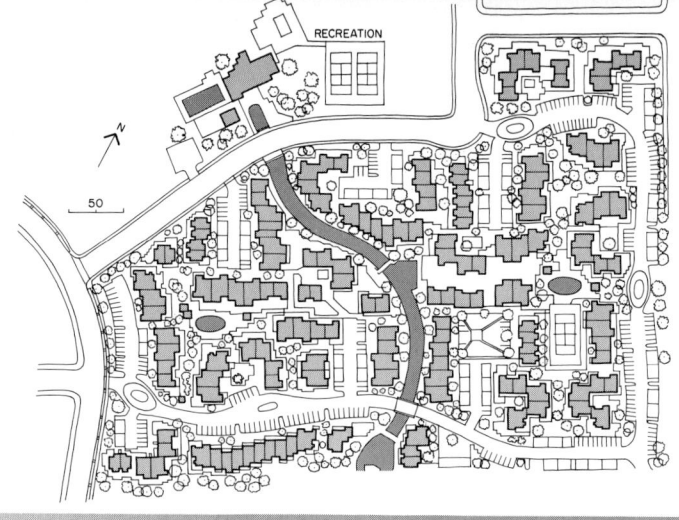

This mixed-use community occupies 150 acres recently released from the long-range expansion plans of two adjacent colleges. It lies at the intersection of two main traffic arteries, one of which has already been strip-zoned for commercial use. In planning the new community, developer and architects wished to exploit the commercial possibilities of the crossroads location without resorting to further strip development. They accomplished this by planning an integrated community with single-family and row housing, recreational facilities, offices, shops and a variety of other community amenities. Chief among these is a continuous system of canals that links all parts of the project with its commercial center—and gives the project its name. References to Venice can be seen in the design vocabulary throughout.

An important part of the open space system is a nine-hole golf course that has been graded and designed with hazards that form a portion of the project's storm drainage pattern. This combined use was important for another reason: it allowed partial funding of the open space through sewer district bonds.

Access to the site is by automobile but the principal avenues of circulation through the site are designed for pedestrians and bicycle riders. As these routes get closer to the commercial hub, they are given more urban form with paving materials and planting appropriate to intensive use. Landscaped berms at the project's perimeter provide an important measure of internal privacy.

At present, all of the first phase commercial, office and residential properties have been sold or leased. Apartment vacancies now run at less than two per cent in a region where the more typical rate is 12-15 per cent. The final phases will include additional housing plus special units for both the elderly and student groups.

Apartment designs include six different unit types which, although repetitive, can be grouped in different combinations to produce a variety of building masses. Finishes vary also in an effort to satisfy a broad spectrum of public tastes.

VENETIAN GARDENS
Architect: Bull Field Volkmann Stockwell
  350 Pacific Avenue
  San Francisco, California
Owner: Schmitz Development, Inc.
Planner: Gary Fong, A.I.P.

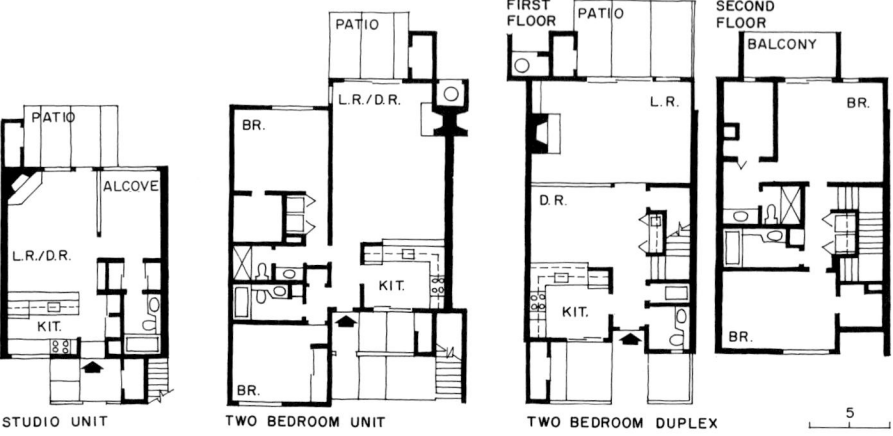

Chapter Four

HOUSING FOR THE ELDERLY

There is a massive need for a new building type that is less an institution and more like home. The living conditions suffered by many people over 65 urgently point toward the need for both construction of better physical facilities and more positive attitudes about a national problem. The fast growing portion of the population that will be pressing their needs on us demands radical change — and better answers. For the design professions, this will mean a re-examination of everything that has been built for the elderly — and it will mean hard work coupled with a search for knowledge.

The current statistics on the aging point to a promising new field of construction. While the 22 million persons over 65 at present form 10 percent of the U.S. population, the average life expectancy of everyone alive today is now well above 70, and increasing. This means that our population will eventually need and expect some type of housing tailored to specifications that have been little met so far. Today, there are only some three million units designed specifically for the aged; and these include everything from apartments to intermediate and advanced medical-care facilities. Yet in New York City alone there are over one million persons over 65.

On the following pages are examples of the best forms of housing now being built. The Monument East Apartments in Baltimore, Maryland (pages 104-105), are located in an imaginatively handled urban renewal area. It is public housing which keeps elderly residents in their accustomed neighborhood — now revitalized — and keeps them active through familiar contacts, aggressive social programs and better design. The Grundy Tower in Bristol, Pennsylvania (pages 106-107), designed for the able-bodied elderly, functions as a self-governing community. The Florida Christian Home Apartments in Jacksonville, Florida (pages 108-109), similar in design to the locally popular "luxury-style" developments in the vicinity, accommodates the needs of a community of elderly in subtle and non-institutionalized ways. Highland Park Apartments in Highland Park, Illinois (pages 110-111), is a tightly disciplined urban solution, while Heaton Court Housing in Stockbridge, Massachusetts (pages 112-113), has some of the qualities of the rambling country resort hotel it replaced. Heritage Gardens in Winthrop, Massachusetts (pages 114-117), was designed to create opportunities for casual social interaction, as was Walnut Hill in Haverstraw, New York (pages 122-123). Maple Knoll Village in Springdale, Ohio (pages 118-121), has the character of a real village where people might choose to live, not an institution where they are sent. It provides for continuous physical care at all levels of need: it does not shuffle its residents off to other facilities when their health conditions worsen. It is truly a place to live — and not just a place to live out time.

1

Monument East is part of a 35-block urban renewal area. But there is little old style "renewal" here. Old Town Mall (photo, opposite) was created by a renovation of existing stores that face onto a previous street, now a walkway. Examples of Baltimore's famous "homesteading" plan are one block away. Many original businesses and residents remain in the neighborhood.

What are the real advantages here? Monument East has 187 apartments, of which more than half have one bedroom (the rest are efficiencies). But the building does far more than just house people. It has been designed to meet the requirements both of its largely black tenants and a very progessive office of the Baltimore Department of Housing and Community Development. The philosophy here has been to keep the elderly in their own neighborhood, close to normal lifestyles, and therefore independent as long as they can manage it. Programs managed by DHCD include organized recreation and housekeeping and medical and therapy services within apartments—all designed to keep those who need such services away from more institutionalized care as long as possible, or indefinitely.

The apartments were planned according to comments by a committee headed by one of the current residents. Spaces are large (by government standards), and made to seem even larger by taking advantage of diagonal views through the relatively open plans. The kitchen was identified by the committee as a major space in previous living patterns, and was accordingly made into a full room—normally with adjacent corner balconies. The round openings from most of these balconies and the correspondingly smaller windows were planned by the architects because they felt that not all of the older residents would feel psychologically comfortable in a tall building without some sense of confinement. Furniture and kitchen arrangements were closely scrutinized by both the architects and the committee during planning.

MONUMENT EAST APARTMENTS, Baltimore, Maryland. Owners: *The Department of Housing and Community Development.* Architects; *Conklin & Rossant—personnel-in-charge: Ray Longwell, George Taft, Gerald Li.* Engineers: *Ewell Finley* (structural); *Charles Creswell* (mechanical/electrical). General contractor: *Leimbach Construction.*

Norman McGrath photos

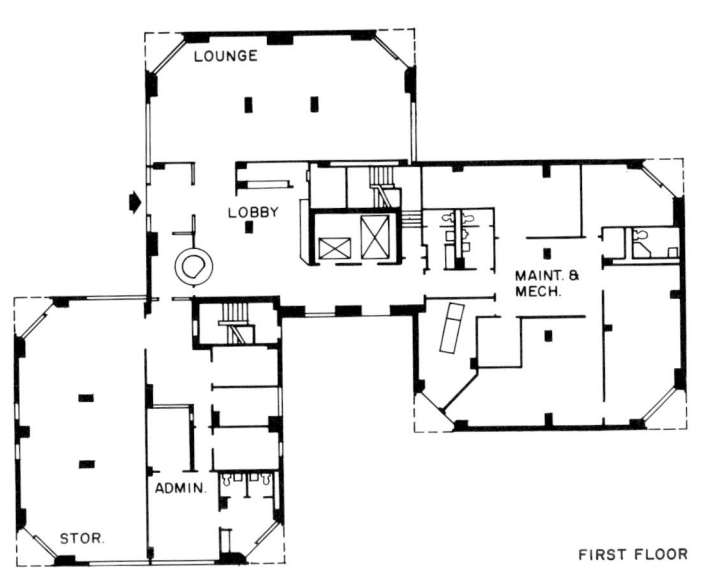
FIRST FLOOR

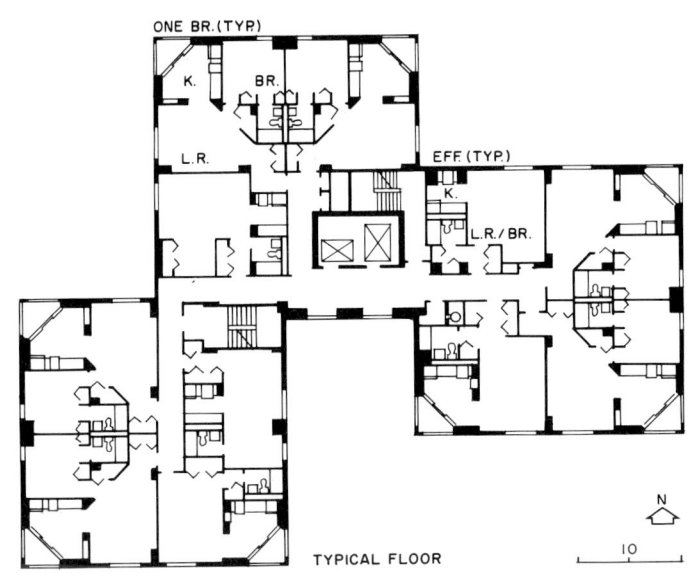
TYPICAL FLOOR

2

Built by a private developer as a turnkey project for the Bucks County Housing Authority, these apartments are intended for able-bodied, low-income persons—many of whom, in this community, had earlier owned their own homes. The Authority does maintain an active social-affairs department, which provides aid during temporary illnesses. According to Executive Director Carl Gabler, the Authority is amending its policies on current projects to include some sort of long-term care, but will continue to consciously avoid an institutionalized environment: "to the residents, these are just good apartments." The building is named after Senator Joseph Grundy, whose foundation supplies extra monies to such projects for amenities not included in the basic government financing.

What are the advantages here? Although many residents may have to look forward to moving on to institutions, while they are at Grundy they have better facilities than they might expect—even under the project's restrictive financing. The apartments are small, but Sauer has tried to overcome this disadvantage by using a stepped perimeter to the building, which visually expands the spaces by providing views in two directions. The fenestration also allows cross ventilation for the majority of rooms which will not be air conditioned. Sauer states that the cost increase for the stepped perimeter was held to 5 per cent. Although the building follows the convention of a double-loaded corridor, the configuration avoids the usual lack of a "sense of location" by providing natural light and recesses for individual apartment doors.

One of the most interesting aspects of the life at Grundy Tower is the way in which social programs and even tenant government are managed—not by the Authority but by a resident committee with elected members from each floor. The common backgrounds of the residents, coupled with the interest in self-government, produce a much more active community than could any imposed program.

GRUNDY TOWER, Bristol, Pennsylvania. Owner: *Bucks County Housing Authority*. Architects: *Louis Sauer Associates*. Associate architect: *Frank Schlesinger*. Engineers: *Joseph Hoffman and Associates* (structural); *Michael Garber and Associates* (mechanical/electrical).

Otto Baitz photos

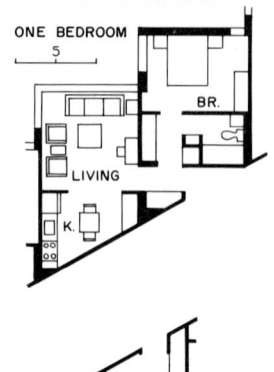

ONE BEDROOM

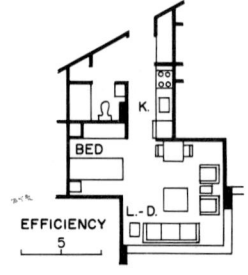

EFFICIENCY

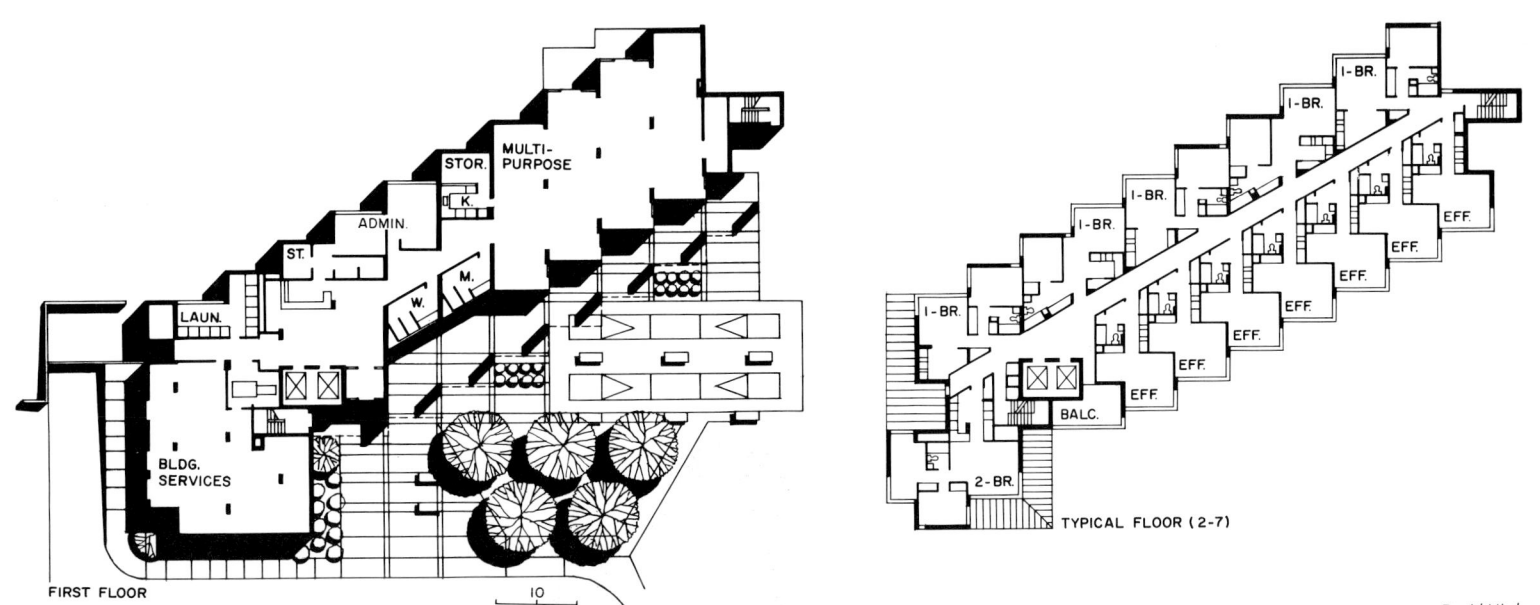

FIRST FLOOR

TYPICAL FLOOR (2-7)

David Hirsh

3

Built under HUD's Section 236 program, this first phase of construction contains 180 apartments. With its six-story height and its segmented mass, it represents something in-between a "home-like" image and that of the many new "luxury" high-rises that dot the area. The angled configuration of the wings (and of a proposed addition, bottom of the plan shown below) conforms to a curved site boundary and provides a smaller scale than the building would otherwise have. Types of apartments are separated in respective wings and—on upper floors—occupy the spaces assigned to common uses on the ground floor plan shown here.

What are the real advantages here? According to architect Peter Rumpel, the FHA 236 financing was not particularly encouraging to the concept of life-long care in a continuing environment. Nor is he certain that the concept is right—when it involves mixing the relatively well with the relatively sick. Still, the 1980 apartments are served by a completely separate nursing unit on the grounds, and a planned second stage of construction (dotted lines on the plan) would accomodate persons with more serious geriatric problems. The building's poured-in-place and precast concrete walls are an unusual departure from normal practice in Florida, and add greatly to the strong sculptural appearance.

The greatest advantage here may be that the building meets the expectations of retired middle class persons with limited incomes. Aside from the building's non-institutional appearance, the apartments contain ample dressing, bath and storage facilities, although the units are not large—in keeping with the FHA restrictions. Natural light and views of activities in the corrdiors are seen upon leaving elevators at each floor, and are among the advantages of the planning of public spaces. The project is within easy walking distance of stores, theaters, churches and public transportation in an urban setting.

THE FLORIDA CHRISTIAN HOME APARTMENTS, Jacksonville, Florida. Owners: *The Christian Church (Disciples of Christ)*. Architects: *Freedman/Clements/Rumpel*—designer: *Peter Rumpel*. Engineers: *H. W. Keister Associates* (structural); *David Bruce Miller* (mechanical/electrical). General contractor: *Wesley of Florida, Inc.*

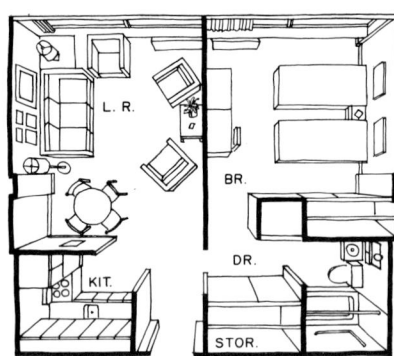

TYPICAL ONE BEDROOM

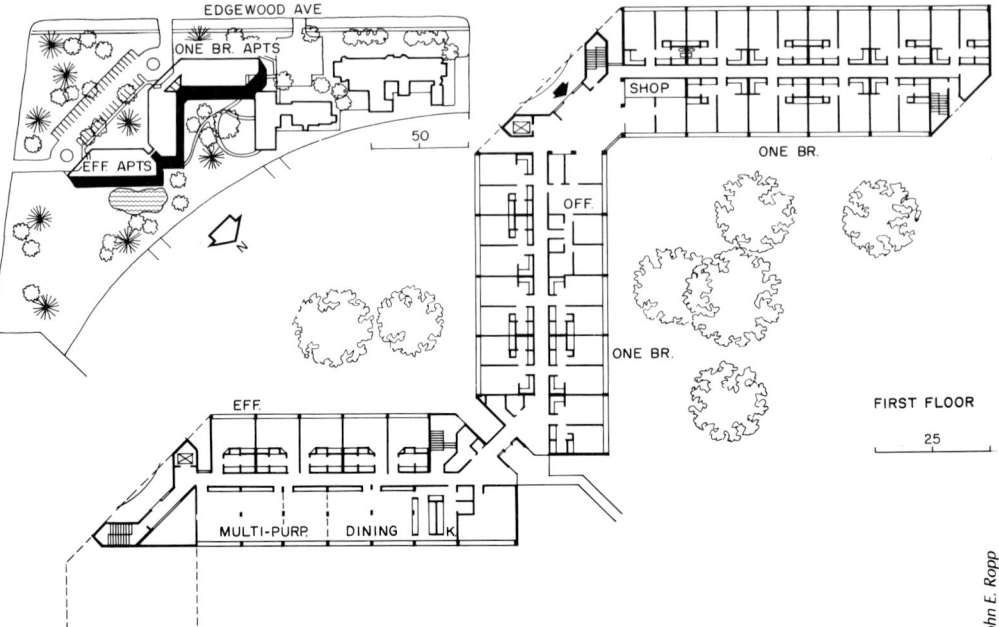

FIRST FLOOR

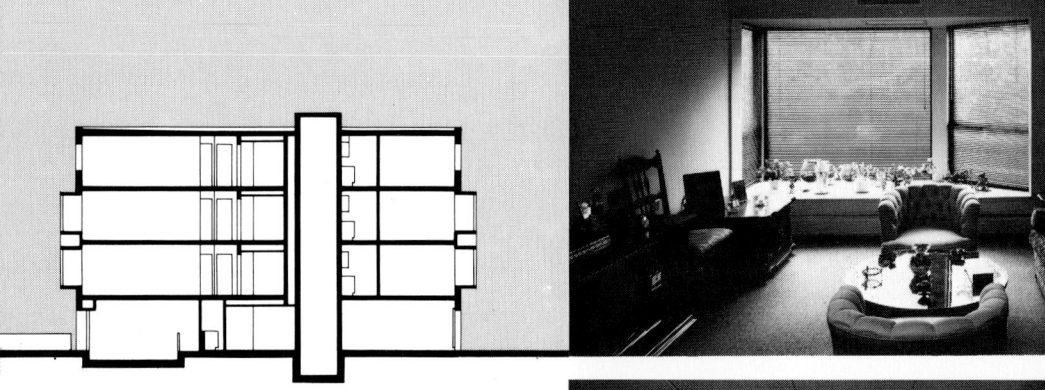

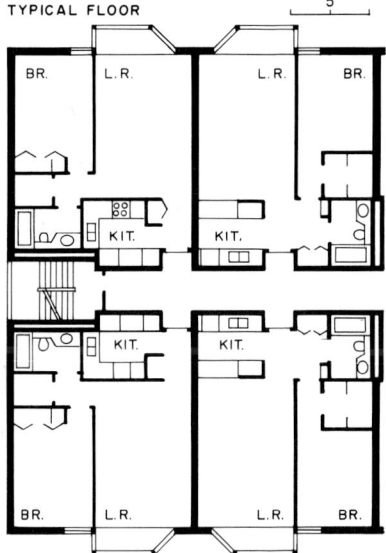

4

An elderly-housing program, a not-for-profit client, a stringent budget: all the ingredients, in fact, that have so often in the past led to callous, institutionalized building. Though they were all present, they led in this instance to something quite different—to an elegant, decidedly non-institutional block of 68 townhouses that respects the scale of its street and neighbors while offering its occupants a pleasant and welcome range of amenities.

The units are constructed using oversized brick, precast concrete plank floors and masonry bearing walls, materials selected for their soundproofing as well as their economic advantages. Though the floor plans are repetitive, the facade is varied to provide a projecting bay window at the intermediate levels for views up and down the street.

The interiors were designed to the needs of the elderly with central elevators, comparatively short corridors, recessed doors, easy-to-maintain finishes and a central commons area off a sunken garden at the sidewalk. A small community room (photo right) and a manager's apartment complete the plan.

The site is a lightly treed parcel at the end of a busy shopping street in a Chicago suburb. In this context, with its height limitations, its setback requirements and its restrictive program, Booth Nagle & Hartray—together with their clients—have succeeded admirably where others before them have too often failed.

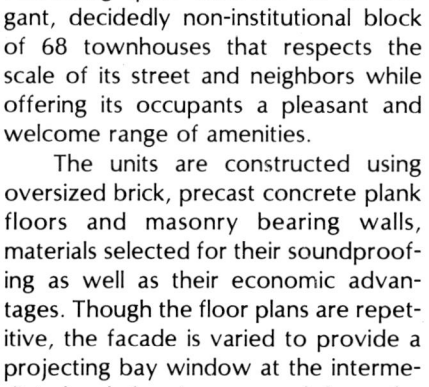
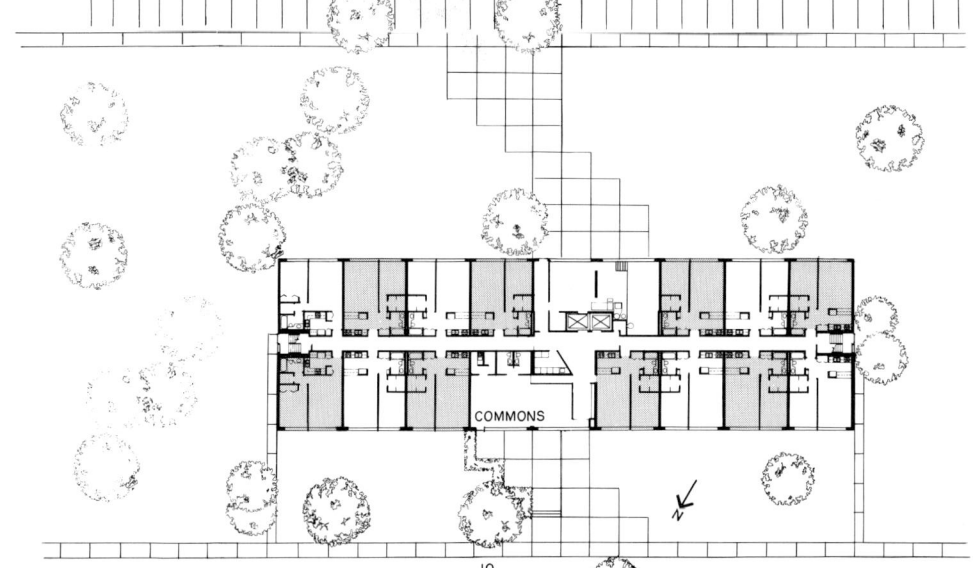

HIGHLAND PARK APARTMENTS
Architects: Booth Nagle & Hartray
  230 East Ohio Street
  Chicago, Illinois
Owners: City of Highland Park
Engineers:
  Wiesinger Holland (structural
  Wallace-Migdal & Drucker (mechanical)
Contractor: E.W. Corrigan Co.
Photographer: Philip Turner

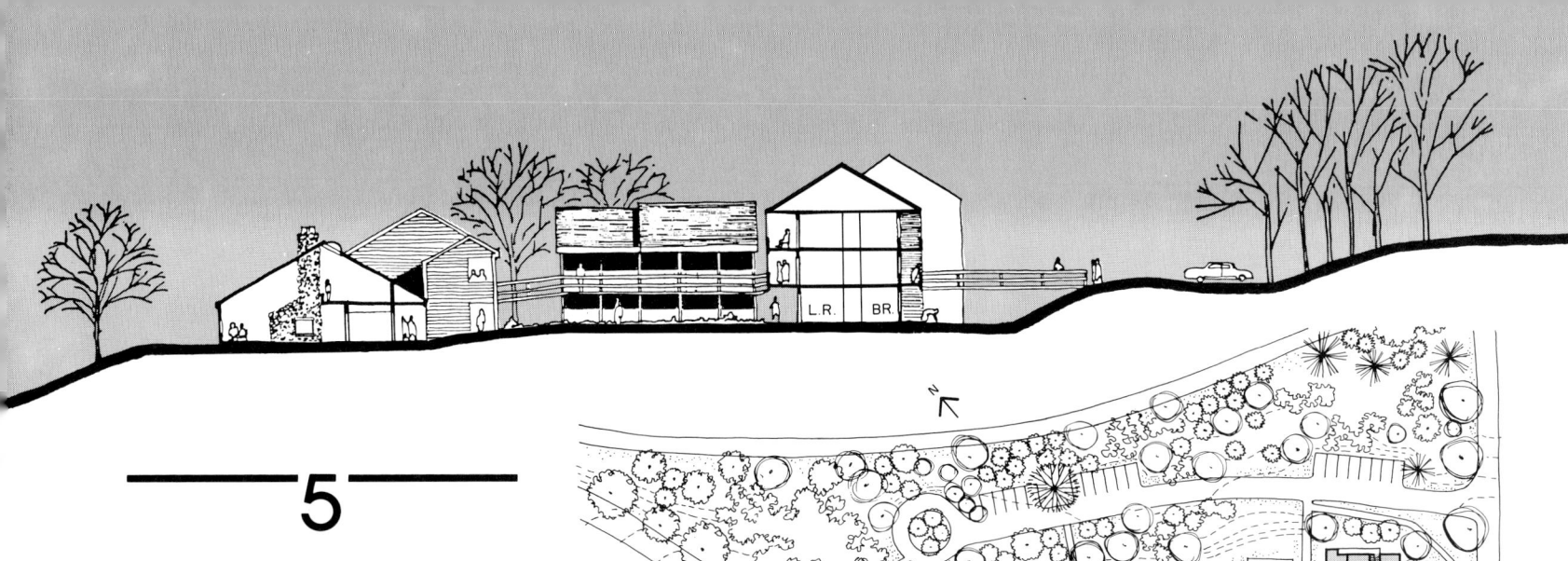

5

This 50-unit housing community for the elderly, located on a site formerly occupied by a rambling resort hotel, is clustered about a landscaped courtyard and surrounded by dense woods. The traditionally shaped, pitched-roof units are linked by continuous porches and galleries that provide covered passages throughout the complex and, in the nice kind of gesture architecture can sometimes make, remind residents of the social porches of the old hotel.

Most of the units are one-bedroom with living spaces facing the gallery, sleeping space turned to the more private rear porch. Parking is provided on the uphill side (see section) and pedestrian bridges provide access at the intermediate level—a device that sharply limits the amount of stair climbing required of both residents and visitors. Further downslope, where residents may wish to stroll, the architects have provided traversing paths that keep the incline to about 1 on 18. Benches and resting spots are provided enroute.

The architects placed the three-story buildings on the north (or uphill) side and kept the single-story structures on the south so that the sun could penetrate the court as fully as possible. This solution also provides the best unobstructed views toward the Berkshire Mountains.

The structure at Heaton Court is standard wood framing finished in cedar clapboard. The gallery areas are surfaced in an all-weather roof deck chosen for its ability to withstand heavy foot traffic and remain waterproof and slip resistant.

HEATON COURT HOUSING
Architects: Goody, Clancy & Associates
  334 Boylston Street
  Boston, Massachusetts
Owner: Stockbridge Housing Authority
Engineers: Souza & True (structural)
  Reardon & Turner (mechanical)
Consultant on the elderly: Steve Demos
Contractor: George E. Emerson, Inc.
Photographer: Clemens Kalischer

6

The Commonwealth of Massachusetts has for many years conducted a vigorous and popular program of housing the low-income elderly. About five years ago, however, it sponsored an architectural competition, partly to attract new blood for the undertaking and partly to stimulate the incorporation in design of recent behavioral thought on the needs of users.

The Boston firm Goody, Clancy & Associates won the competition with the design shown here, and the city of Winthrop executed the competition winner "faithfully and economically—$17,800 per unit," reports architect Joan Goody.

More important, Mrs. Goody thinks, the project "fulfills behavioral criteria established for this kind of housing by maximizing opportunities for casual social interaction and providing interest-provoking views."

The project provides 100 one-bedroom units ("double" units for couples have larger bedrooms) in two-story buildings. A major opportunity for casual, and inevitable, social encounters occurs at the building entrances, where four units share a common outside door and foyer. This opportunity answers one of the most serious problems faced by the elderly: loneliness, caused by the deaths of spouses and old friends and aggravated by

©Steve Rosenthal photos

diminished physical powers and a tendency to withdraw from both social and physical activity.

The floor-through units are separated by halls and stairways or by party walls. The living and dining areas occupy the front of the clustered units, where residents can see activity along the four "malls" that traverse the site and connect the buildings. On the second floor, the stair hall gives onto a shared balcony that overlooks the mall. Bedrooms and bathrooms, on the other hand, are located at the rear, quieter and more private. Units for handicapped tenants—the law requires that five per cent of the space in projects for the

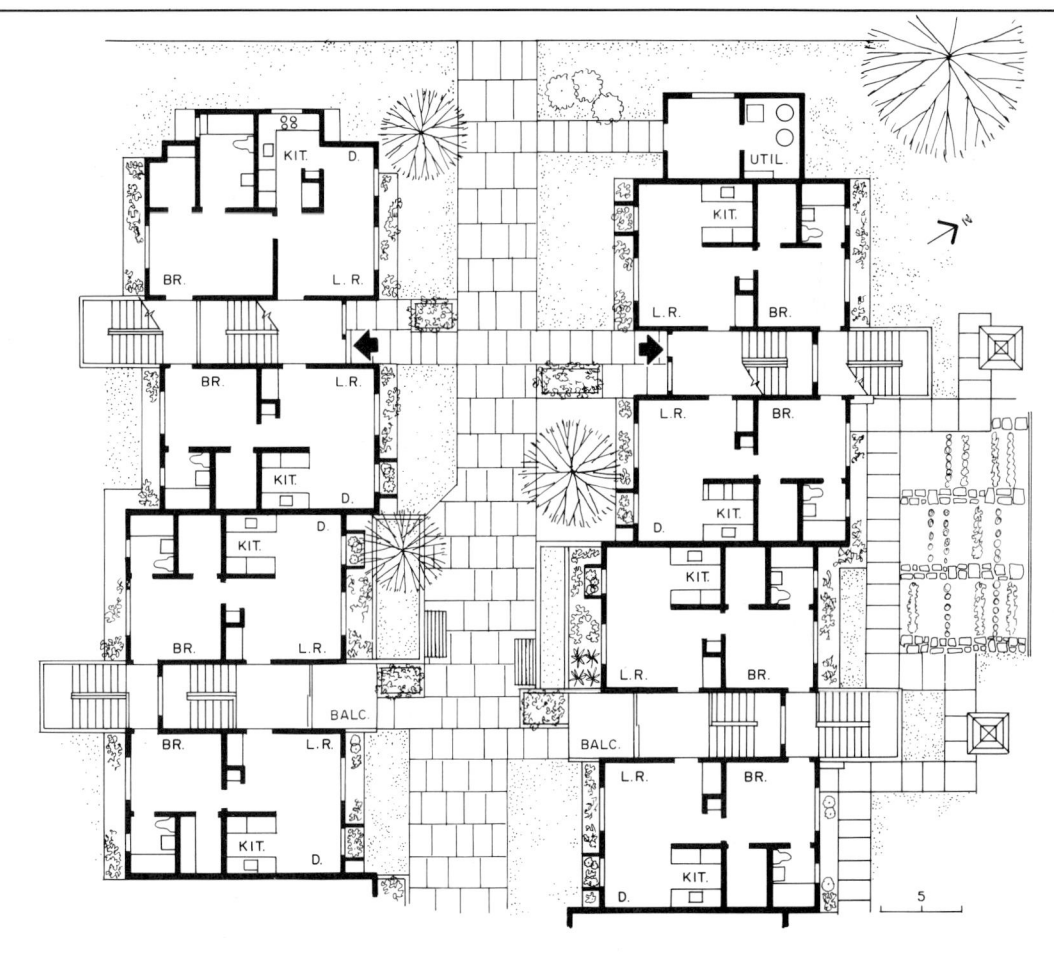

elderly be allocated to the handicapped—have stair-less entries on grade.

In addition to the common entries, the site plan itself was designed to make social meetings easy. The site is located in an area of one- and two-family houses formerly occupied by many Heritage Gardens tenants. The four malls act as streets connecting the housing to the neighborhood. Along them, residents doing errands such as grocery shopping can expect to run into their fellows.

An existing apartment complex for the elderly is adjacent to, but well downhill from, Heritage Gardens. The new design joins the two with a community center that houses lounges, space for crafts and hobbies, and a laundry (more casual contact).

Because the site is so steep, the three-story building follows the hillside. Residents from Heritage Gardens enter on grade at the third floor, residents from the older development enter on grade at the first level, and visitors from either project can reach the other by elevator within the building. Surrounding terraces joined by steps offer outdoor access to the physically mobile and visual connection for the infirm.

All bathrooms and bedrooms are equipped with an emergency call system: if a tenant throws a switch, a bell rings and a bulb lights outside to notify neighbors that assistance is needed. Kitchens and baths include safety features—low cabinets, front-control ranges, grab bars—but use traditional materials for comfort of association.

HERITAGE GARDENS, WINTHROP HOUSING FOR THE ELDERLY, Winthrop, Massachusetts. Owner: *Winthrop Housing Authority*. Architects: *Goody, Clancy & Associates, Inc.*—partner-in-charge: *Joan E. Goody*; project architect: *William E. Warren*; architect for community building: *Paul H. Dudek*. Engineers: *Sousa & True* (structural); *Joseph Schneider* (mechanical/electrical). Contractor: *Bick-Com Corporation*.

The Heritage Gardens project includes a new community center that joins an older housing project for the elderly. The three-story center climbs a steep hill between the two, offering access at grade to the older housing at the base (photo at left). Visitors from Heritage Gardens also enter at grade—on the top floor. The main entrance is on the first floor in an alcove behind the central exterior stair. At the lowest level, a large lounge and game room (upper right) faces the older development through a glass wall. The second story contains laundry and television rooms, the top floor rooms for crafts and maintenance, and an elevator provides a protected connection between these floors and between the two complexes.

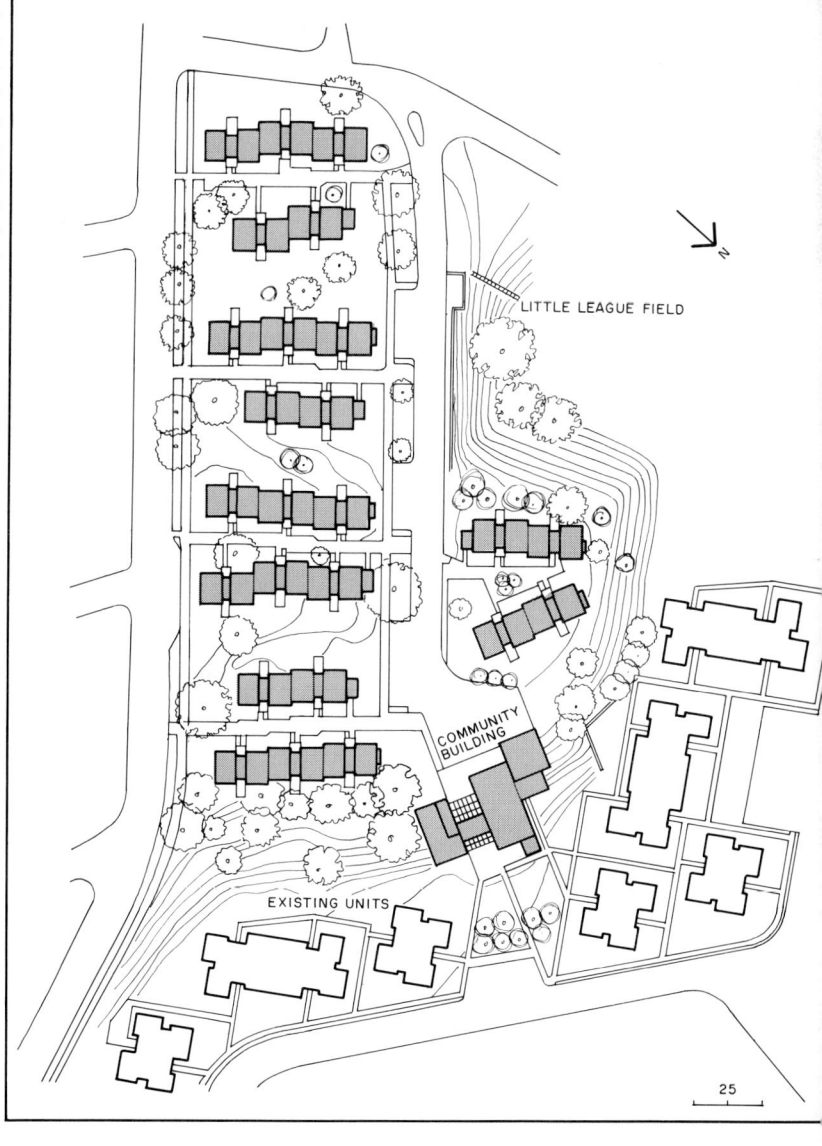

117

7

Intimate in scale and more like conventional housing than an institution, suburban Cincinnati's Maple Knoll Village encourages the sort of living—and not just custodial care—for the elderly that one hopes is the wave of the future. With a steadily growing part of the population in old age, and with the decreasing number of close-knit families that once provided ongoing care in the home, architects Gruzen & Partners have found good answers to what the alternative—communal living—can be. It may often have to be communal because of common specialized physical needs—and according to some gerontologists, because of psychological needs as well. But Gruzen has proven that such living need not be in the inhumane hospital-like atmosphere that has sapped vitality from so many older people in the past.

Maple Knoll clearly resolves what often has been regarded as a contradiction: an at-home atmosphere *and* provision on a continuous basis for medical needs that have normally been met by transferring ailing residents to institutional environments.

At Maple Knoll, three levels of care are accommodated in four types of buildings. At the most independent level, persons with limited medical needs live in town-houses of one and two bedrooms, clustered at the northwestern corner of the site. The other buildings, linked together by a wide street-like corridor, have one bedroom or efficiency apartments for the relatively independent in the northernmost block, communal facilities in the central block and nursing care in the southern. These linked buildings are arranged around a large "village green" of lawn and mature trees that occupied the site before the new construction (photo opposite).

While there is some natural segregation of facilities for the various levels of care, there is also a strong interaction of all the residents that is encouraged by the interior "street" and the large number of shared activities that it connects (see plan overleaf). Because of the constant traffic along the street, the lounges dispersed along the street's length offer the same appeals to the more sedentary elderly that are gained in other projects by such persons clustering around the main entrances just to "see what is happening." And to counter the idleness that makes residents cluster, there are the many opportunities to develop busy hands and minds that are discussed further on.

Maple Knoll's 32-acre site was occupied by an older structure, and its foundations were retained as a partially covered terrace and a central focus of the "village green." Because of the desire to make a direct contact between the buildings and the green, the site's access road was located on the outside of the ring of connected buildings. And to create another variation on the scale of exterior spaces, the northernmost apartment block encloses courtyards that open onto the green.

Both the townhouse units and the apartments are large by institutional standards, and could well be like smaller apartments that residents might have occupied in their more active years. The concept is to ease the transition to a new life style. The town houses have individual garages and many of the 150 apartments have balconies. It is only in the nursing rooms that a more practical, institutional character predominates.

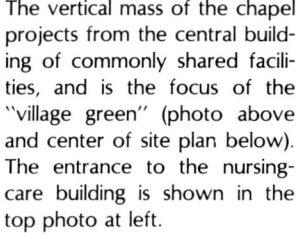

The vertical mass of the chapel projects from the central building of commonly shared facilities, and is the focus of the "village green" (photo above and center of site plan below). The entrance to the nursing-care building is shown in the top photo at left.

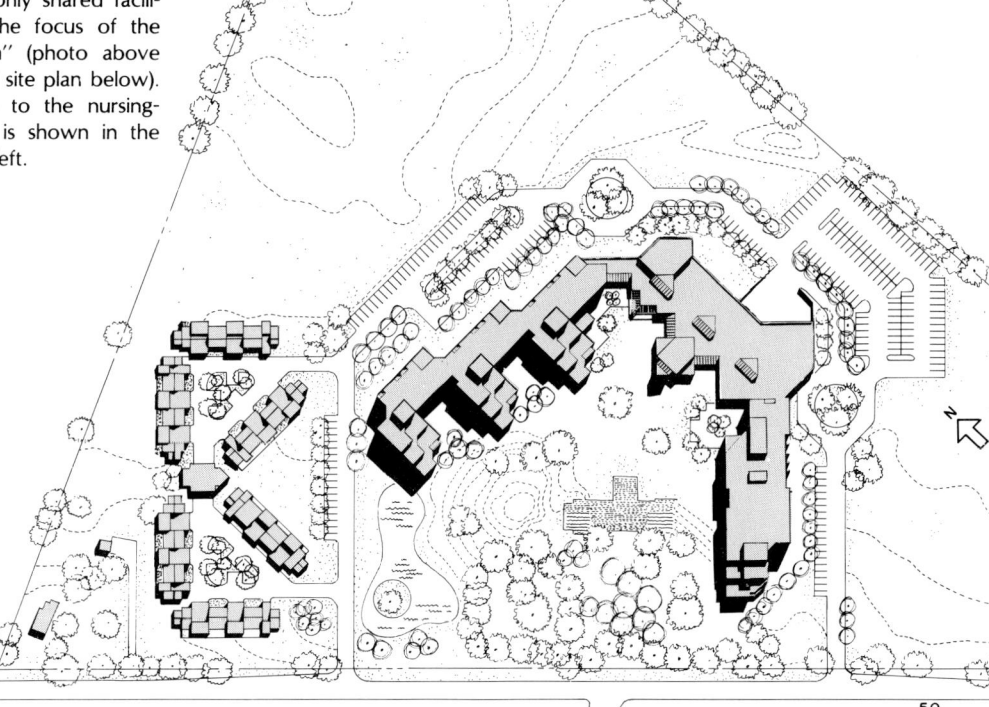

Bo Parker photos

But even in many of these, there are balconies, and a large proportion of the 165 beds are one to a room.

But of course, the object is to keep residents out of the nursing units in the first place, by stimulating their all-important psychological drives. In accomplishing this stimulation, the programs and the attitudes of the administration become as important as the physical surroundings. At Maple Knoll, residents are offered a number of activities beside the usual social programs. Most striking is the opportunity of teaching either in the pre-school facility or in the day-care center, that are both located on the ground floor of the nursing unit. (These are intended for the younger children in the neighborhood.) It is well established that the elderly can be extremely effective in working with the very young. Another unusual opportunity is the ability to make various craft objects, which are sold in Maple Knoll's gift shop. Both activities keep interest and a sense of responsibility high, while allowing for the opportunity to produce income.

To house the many activities, there are—besides the facilities already mentioned—craft rooms, a machine shop, a therapy room, a beauty shop, a snack bar, a library, a gift shop and a chapel. The chapel is located at the focus of the common facilities building, and its importance on the village green is accentuated by its high roof and vertical mass. Round windows near the altar further enhance its special character. All of the stained glass in the chapel was designed by artist Harriet Hyams.

The ambitious and vital nature of both Maple Knoll's programs and the facilities to house them are a result of the special natures of the clients and of the architects. The client, Southwestern Ohio Senior Services grew from an organization once called the Widows and Old Men's Home, founded more than 100 years ago by Harriet Beecher Stowe's mother. Up to the recent past, the group had a traditional custodial attitude, which has been radically changed by a new administrator, the Reverend Jerry Smart.

According to Gruzen partner-in-charge Peter Samton, it is vitally important that the architects are involved in the planning for such facilities right from the initial programming stages. This is especially true when the architects have had as much experience as Gruzen's, which began in the early 1950's. "In a specialized but relatively unresearched field, there is much to be learned from repetitive experience. This ranges from improving hand rails to the location of lounges."

Maple Knoll currently houses 315 residents, and expansion around the perimeter of the site is planned for up to a total of 700. The buildings now contain 290,000 square feet. The basic structural system is precast concrete plank on masonry bearing walls, and the cladding is brick.

MAPLEKNOLL VILLAGE, Springdale, Ohio. Owner: *Southwestern Ohio Senior Services, Inc.* Architect: *Gruzen & Partners—partner-in charge: Peter Samton; project architect: Benedetto Puccio; design assistant: Robert Evans.* Associated architects: *Glaser & Myers & Associates, Inc.* Engineers: *Robert Silman Associates* (structural); *Syska & Hennessy, Inc.* (mechanical/electrical). Landscape architect: *M. Paul Friedberg & Partners.* Cost consultant: *Amis Construction & Consulting Services, Inc.* Construction manager: *Gruzen/Amis*

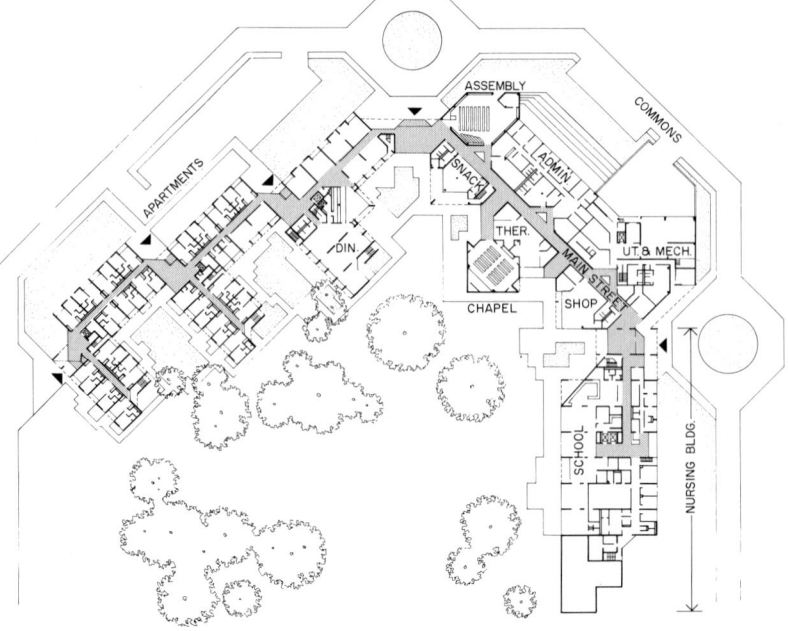

8

Financed under Federal Section 236, this 180-unit cluster housing project is designed for low- and moderate-income families (the majority of them elderly) and is located on 7.75 acres north of New York City.

The eight two-story structures that make up the project step down the sloping site in a linear pattern that generally parallels the contours so that each ground floor unit has an on-grade entrance, convenient access to automobiles, pedestrian ways and community facilities. This arrangement also provides views of the Hudson River Valley from most of the upper-level apartments.

The units themselves consist of an upper and lower apartment; the upper apartment provided with a bridge entrance and a balcony, the lower with a small garden area to be planted at the tenant's option. All units have through ventilation.

A prime concern for designers—and one they solved with considerable success—was the establishment of a community identity and a village scale. The ring road, the pedestrian spine and the community building (photos below right) all contribute to this success. The design vocabulary is simple but used so consistently that the project "reads" as a village—and a nice one. The repetition of units does not pall because the designers have maximized their opportunities to articulate differences in grade and landscape form.

The principal exterior finish is plywood over a wood frame structure.

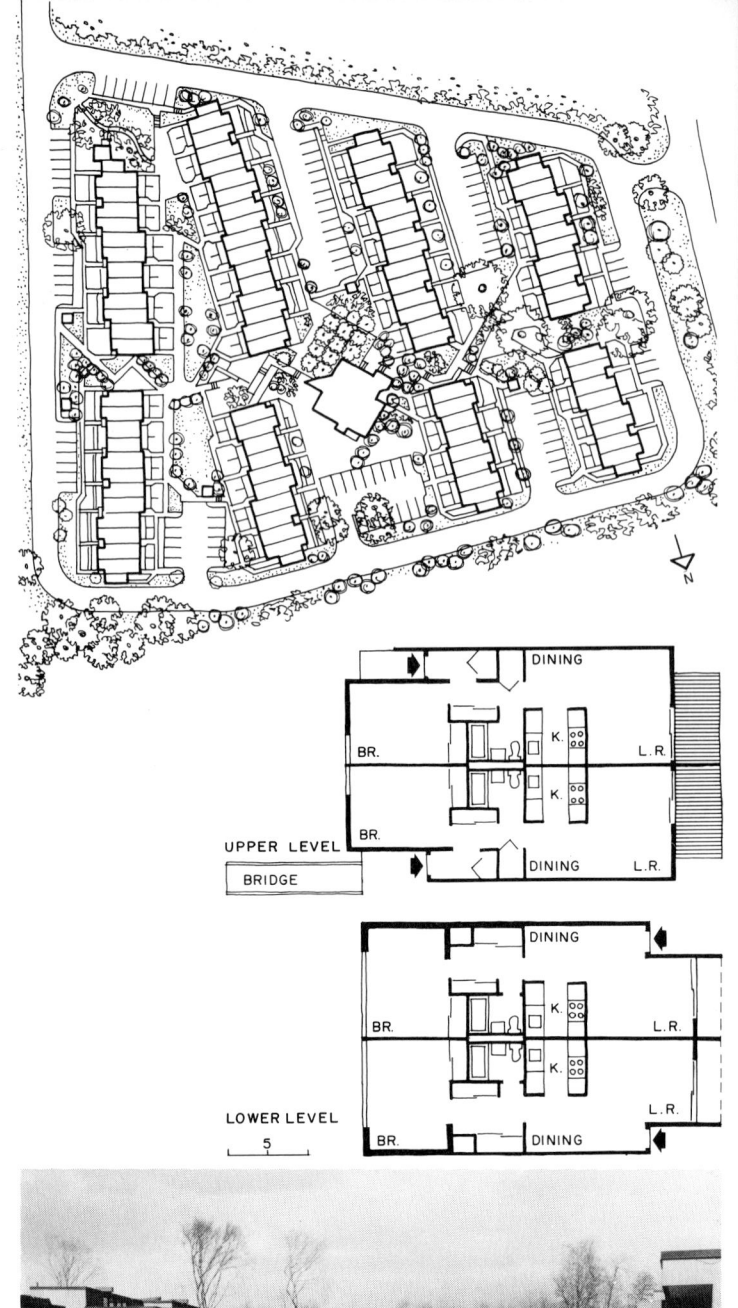

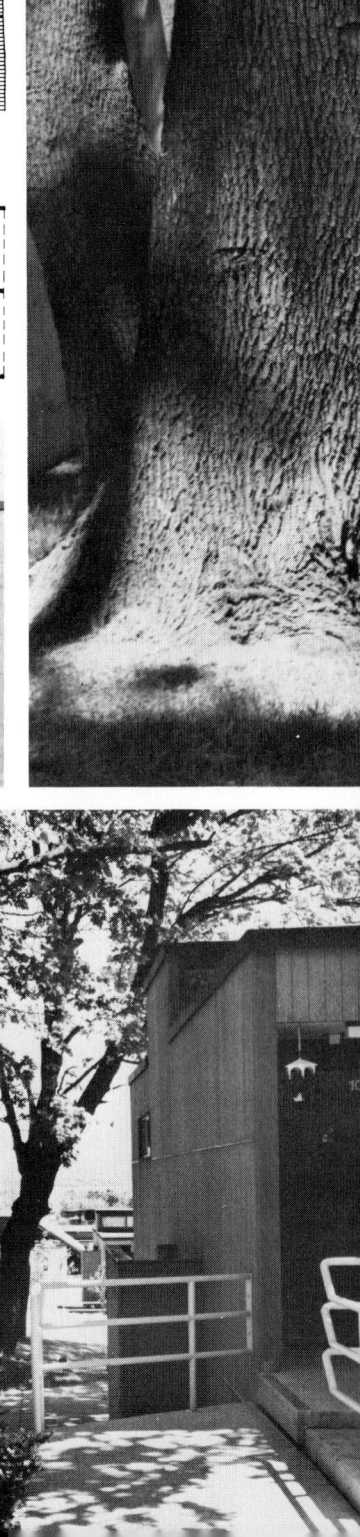

WALNUT HILL APARTMENTS
Architects: Smotrich & Platt
  12 East 44th Street
  New York, New York
  William Eisenberg, project architect
Owners: Haverstraw Associates
  with New York State Urban
  Development Corp.
Engineers: Atlas/Balogh Associates (structural)
  Woodward Clyde (soils)
  Robert Ettinger Associates (mechanical)
Landscape design:
  Environmental Systems Planning
Contractor: Helmer/Cronin Construction
Photographer: Thomas P. Palmer

Chapter Five

HOUSING FOR SKI RESORTS

Apartments and condominiums built for snow country must be designed with common sense. Architect Henrik Bull, head of the team of architects who designed Northstar Village at Lake Tahoe, California (pages 130-131), points out that it takes more than extra insulation and a larger furnace to make a warm and good living space for skiers. Too many architects, he claims, provide only that and add architectural cliches of shape and form with no relevance to mountain climates. Such architects expect the weather to adapt to their designs instead of the other way around.

For an example, everyone knows that melting snow will slide on an inclined surface, but not enough designers give any thought to where that snow will end up and often it plunges over a doorway and onto a deck or path. A good first rule, then, for the design of housing in the mountains is to pitch the roofs away from where people are expected to be.

Ice dams, formed at the eaves when the heat indoors melts the snow and sends it coursing down to the cold eave where it freezes, will eventually cause leaks inside or damage to the roof outside. A good second rule, therefore, is to design so that ice dams can't form. This is accomplished either by using the European "cold roof" — two separate layers between which outside air flows, preventing heat transfer — or by introducing warm air into the eaves. A good third rule in snow country is to design for a respectable snow load: at Northstar the architects used 240 pounds per square foot to take the very heavy snow loads of the High Sierras.

Each complex shown in this chapter consists of a varying number and type of modular units, concentrated in clusters. In Northstar four plans were used to create twenty different buildings. The units were stacked vertically or linked horizontally as needed. Three-story and two-story units were placed next to each other with the same roof pitch serving both.

Thus all the housing in this chapter consists of simple modules arranged in complex ways. The clusters, however, share a common simplicity of construction — wood frame with wood siding and standing seam metal or wood shingle roofs.

The housing complexes also share evidence of the concern of their architects for the beauty and ecology of their surroundings. All were designed for minimum disturbance to the terrain and most even enhance it.

1

Located near Sugarbush, one of Vermont's famed skiing resorts, this group of 48 condominium apartments is divided into eight house-like buildings that are separated from each other by generous distances and trees. Still, the condominiums occupy only a small portion of a large natural site of 101 acres. And their presence offers an interesting financial means for maintaining the bulk of that site in its sylvan condition—which is doubly important because of its location adjacent to a large state forest. As the condominiums themselves produce a viable density for the amount of land the remainder can be divided into 24 acres of totally undisturbed common space and 15 parcels for single houses on at least five acres each.

Each of the house-like units shown here contains six apartments—not large, but in keeping with their intended use for vacations. Sizes range from 600 square feet in a studio to 1050 square feet in the largest two-bedroom unit. Every unit is given visual interest and a feeling of more expansive space by changes in the floor levels or by double-height ceilings (see sections). Each is entered from grade—the upper units being entered by bridges from the nearby uphill slope. Siting for each of the buildings has been carefully considered to make natural conditions work to advantage.

Commonly owned facilities include a community building, tennis courts and a swimming pool. Construction—while mostly of standard wood framing—was accomplished by the prefabrication of parts in an on-site factory. The factory was built in recognition of the short construction season in the locale, and allowed non-seasonal work—as well as a speeding of the whole process. Concrete block walls between the units act as fire barriers and deaden sounds. They also support the light weight concrete floors. Windows are double glazing in wooden frames, and roofs are galvanized steel sheets with standing seams.

Butternut Hill Condominiums
Architects: Design Five, Inc.
  806 Massachusetts Avenue
  Cambridge, Massachusetts
Owner: Great Eastern Building Company, Inc.
Contractor: Great Eastern Building Company, Inc.
Photographer: © Steve Rosenthal

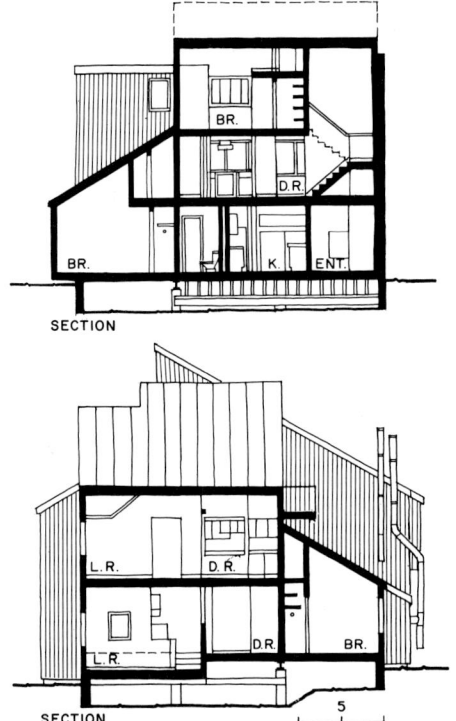

Forty-eight apartments are designed for vacation living. Half contain two bedrooms. The remainder have one bedroom or are efficiencies. The upper living rooms are double-height, while visual interest in the lower-level living rooms is provided by a change in floor levels (see smaller photos and sections above).

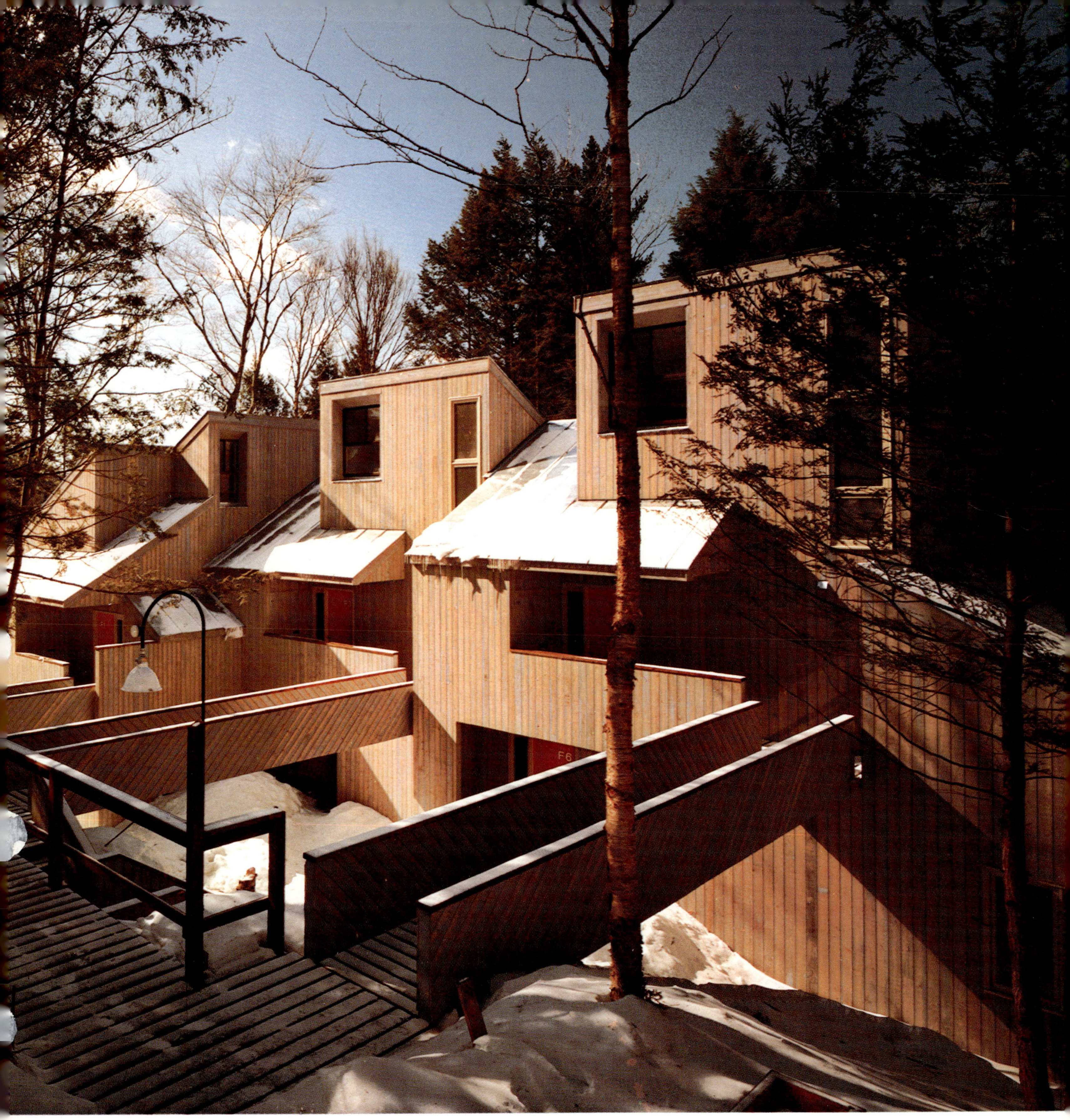

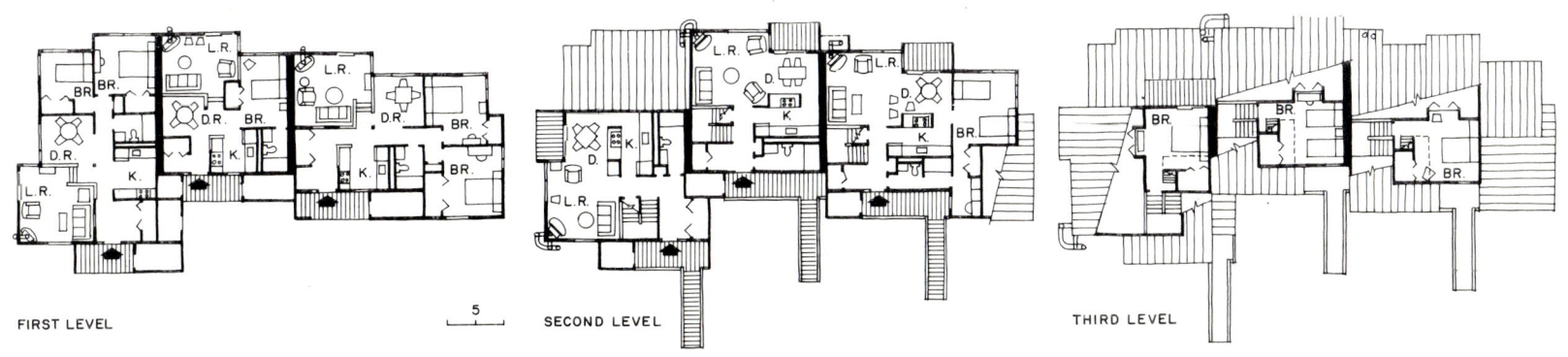

FIRST LEVEL   5   SECOND LEVEL   THIRD LEVEL

127

2

Even in summer, when it blends visually into the background of mountain grasses leading to a high ridge, Village Point is a powerful megastructural solution well suited to its Rocky Mountain setting. In winter, set against a mantle of white, it is a ski center and filled with the colors and activity that skiing equipment and clothing inevitably produce.

The buildings are stepped back in section to make them conform to the site profile and extend inward to provide covered parking (see section). The 33 apartments in this first phase of the development are built on a 12-foot planning module, are typically two- and three-bedroom duplex condominiums. The standard modular unit plan can be combined and arranged on the site to satisfy the program requirements. Covered passageways, stairs and bridges (photo below) provide easy avenues of circulation between apartments while protecting the privacy of individual units. Design architect Arley Rinehart has used these bridges as ligaments to bind together the project's very considerable masses. The massing is also enriched by a system of earth berms into which the project's foundations are carefully keyed. A swimming pool, located at the juncture between the two long structures, offers owners a fair weather option.

The structure includes wood posts and laminated wood beams left exposed inside for visual continuity. Roofs are sheathed in copper. Anticipating a copper patina, the exteriors are clad in cedar siding stained to a soft brown.

Village Point Condominiums are vigorously conceived and executed without noticeable compromise to the important planning principles that form the project's conceptual core.

SECTION

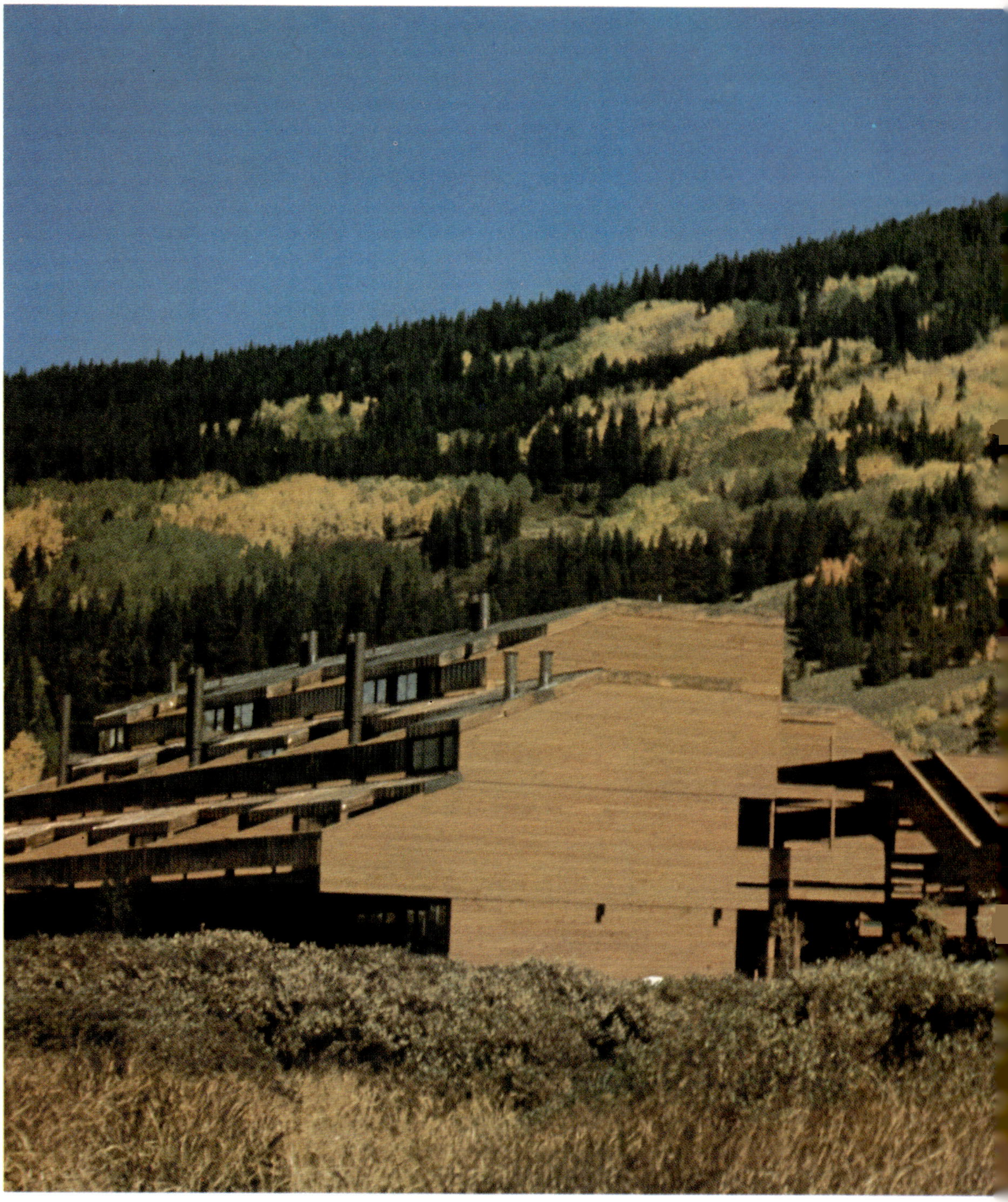

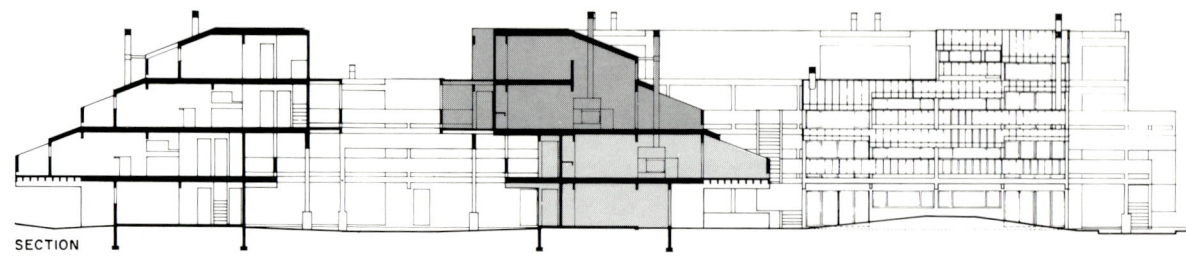

VILLAGE POINT
Design architects: Arley Rinehart Associates
Richard Henry, associate
2345 Seventh Street
Denver, Colorado
Associated architects:
Seracuse Lawler and Partners
Project name: Village Point
Owner: Broker House Ltd.
Engineers: AD&C Group (structural)
J. J. Blank (mechanical)
Garland Cox & Associates (electrical)
Interiors: Associates III
Landscape architects: Dennis Miller Associates
Photographer: Richard Henry

1 LOWER FLOOR 2 UPPER FLOOR 3 LOWER FLOOR 4 UPPER FLOOR

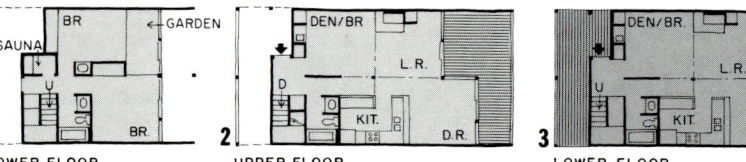

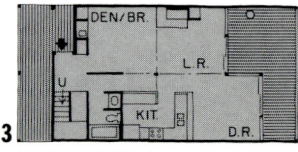

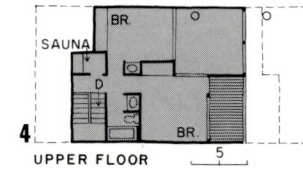

3

When the snows come to Lake Tahoe so do the skiers—and in increasing numbers each year. Not all of this beautiful region's recent development has been praiseworthy, but Northstar Village, by architects Bull Field Volkmann Stockwell, has been designed and built with sensitivity to its surroundings as well as to the recreational needs of its users. It is also built on a European resort model, employing tidy, compact planning principles that emphasize a sense of community rather than individual spatial amenity. Most living spaces (see plans) are minimal when compared to other second-home developments, but the first phase of this project has sold well and another grouping of similar units is now in planning. When it is complete, the two groupings will enclose a central plaza that will act as a gathering point and focus for the whole development.

The section at right reveals the planning scheme concisely. Residential units, located on the upper levels, have their own access and parking underneath. Linking all the units is a low arcade on the plaza level lined by shop windows and restaurants. Balconies over the arcade give condominium owners views into the central plaza or to the slopes beyond.

The structures are heavy wood frame clad in cedar siding. Only the roof, finished in blue metal, adds an accent of color to contrast with the natural tones of wood. The characteristic roof form is designed to protect against ice slides caused when the relatively warm interior spaces melt the snow by day and sub-freezing temperatures refreeze it at night.

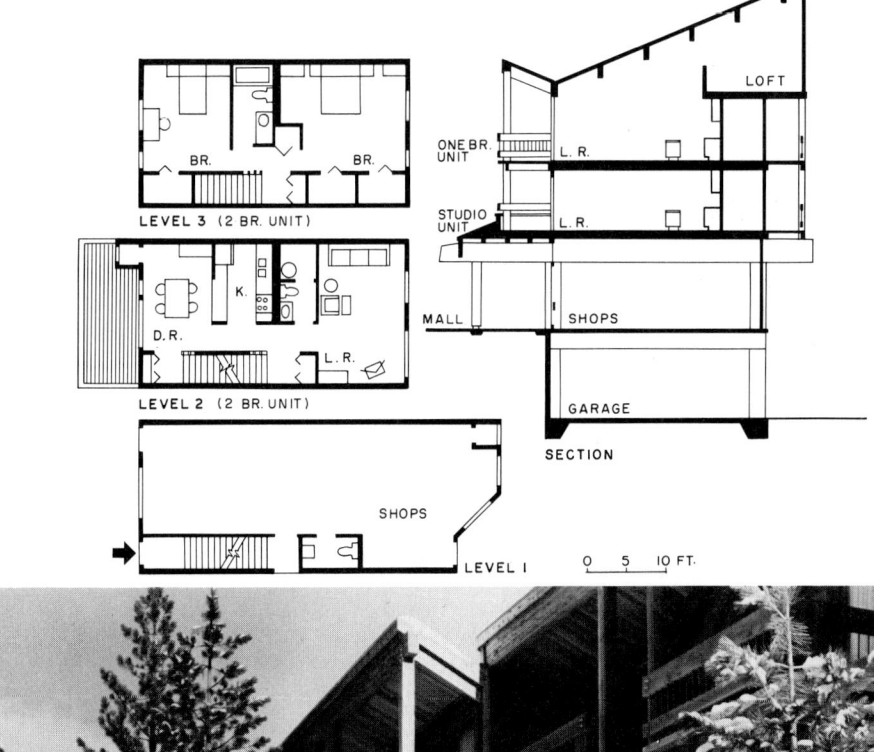

NORTHSTAR VILLAGE
Architects: Bull Field Volkmann Stockwell
  project architect: Steven Kodama
  designer: Serge Bicking
  350 Pacific Avenue
  San Francisco, California
Project name: Northstar Village
Owner: Trimont Land Company
Location: Placer County, California
Engineers:
  Gilbert, Forsberg, Dickmann & Schmidt (structural)
  Dames & Moore (foundation)
  Marion Cerbatos & Tomasi (mechanical)
Contractor: Murchison Construction
Photographer: Tom Lippert

4

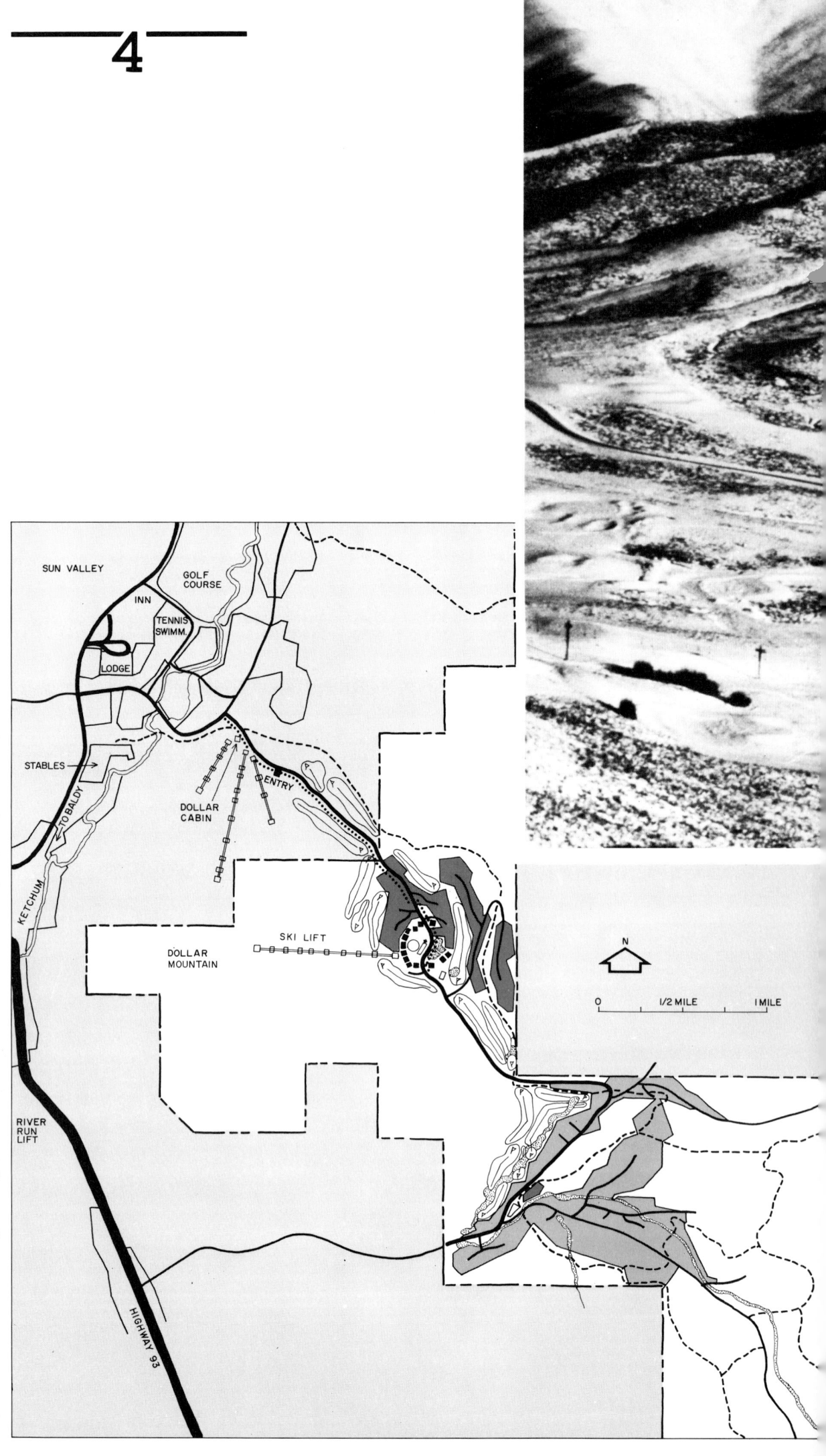

Elkhorn Valley, a mile and a half south of Sun Valley and just over the saddle of Dollar Mountain, is a sunny, almost windless, completely treeless and —until 1972—untouched place in Idaho, known mostly to skiers and hikers. In 1972, Bill Janss, owner of the Sun Valley Corporation, joined with Johns-Manville Corporation in a plan to develop 2,950 acres of Elkhorn Valley as a new ski resort area to complement the resort at Sun Valley.

Fortunately, Janss and his co-developers were aware of the need to handle such an area with great care. Development at Sun Valley had extended that resort town to its furthest limits as a walking village, and further development would encroach on the character of the place, which, along with its splendid powder snow, had made it an internationally attractive area since 1936 when the Union Pacific Railroad began its development.

Site planners Sasaki, Walker & Associates were called in to master plan the new resort for phased development over a 10-year period. They studied every aspect of the valley's environment—climate, soil structure, geology and soil relationships, topography, vegetation—in order to know how to develop the land and at the same time maintain its natural relationships. A slope inventory was also made and— since the visual quality of the place was of great importance to its success—a visual analysis was made of the views and vistas of the site, from the site, and within the site. From this data, a physical and visual summary was made as the first step toward a conceptual plan for the valley.

To intrude upon the untouched grandeur of this open valley may have seemed a sacrilege, but its openness made it vulnerable and a sure target for development at some time. The decision to make of Elkhorn a human-scaled village within the vast scale of the valley and mountains at once brought it into the context of similar situations in the Alps. Indeed, there is a feeling of a Swiss mountain village in the location of Elkhorn in a valley below a lofty mountain. The man-made village seems tiny, drawn into itself, alone—especially in the snow. What makes it uniquely American and particularly Western American is its containment within, its circumscription by, a space vastly larger than itself and destined to remain so.

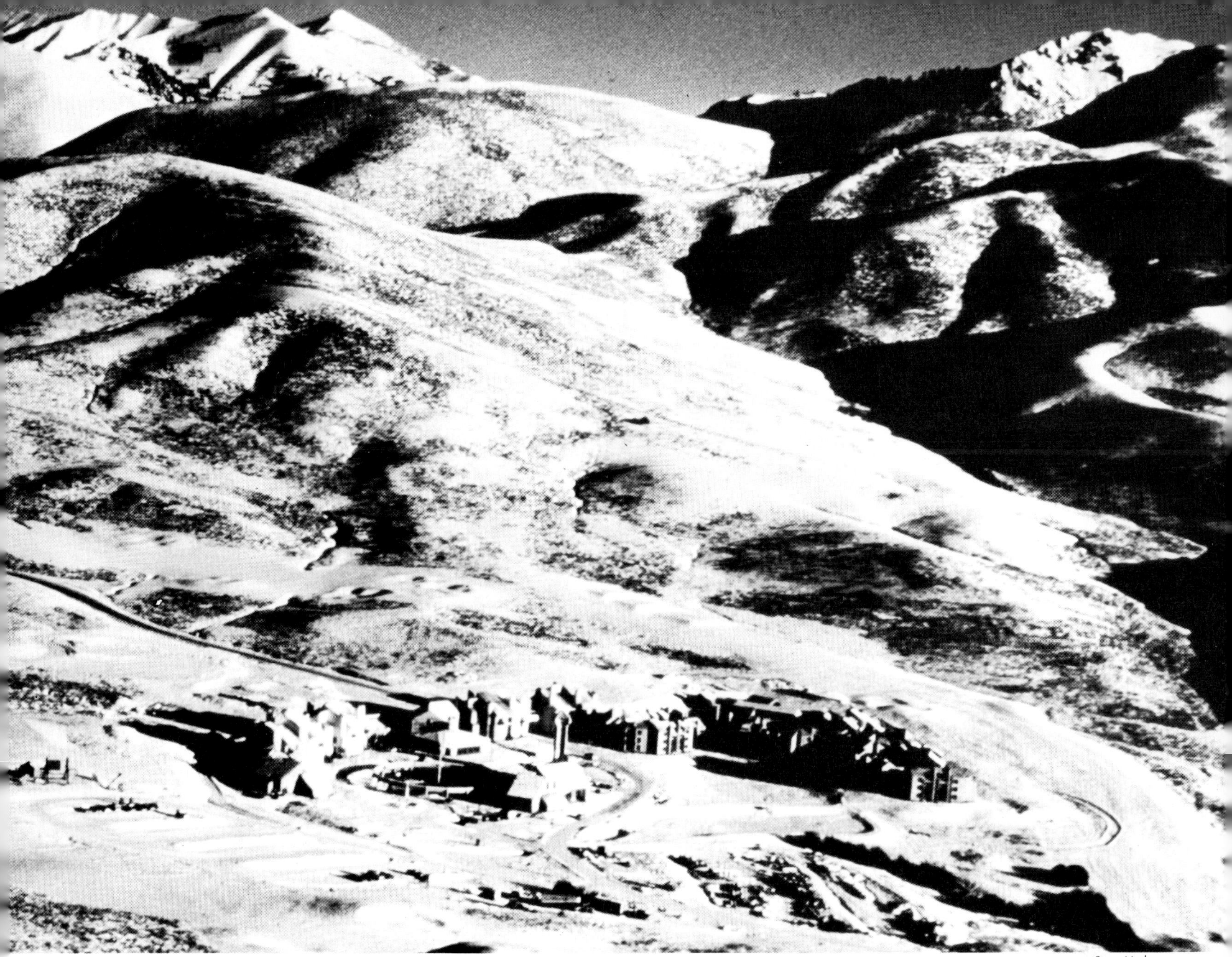

Steve Marks

Elkhorn's master plan was developed by the land planners as part of the over-all long-range plan for the city of Sun Valley (left) of which it is a part, so that the same standards—though not the same architectural style—will control development in each. The total development plan for Elkhorn (right) shows density of future condominium development around village center.

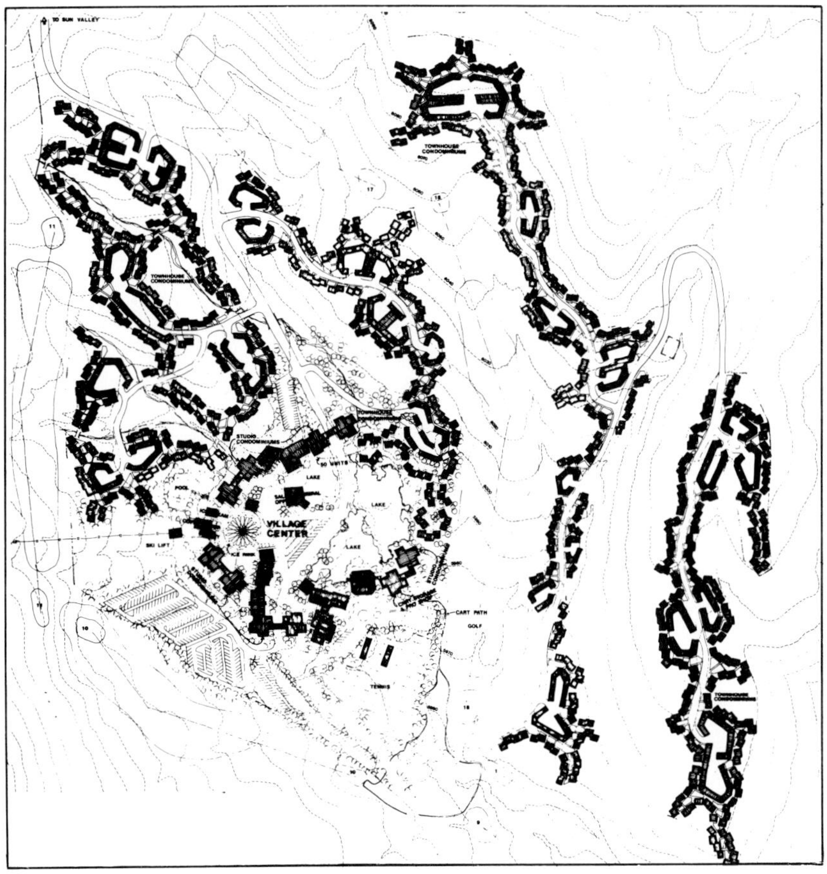

TO SUN VALLEY
TOWNHOUSE CONDOMINIUMS
VILLAGE CENTER
LAKE
SKI LIFT
CART PATH
GOLF
TENNIS

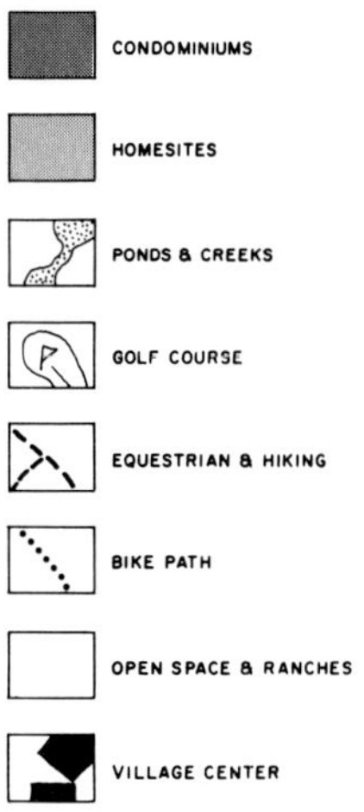

CONDOMINIUMS
HOMESITES
PONDS & CREEKS
GOLF COURSE
EQUESTRIAN & HIKING
BIKE PATH
OPEN SPACE & RANCHES
VILLAGE CENTER

At Elkhorn, the view is up to the mountains, rather than, as more frequently happens in this country, from the mountain to a panorama of the valley.

Of the 2,950 acres of Elkhorn's site, only 300 will be covered by buildings. Approximately 400 will be paved and landscaped, and the remainder—75 per cent of the site—will be preserved as natural open space.

In the village center are community and commercial facilities, less extensive than a self sufficient village might require since Sun Valley's older and more extensive commercial development and its two large hotels are easily accessible by car or free bus service.

In developing an architectural expression for this new resort, Killingsworth, Brady & Associates, architects for both condominiums and commercial areas, studied mountain villages in various parts of Europe—not to borrow their forms but to analyze the characteristics which were common to all, and, using these basics, to devise a contemporary and individual style which would be distinct to Elkhorn. The pitched roofs, deep set windows and balconies, and stenciled patterns (in blue) catch the whimsical and the practical aspects of Alpine buildings but look little like them.

"Old villages," says Edward Killingsworth, "aren't precise and well-ordered; they just sort of happen." The analysis by Killingsworth and his associates netted good results: Elkhorn is no self-conscious putting-together of forms for a studied variation, but has a feeling of natural difference which comes from the siting of the groups of condominiums and from disciplined use of materials.

The valley's landmark is the village bell tower, a distinctive form which is the focal point of the village center, marking the location of the community hall. Nearby, and complementing the tower with its strong circular form, is the ice rink, used year-round. Ranged in a semi-circle about the rink is a terrace on which are located shops with condominiums above, and a hip-roofed restaurant building (bottom, right).

When it is completed in 1982, Elkhorn will look only slightly larger than it does now. More condominiums will be built around the village, but private residences and ranches (lots up to two and a half acres) will be located in the "finger valleys" off the big valley, preserving the unity of the village.

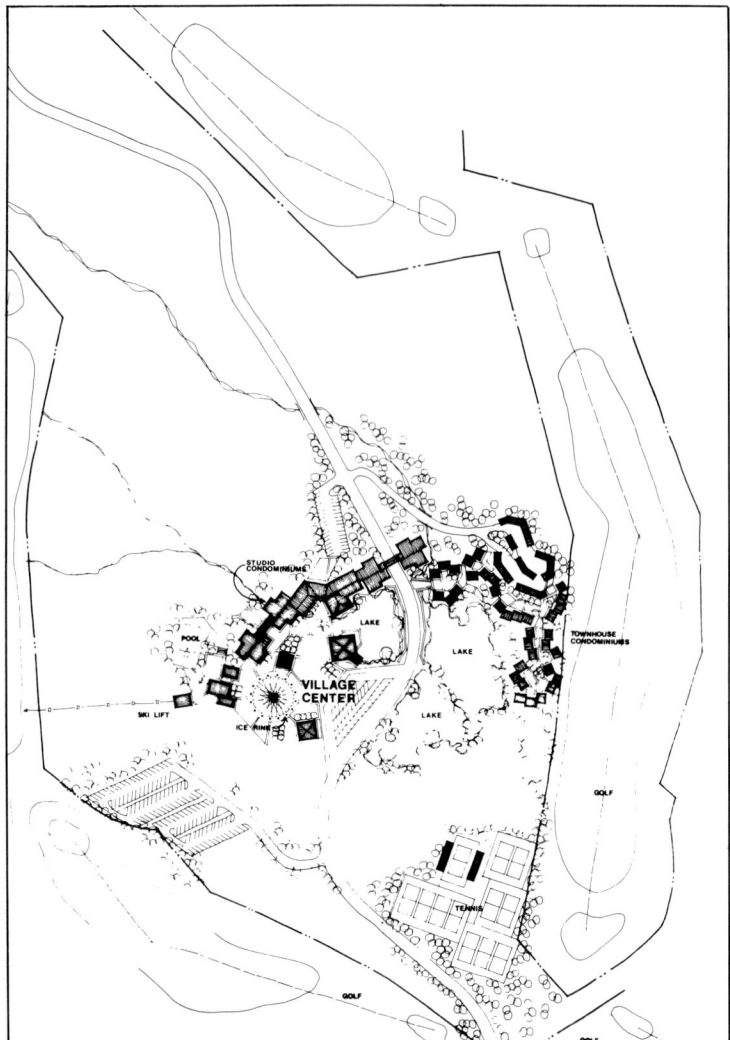
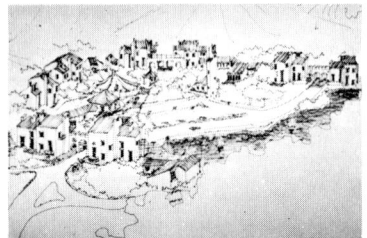

Lars Speyer

The village center concentrates community activity in a small area of shops, restaurants and recreational facilities, like the ice rink (top, across page). Although cars are not permitted in the center, ample parking is provided for visitors and skiers (the Dollar Mountain ski lift is just outside the center) on the periphery. The first phase development (plan, above, left) included the commercial area and village condominiums, Bonne Vie condominiums, the ice rink and some tennis courts. Actual buildings in the village show some changes from the early studies of architectural character, particularly in more formal proposals for Village entrance (above, center sketch), and in use of stencilling on the village buildings. The Bell Tower's strong form dominates the village center and is visible from all parts of the valley.

All photos by Lars Speyer except as noted.

The essay on Elkhorn which begins on this page is by Edward A. Killingsworth, FAIA, Killingsworth, Brady & Associates

A new resort town, however small, deserves its own architectural character as much—perhaps more, because it is small and more easily seen—as any larger development. Sun Valley, in the next valley, had chosen years ago to use an eclectic, unspecific European approach for its buildings, but we determined that Elkhorn should be completely modern. We knew, however, that we wanted it to have as much charm as an Alpine village, so we studied European mountain villages and towns, establishing those basic elements that are so universally appealing to people.

Reduced to their basics, many villages—Swiss, Bavarian, Austrian, Italian: it makes little difference—are essentially identical. The towns have many common denominators, all of which contribute to an impression of inviting variety, carefully balanced by great discipline in the use of materials and details: a play of spaces; narrow curving streets, enticing the pedestrian, that spill out into squares; narrow slits between buildings through which shafts of light penetrate; a feeling of containment derived from tall buildings and restricted vistas. All contribute to a comfortable pedestrian scale and to the delight which spells success in any destination resort.

We determined to base our design for Elkhorn on these principles, but to develop only the subtlest resemblance to buildings of earlier periods so that a unique identity could develop for Elkhorn. We adopted and adapted the Tyrol's exterior surface stenciling using our own designs in a bolder contemporary way. (Stenciling proved economical and is easily maintained.) Deep wall recesses and double doors suggest but do not imitate old world details. Steep-pitched roofs became the strongest element in the village, marking it against the stark valley landscape as a place of unique and individual character.

In its initial development, Elkhorn is small, perhaps too small to have the scale needed to make an impact in the beautiful openness that surrounds it and is there forever. As it develops to its full size—1400 condominium units, 700 single-family houses and ranches—that scale will change.

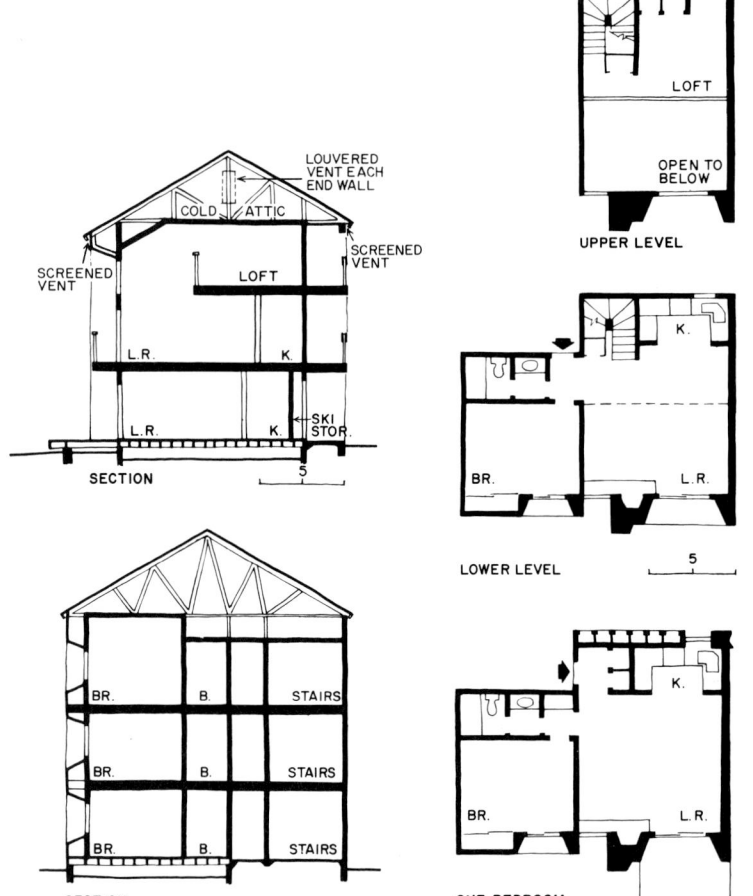
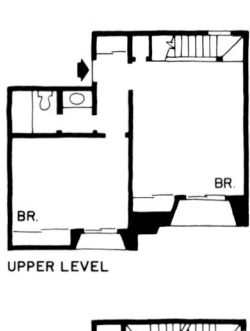

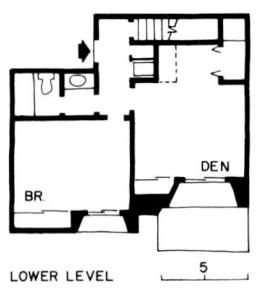

Elkhorn's master plan premises a total of 1400 condominium units (and an overall total of 2100 housing units, including ranches and single-family houses). There are three groups of condominiums: the Village Group (bottom, across page) is European-style, above shops and restaurants. The Bonne Vie (top, across page) is northeast of the Village, across the road from Sun Valley. Another group, Indian Springs (not shown) is northwest of the village. Bonne Vie units have garages as well as open parking; Indian Springs has open parking. Village units have parking on the periphery, near enough but well outside the actual village where no cars are permitted. Warm air is circulated under the pitched roofs of condominium buildings and to the eaves so that snow rarely builds up on them. Icicles do form, however, at roof edges and are removed with long poles (bottom left). Wood shingles, boards and plaster are used on condominium building exteriors.

Lars Speyer photos

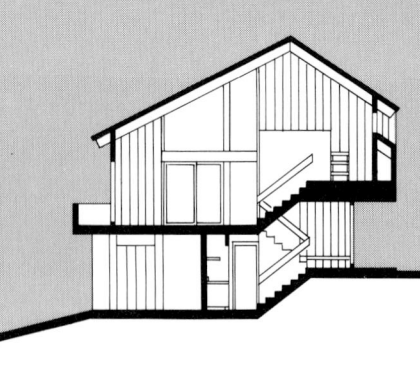

5

On this 800-acre parcel that faces the Loon Mountain Ski area in the White Mountains, the architects have completed the first phase of development that includes 200 hillside townhouses grouped around an attractive Village Center. The Center is a pedestrian shopping/recreation street complete with restaurant, grocery stores, skating rink, swimming pool (photo below) and indoor-outdoor tennis facilities. Up from the Center, along the flanks of the mountainside, are 1-, 2-, and 3-bedroom condominiums clustered as topographical conditions dictated in groupings of various sizes. Each cluster is sited so as to disturb the terrain as little as possible. Close-in trees, as the photo at right indicates, were retained and the natural vegetation of the earth floor was left as is. These things, together with an active but unassuming massing and choice of finishes, produces about as gentle an intrusion as any architecture can make into a forest setting while still providing a full array of domestic amenities.

The floor plans of individual units vary by type but all are arranged in a lively series of half levels keyed to the slope of the site. Living, dining, and kitchen spaces typically occupy the intermediate level with master bedroom and sleeping loft a half level below and above respectively. The entry, which leads to the split level stair, is designed and outfitted as a ski storage space.

The delight of this project is in the site relationships and in the manner in which the architects have responded to them. Without noticeable sacrifice to environmental values, this community offers superb access to some of the best and least developed recreational lands in the Northeast.

VILLAGE AT LOON MOUNTAIN
Architects: Huygens and Tappé, Inc.
   462 Boylston Street
   Boston, Massachusetts
   Francis Di Mella, partner-in-charge
Developer: Herriot, Eaton, Keating
Site planning: Sasaki, Walker, Roberts
Engineer: Steco Engineering Corp. (structural)
Contractor: Martin Carrier
Photographer: ©Steve Rosenthal

The pool complex, at left, is a portion of the Village Center—a Center that is being built in stages to correspond with the over-all growth of this recreational community. What is emphasized by these designs in the impression of ``village'' rather than development.

The townhouses are of wood frame construction with rough-sawn, shiplapped pine siding on exterior walls and spruce clapboards on balcony parapets. Metal roofing has a bronze-colored, baked enamel finish. Inside, floors are carpeted except for sheet vinyl in kitchen and bathrooms, and 4- by 6-in. wood blocks with end cut exposed in the entry ski rooms. All units have fireplaces and electric heating.

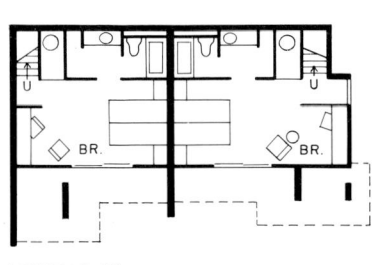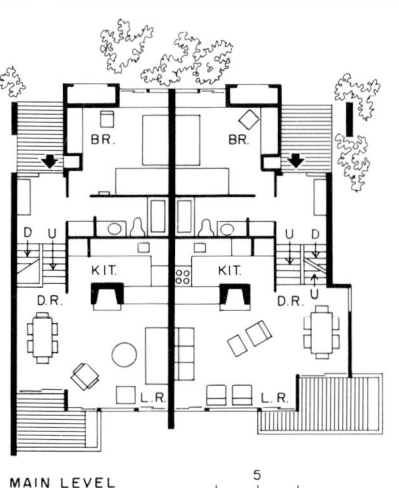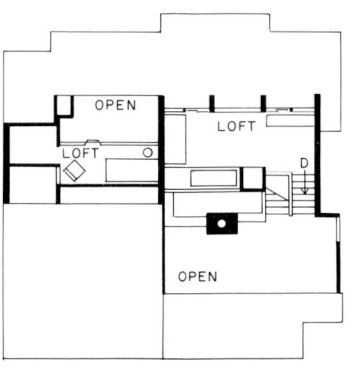

LOWER LEVEL　　　MAIN LEVEL　　　UPPER LEVEL

141

6

This 60- by 100-foot corner lot was the last undeveloped property in a residential neighborhood largely characterized by small scale, late-19th-century Victorian buildings. The architects' task was to provide six studio apartments of simple and economic design that were compatible with the Victorian "feel" of the community.

The six units at 600 square feet each are minimal in program but are designed with concern for both site and occupants. The plans are staggered along the front facade to heighten its sense of three-dimensional depth and to preserve an open space of modest scale at the corner of the site. Within the severe restrictions of budget, each apartment has a measure of outdoor space as well as a fireplace and a 13-foot ceiling.

The structure is concrete block bearing walls, exposed inside and out, wood floor and roof joists and a built-up roof. Gypsum board is used inside for ceilings and some wall surfaces, and outside cedar siding is used to contrast warmly with the block. Painted metal railings and flues provide added visual interest.

What seems especially commendable—and perhaps this is the lesson—is that the restrictions of program, budget and site did not become excuses for a design devoid of any interest. Instead, the architects achieved considerable sculptural interest, significant and welcome interior comfort and a building cluster that sits well on its site—a site near the ski lifts and only a short walk from shopping.

COOPER STREET LOFTS
Architects: Copland Finholm Hagman Yaw
  Box 2736
  Aspen, Colorado
  William Campbell, project manager
Owner: Cooper Street Partners
Engineers:
  Anderson & Hastings (structural)
  McFall and Konkel (mechanical)
Contractor: Wilbur, Carlson, Inc.
Photographer: William Lukes

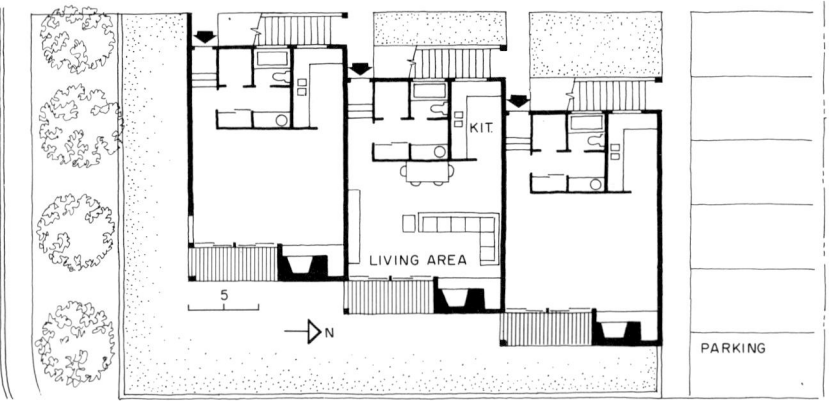

Chapter Six

RECYCLING AND ADAPTIVE RE-USE

The dollars being spent for restoration and remodeling for re-use are multiplying. More and more architects are converting all kinds of buildings into housing for an obvious reason, the downturn in new housing and apartment construction. But there are other important influences as well.

The downturn in new housing construction was preceded by a new public and client awareness of the economic value of older buildings and their interior spaces. Often remodeling makes more sense in dollar terms than new construction. Further, there is a deepening awareness on the part of the public and the client of the esthetic as well as the practical value and potential of older buildings that have aged well, in older neighborhoods which carry their years with grace. The examples included in this chapter prove the point. An old granite wharf building in Boston which once housed ship chandlers and sail makers now contains 121 mixed-income apartments ranging from duplexes and triplexes with lofts and skylights to one-bedroom apartments (pages 146-147). An outmoded tannery complex in Peabody, Massachusetts has been recycled into housing for the elderly (pages 148-151).

A six-story former toy factory with one of the finest cast iron fronts in New York City's SoHo district has been wittily restored by architect Hanford Yang who lives and works in two of its loft floors (pages 152-153). Another loft building — a five-story former cord factory in lower Manhattan has been transformed into three spacious apartments and rentable commercial space (154-157). And only minor structural changes were required to transform an old blacksmith's shop with a rooming house above into middle-income apartments (pages 158-159).

Streets as well as buildings can of course be recycled and so-called infill housing has an important role to play. On Boston's Beacon Hill, fire destroyed one of a pair of rowhouses which was sensitively replaced by a fifteen unit condominium. It fits snugly into the street and respects the scale, form and finish of its neighbors (pages 178-179).

Surplus urban schools are now being converted into housing and their nearness to libraries, churches and shopping make them ideal for the elderly (pages 162-163). Hotels are being recycled (pages 164-165), as are office buildings (pages 166-169). And older townhouses and apartments within old and new high-rise apartment buildings are being renewed or adapted to meet today's standards of luxury and to provide additional saleable units.

© Steve Rosenthal photos

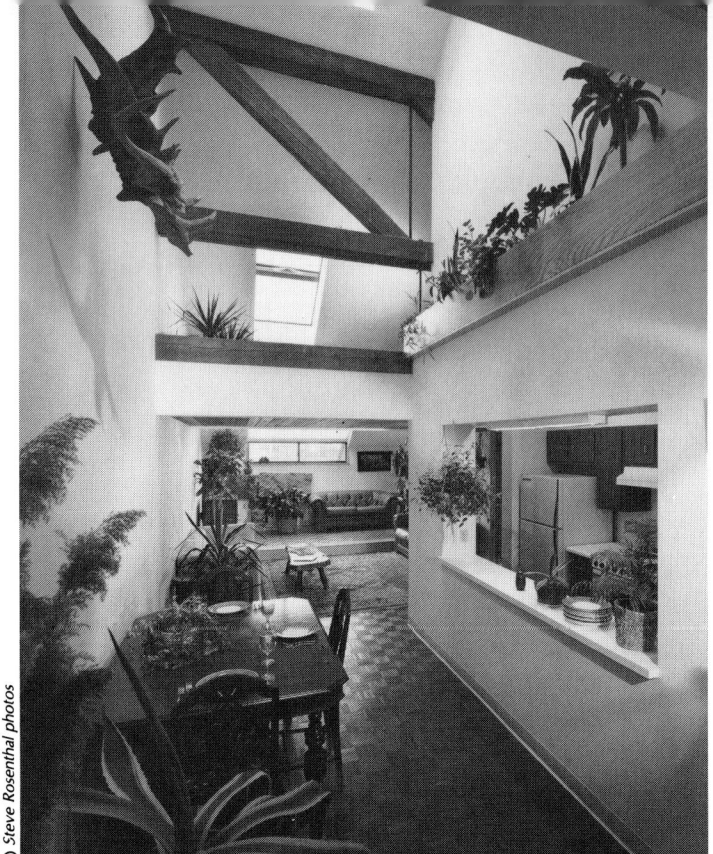

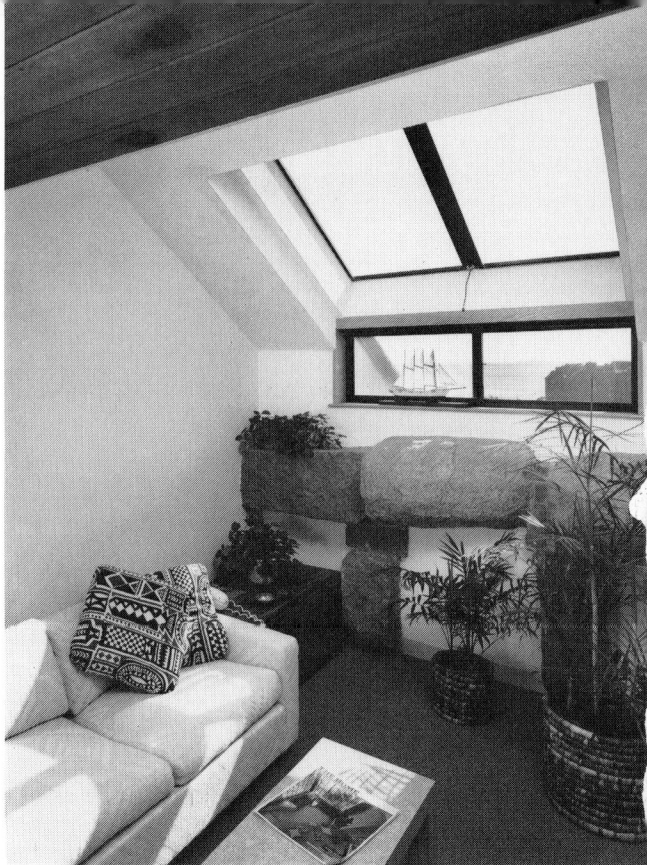

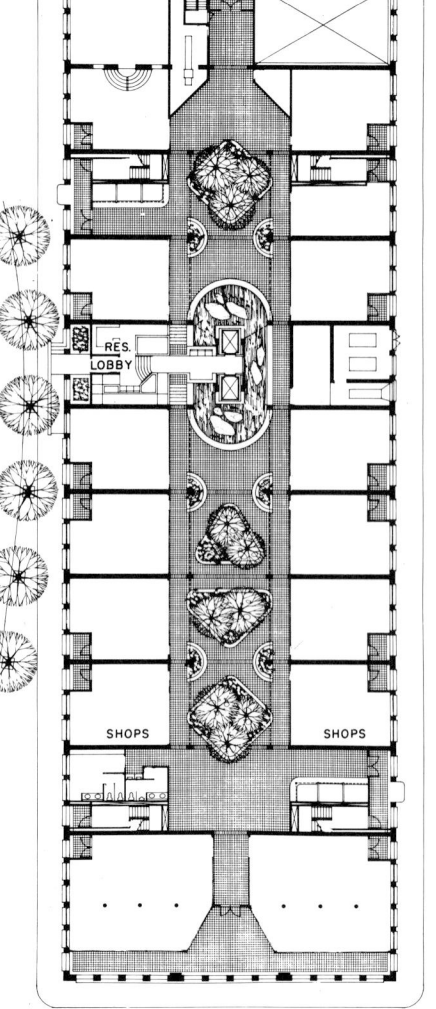

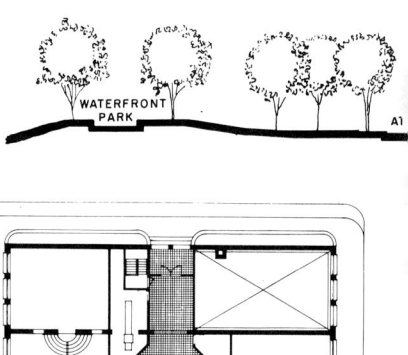

GROUND FLOOR

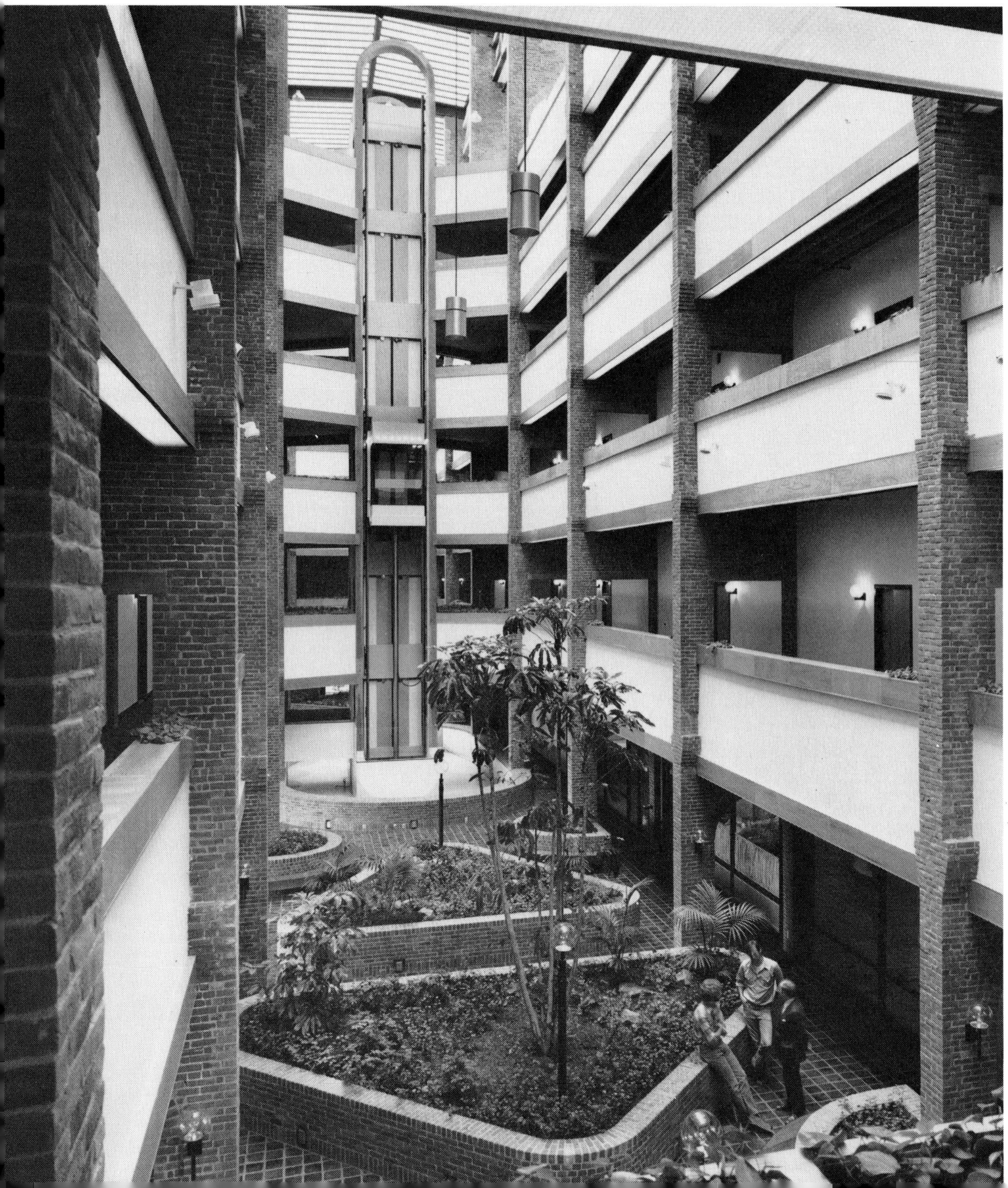

1

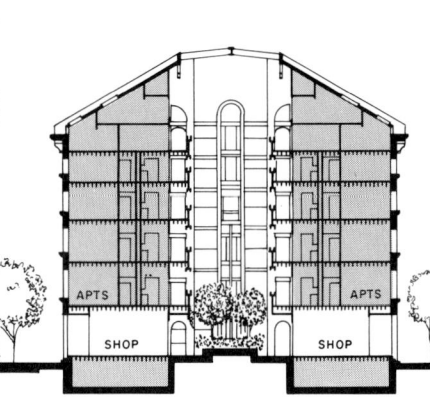

The Mercantile Wharf Building was not developed by one of Boston's poor communities. 16-21). The excellent collaboration

Sharratt got the job to renovate the Mercantile Wharf Building by winning a developer/architect competition sponsored by the Boston Redevelopment Authority in 1972. The successful developer was Peabody Construction Company, which earlier built "Torre Unidad" for the elderly in Viviendas La Victoria in Boston's South End, designed by Sharratt (pages 16-21). The excellent collaboration between Sharratt and Peabody led to their joint proposal.

The BRA had opposed Sharratt as "a trouble maker" during his early years as an advocacy planner. By 1972, however, leading officials of the BRA were calling the remodeled row houses of Viviendas La Victoria (photo, page 17) "the best residential rehabilitation in the city." And by the time Sharratt won the competition to rehabilitate the Mercantile Wharf Building, the BRA had begun recommending him to developers.

The BRA did no preliminary work on the building to get it ready for the developer. According to Sharratt: "it was full of dead animals, garbage, and rusted-out appliances—but it was very solid and well built." Originally designed in 1857 by Gridley James Fox Bryant in the French Second Empire Style, it once housed shipchandlers and sailmakers.

Sharratt's design preserves the original character of the building from the outside. Inside he has carved out a spectacular six-story atrium with a skylight extending its entire length. Two glass enclosed elevators descend to a pool.

The building contains 121 apartments ranging from duplexes and triplexes with lofts and skylights to one-bedroom apartments. Thirty-six of the apartment units are leased at market rents. Forty-two are for moderate-income and forty-three are low income. The subsidy program is HUD Section 707, and HUD Section 236.

MERCANTILE WHARF BUILDING, Boston, Massachusetts. Owner: *Mercantile Associates*. Architects: *John Sharratt Associates, Inc.—project architect: John Sharratt; project manager: Robert Meeker*. Consultants: *Engineers Design Group, Inc. (structural); William R. Ginns (mechanical); Sam Zax (electrical)*. General contractor: *Peabody Construction Co., Inc.*

2

An outmoded tannery complex has been recycled into housing for the elderly and has demonstrated the potential worth of such actions for smaller communities and for buildings that are less than landmark structures. The project has also brought new life to the neighborhood and a bit of history.

The complex was abandoned in 1971 because the buildings did not meet current industrial standards. The architects pinpointed and selectively demolished deteriorating structures, retaining three buildings (two six-story masonry and one three-story reinforced concrete building). Each was gutted and 284 apartments were constructed in a combination of efficiency, one- and two-bedroom apartments and duplex designs. Ten per cent of the units are specially equipped for handicapped tenants. Spatial variety in the original was maintained; in one instance, the roof of one building was jacked-up to provide space for duplex apartments. The exterior walls were cleaned and interior wooden beams and ceilings sandblasted to complete the recycling. Glass-enclosed bridges connect the two large apartment houses to the community center.

The project was financed in the early seventies by a $6 million mortgage from the Massachusetts Housing Finance Agency. It was the first time such funds were applied to recycled construction outside the Boston area. Twenty-five per cent of the units are low-income housing and subsidized by the state or are at full market rentals.

THE TANNERY, Peabody, Massachusetts. Owner: *Crowninshield Corporation*. Architects: *Anderson Notter Associates, Inc.* Engineers: *David M. Berg, Inc.* (structural); *Samuel Lesburg Associates* (mechanical); *Goodall Shapiro Associates, Inc.* (electrical). Landscape architect: *John G. Crowe*. Architectural historian: *George M. Wrenn III, Society for the Preservation of New England Antiquities*. General contractor: *Taylor Woodrow Blitman Construction*.

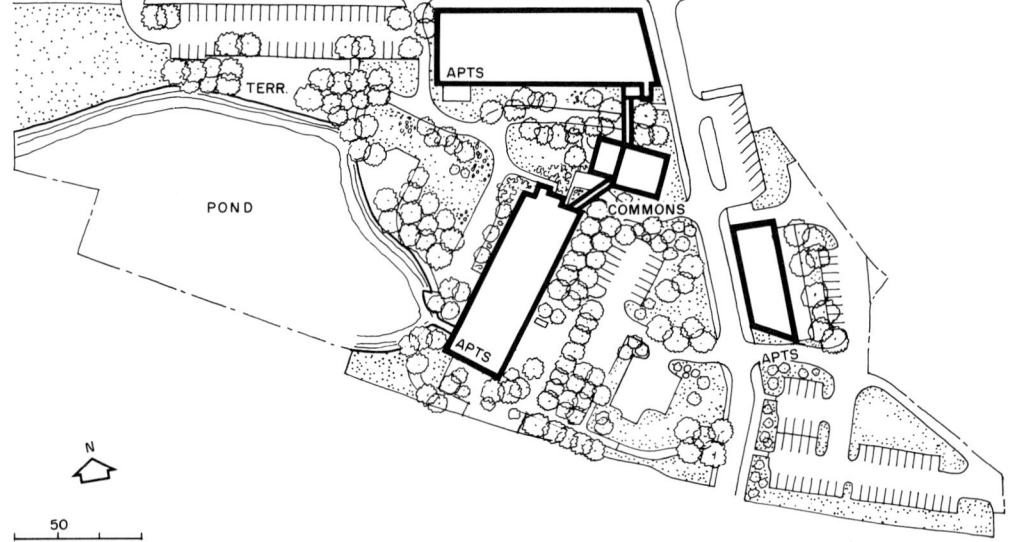

Remnants of the former tannery have been saved and reused, to provide "historic continuity" to the compex and site. Old tannery vats and drying wheels are now used as planters, including in the parking areas. Some foundations or walls (overleaf) are other than functional, lending an element of surprise or delight while retaining a special quality to the old structure. The pond was also cleaned-up to make a pleasant spot.

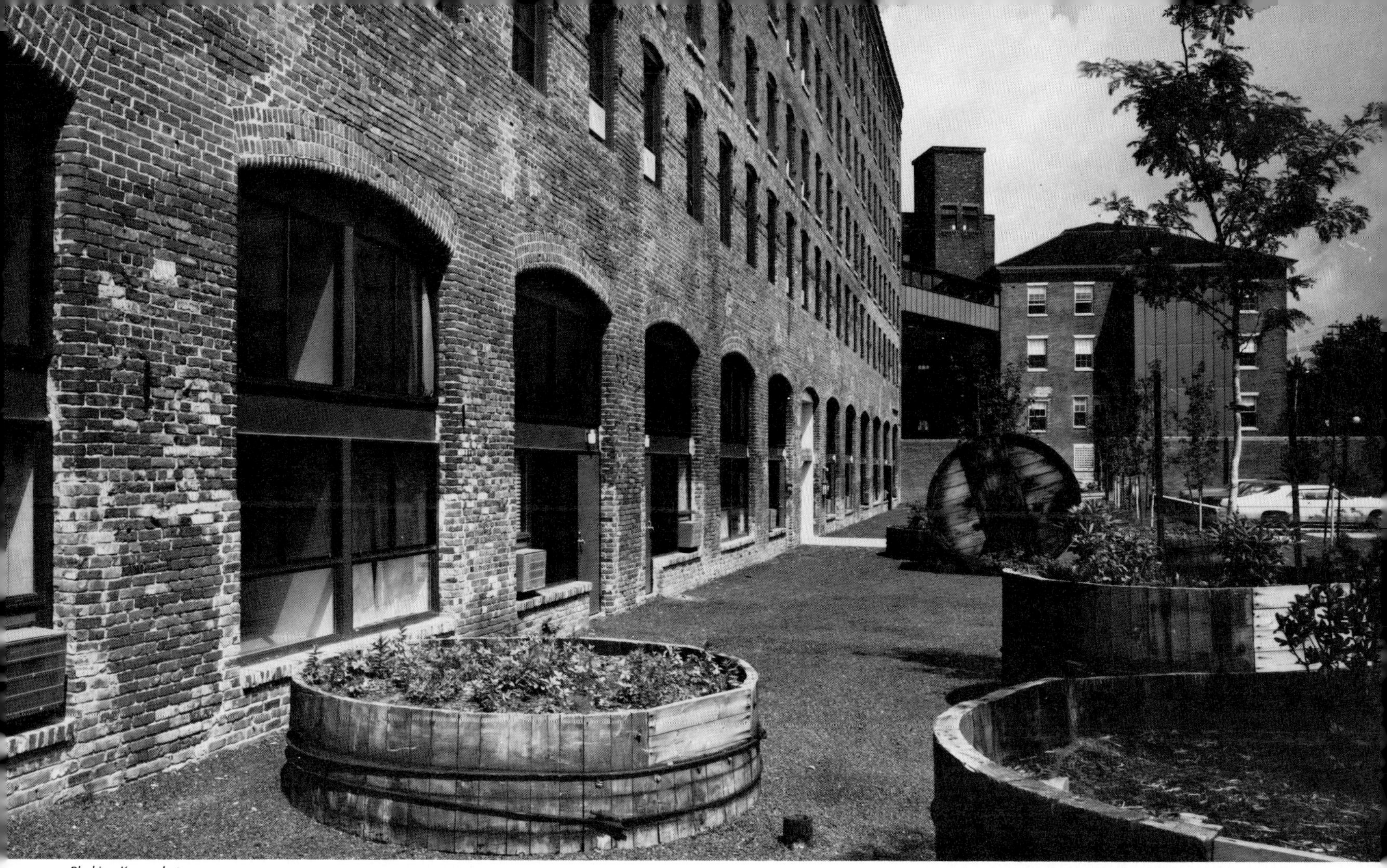

Phokion Karas photos

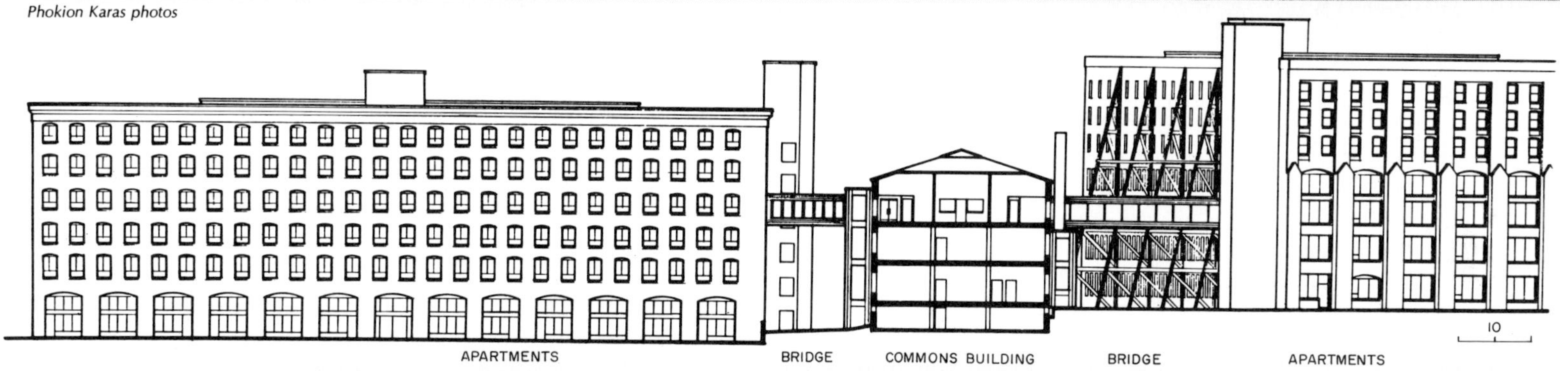

APARTMENTS | BRIDGE | COMMONS BUILDING | BRIDGE | APARTMENTS

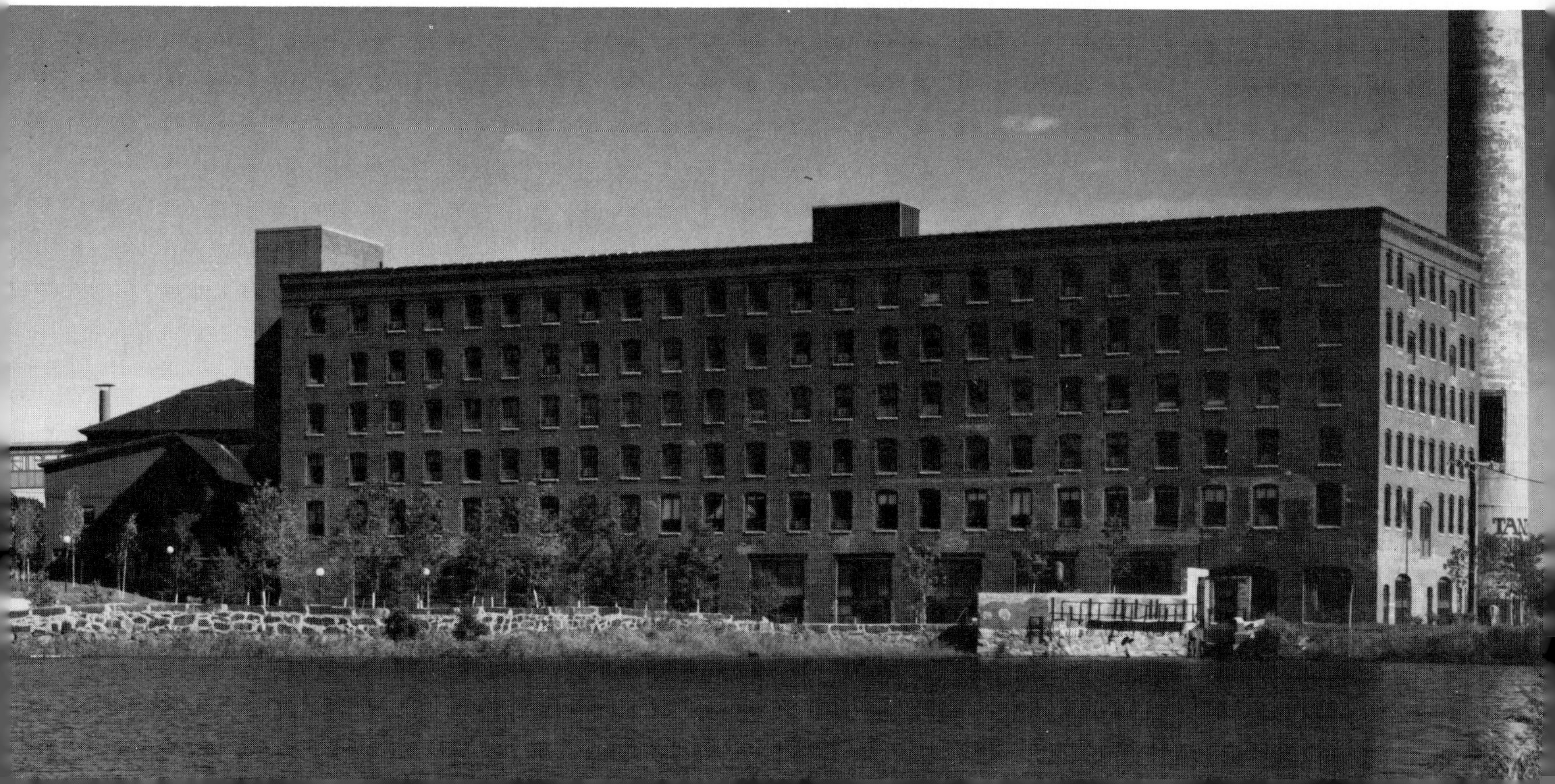

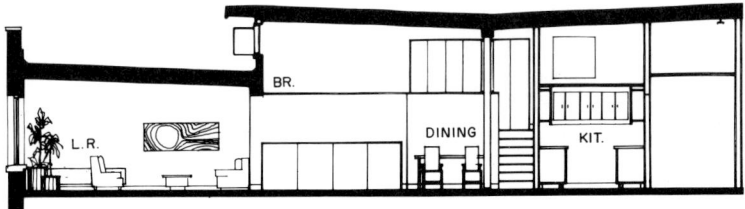

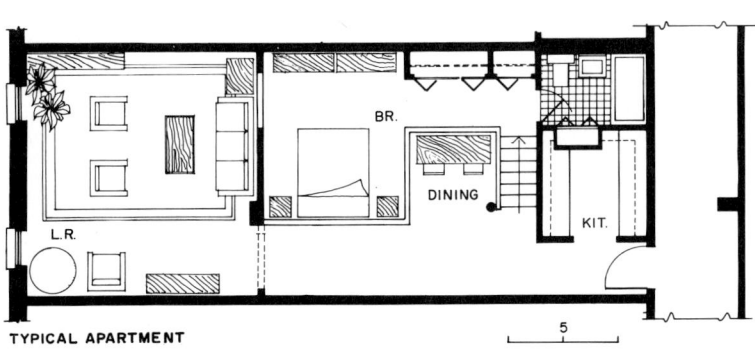

TYPICAL APARTMENT

Community facilities, at the Tannery, including the management's offices, laundry and meeting rooms are housed in an old mansion on the site. Due to varying structural and dimensional conditions, interior features such as high ceilings, heavy timber beams, exposed cast iron details provide attractive living and meeting spaces.

Laura Rosen

The dummy window (above) has a painted cat on its sill. Yang's apartment has been designed primarily for entertaining and the contemplation of art. Books, records and miscellany are concealed in extensive cabinet work, and surfaces are kept clear. His office (not shown) is on a lower floor.

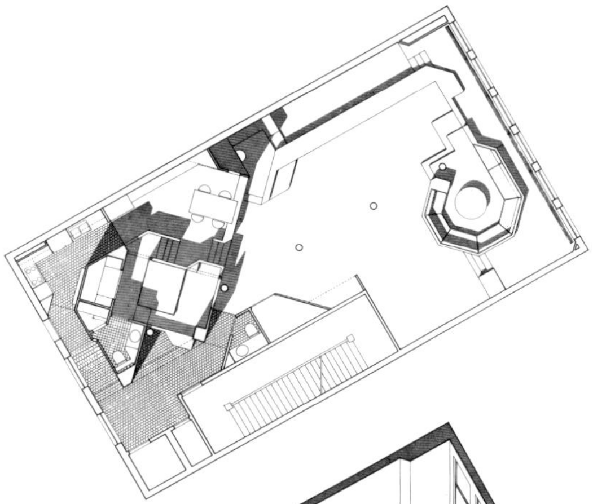

3

New York City's Soho district is the place to go to admire its cast iron fronts and to look at paintings in its burgeoning art galleries. On their way down Prince Street, however, some art lovers may miss a remarkable *trompel'oeil*—a mural of a cast iron front at right angles to a genuine cast iron front. This witty deception was instigated by architect Hanford Yang (who owns the landmark building), the New York City Landmarks Commission, City Walls Inc. (which has promoted other murals on the exterior walls of old buildings), and the National Endowment for the Arts (which provided the money). The mural was designed by Richard Haas, a photorealist painter for whom cast iron buildings are a frequent subject. He made a carefully dimensioned drawing which was scaled up, transferred to the wall and filled in by professional sign painters.

The real cast iron front is one of the loveliest in New York. It is one of the few that is not criss-crossed by a fire escape, so the proportions can be clearly seen. As the photographs (opposite page) indicate, the floor heights decrease by 18 inches each as they go up, an optical device to make the building look taller. Architect Yang bought the building for its looks and set about transforming it into an office and home for himself.

It had once been a toy factory with tin ceilings, and was in very bad repair when Yang acquired it. After making basic repairs and installing a new mechanical system, Yang began to experiment with the interior spaces. His workmen were local artists who were willing to change the heights, sizes and positions of the various design elements, as Yang tested them. Much attention was paid to the placement of his art objects. As can be seen in the photograph above, all the cast iron columns are articulated. The partitions have been cut and turned to accommodate them. Walls are white, the carpets are grey and the natural wood surfaces have a high-gloss finish. The only color is provided by the art.

4

At the time of purchase, this five-story loft building—a former cord factory—in Lower Manhattan showed many of the signs of neglect that make this kind of building economically attractive and certain design idiocyncracies that might be turned into architectural virtues. The floors were in poor condition and needed patching. The stamped tin ceiling, nailed right to the wood joists, was in sad disrepair. Transverse partitions, some of them awkwardly positioned with respect to the structural grid of heavy timber, chopped up the space wastefully. In addition, all the mechanical and plumbing services were at one end of the 25- by 90-foot floors.

The architect/owner Alan Buchsbaum removed the partitions and made repairs to finish. He opened the space to its full length. In plan, he zoned out the principal functions, being guided by obvious requirements for light and privacy. The kitchen, needing large amounts of neither, was placed near the center of one of the long walls. But to bring the services to it from the rear wall, the bedroom and dining areas had to be raised up to create a false floor. Across from the kitchen, Buchsbaum set up a work area with drafting tables, tack space and supply cabinets. The plan is completed by living space and bedroom at opposite ends.

In general feeling, the loft is casual and unselfconscious, although sculptural accents—as at the long kitchen counter—betray an abiding concern for form. Most of the furnishings are simple, informal, and selected for their potential for easy rearrangement. Buchsbaum has gotten considerable design mileage from subtle contrasts in textures.

BR.
BR.
DINING
KIT
LIVING
5

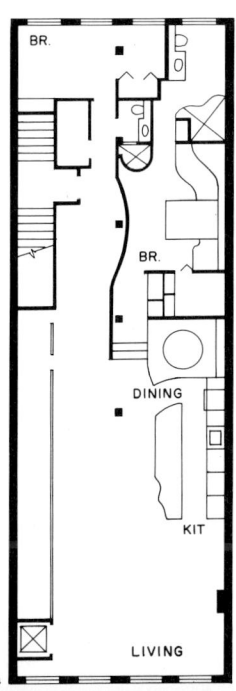

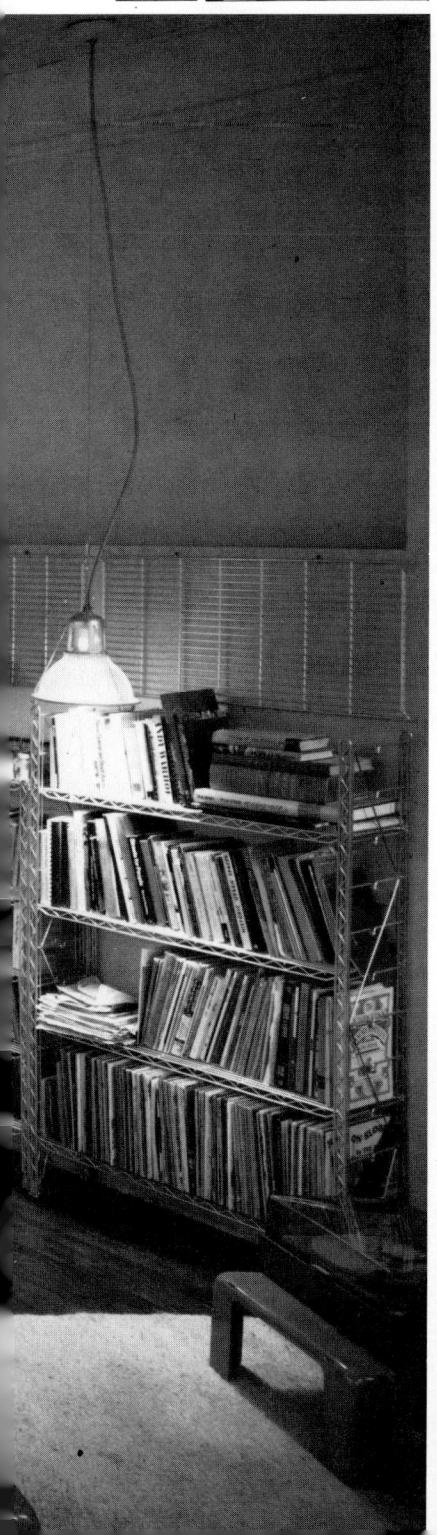

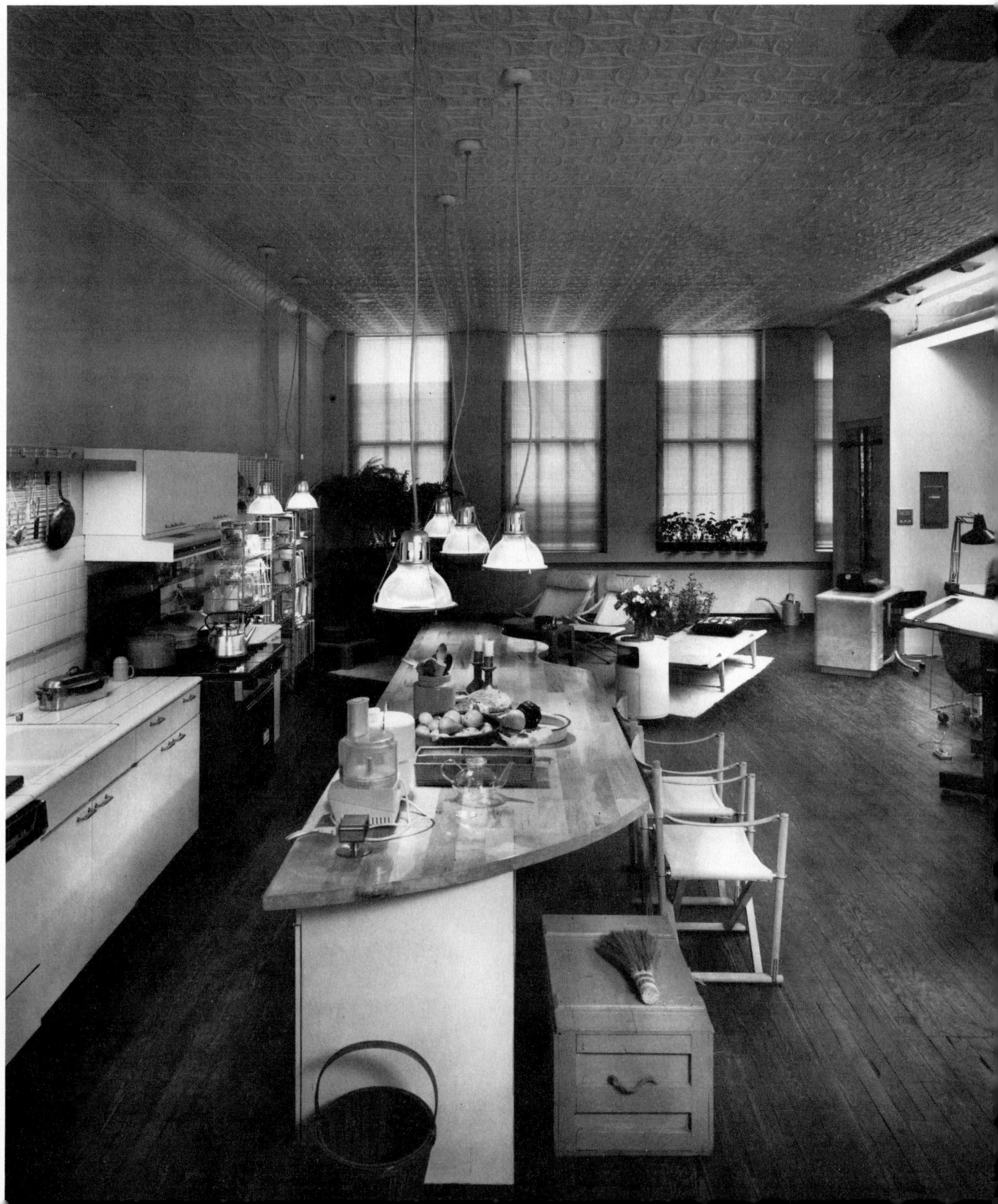

The raised platform—required for plumbing—provides carpeted seating for the dining table which is set in a circular cutout. Over the dining area (photo at right) is a tapestry/sculpture executed in felt and designed by Robert Morris. The bath, with its open shower, is shown reflected (photo below). It is finished, like the bedroom, in reflective materials.

The bedroom however, presents a somewhat different vocabulary of form and finish—a vocabulary of more studied elegance and more dramatic contrasts. The raised floor is finished in a smooth, high glaze, off-white tile that turns up at the built-in bed to form an enclosure for the mattress. The closet has mirror-glass doors and the whole space is defined in the long axis by a gently undulating glass block partition that slaloms leisurely around a pair of heavy wood columns. The lighting is subdued in the bedroom although the glass block partition is actually lighted from both sides. A row of airport fixtures, floor mounted with rigid conduit and fitted with blue bulbs, lends the space an unexpected trace of mystery.

The building has three owners (Buchsbaum is one) and each occupies a floor. To put the project on a sounder economic footing, the remaining space has been turned into rental property.

LOFT FOR ALAN BUCHSBAUM, New York City. Architects: *Alan Buchsbaum and Stephen Tilly.* Lighting design: *Paul Marantz.*

Norman McGrath photos

5

An imaginative design concept for the renovation of an old blacksmith shop and rooming house into modern apartments has created a special living experience in the heart of New York City. The original structure had three distinct sections with varying roof heights—a four-story section at the front, a one-story section at the middle of the lot, and a two-story portion in the rear.

The four-story portion was a rooming house, now modernized as one-bedroom and studio units. The blacksmith shop had occupied the entire first floor, but in order to create an inner courtyard the one-story section (which housed the forge) was removed. The rear area was converted into apartments which overlook the courtyard.

Only minor structural changes were required. A new six-foot-high party-wall was erected and a new outside stairway, designed with special railing details, was installed to increase efficiency of circulation.

Recycling this building has helped to preserve the character of the neighborhood and encouraged business expansion through the inclusion of commercial space on the ground level.

The owner was able to take advantage of New York City's J-51 tax abatement program which encourages apartment conversions. In this case, a tax abatement for ten years has been exchanged for compliance with all the program's regulations, including rent qualifications and the proper ratio of bedroom apartments to studios.

There is a total of eight apartments on the 20- by 100-foot lot—a high density.

---

240 EAST 26TH STREET APARTMENTS, New York, New York. Owner: *Barry E. Fallis/Arida Properties, Inc.* Architects: *Marvin H. Meltzer Architects—Marvin H. Meltzer designer; Len Pitkowsky, project architect.* Engineers: *Antony Vairamides* (structural/foundation/soils); *Hecht, Hartmann & Concessi* (mechanical/electrical). General contractor: *Malor Construction Company.*

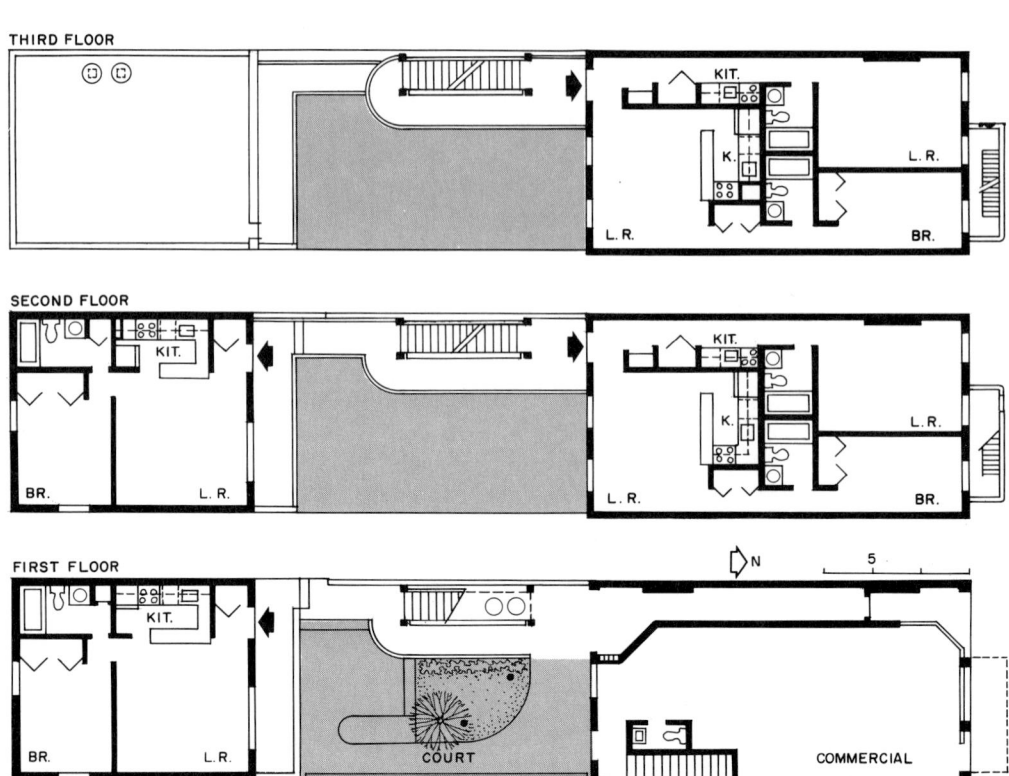

Elliot Fine photos

The courtyard is the main focal point of the complex (right). There is a contrast between the interior landscaped court and the street elevation—dramatically highlighted after entering through a covered walkway (bottom). The courtyard also serves as the main organizing and circulating space, while being a pleasant respite. Nearly all apartments have some view of the courtyard.

159

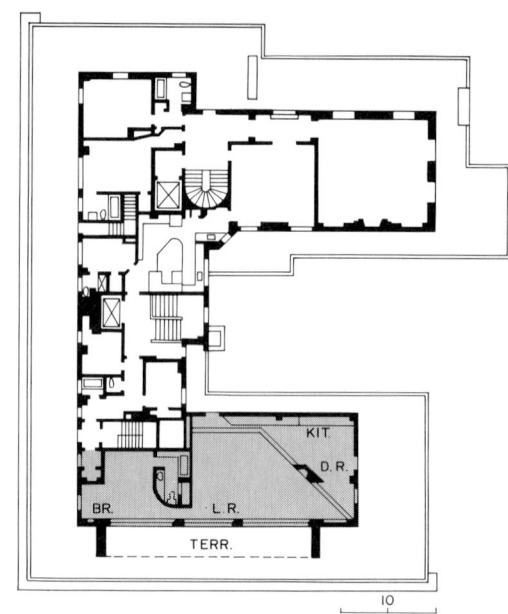

6

When the small rooftop structure next to the upper level of their own duplex apartment became available, the owners purchased the space with the eventual aim of selling the lower portion of their duplex and consolidating their space on the roof level of this Manhattan highrise. They commissioned C.C. Pei to transform what had been laundry and maid quarters into an efficient, self-contained guest house.

Pei gutted the small space, raised the floor to match the level of the surrounding terrace and used the underfloor space to run mechanical services. Even with the raised floor, Pei maintained ceiling heights between 9 and 10 feet. By opening the wall to the west, then protecting the sliding glass with awnings and drop screens, long views from the living room and bedroom could be achieved without either loss of privacy or unmanageable solar gain. Working within existing structure, Pei designed spaces that are not large but are finished with elegance and the furniture has been selected with close attention to scale and texture.

The guest house is ringed on three sides by terrace strips of variable width. Landscape designer Graham Gordon sensitively developed these areas with planting, using simple devices—containers of various kinds plunged into beds of gravel—to form a more or less continuous green belt around the outdoor areas. Though lush in feeling, the planting beds are easily maintained. Plants can be added, subtracted, moved and tended with comparative ease.

ROOFTOP APARTMENT, New York City. Owners: *Mr. & Mrs. Peter Millard.* Architect: *C.C. Pei.* Landscape design: *Graham M. Gordon.* Contractor: *Albert Disser*

7 AND 8

The Boston architectural firm Anderson Notter Finegold has, as both architect and developer, cultivated a trend within the trend of adaptive use—the conversion of surplus schools to housing for the elderly.

The architects point to siting as one of the major advantages to elderly tenants in this kind of re-use. Older schools typically occupy space close to central districts that can provide necessary services, along with the comfort of familiarity to residents.

Another advantage: floor space and volume, which offer amenity to the elderly and their lifetimes' accumulation of belongings and which, in the shape of classrooms, provide a ready-made area for apartments. Moreover, "hidden" space in the old buildings, such as large attics, gives room for additional units. Indeed, Anderson Notter Finegold emphasize hidden spaces as essential in judging whether adaptive use is financially or architecturally practicable.

At Central Grammar School (this page), powerful local sentiment militated for adaptive use: hundreds of citizens had studied, and taught, there since its opening in 1889. Its location was a major plus for housing for the elderly—next to the library, across from the post office, within walking distance of shopping, churches and services.

By dropping bathroom/kitchen cores into the middle of 30- by 30-ft classrooms, the architects established ample apartments, with variable planning possible around the cores. Consultants for the design of the core included senior citizens' groups who commented on early mock-ups. (This may have had something to do with the project's complete rental within 12 days of offering.)

Elsewhere in the building, the architects found "hidden" space for new units, notably in the volume that had accommodated the gym and in the attic.

Although the costs of renovation and re-use are tricky to assess, Central Grammar

Phokion Karas photos

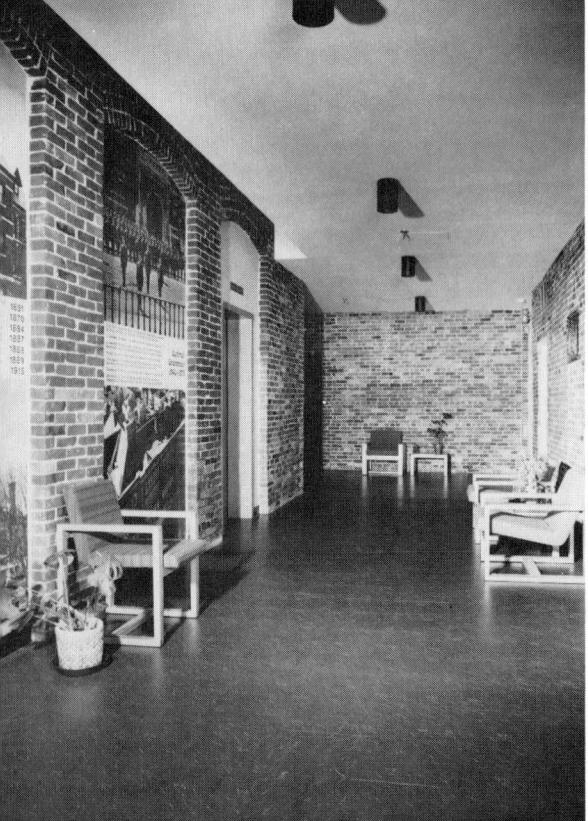

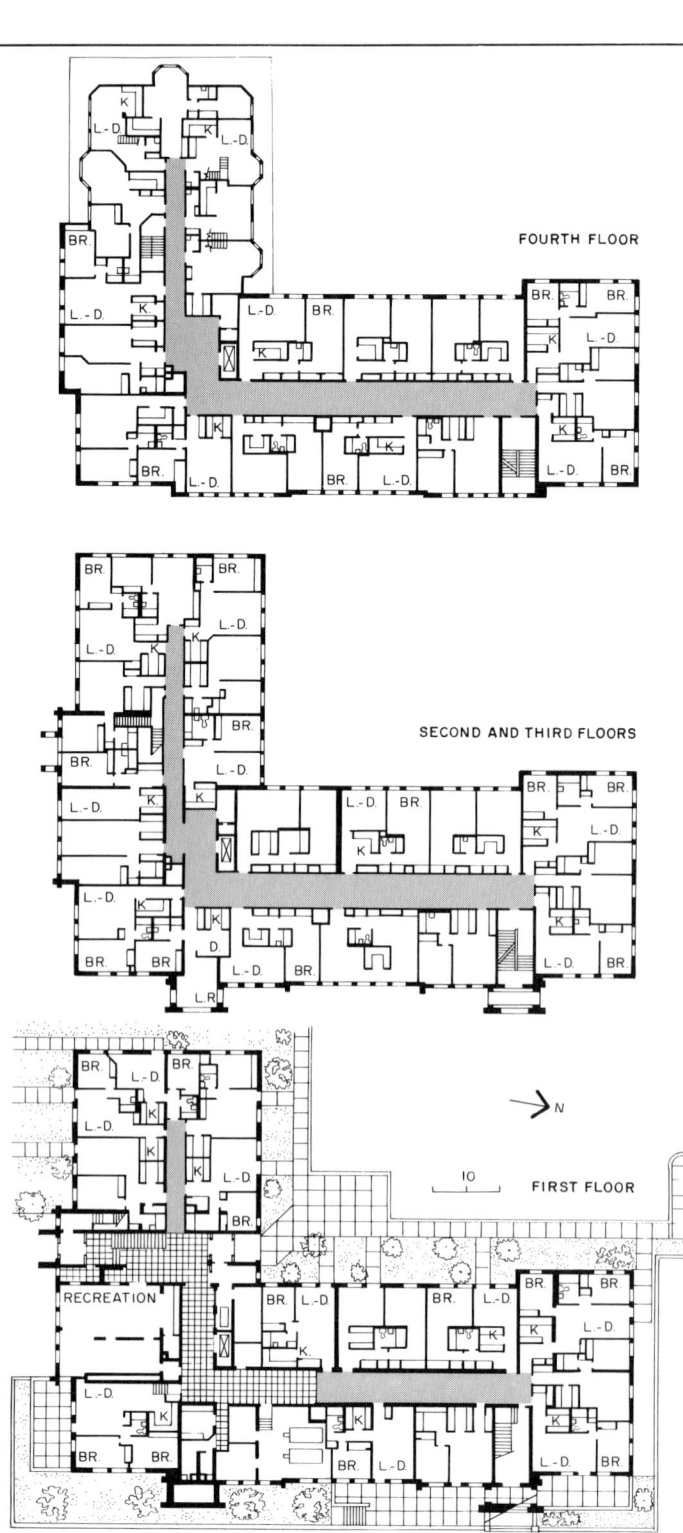

has been compared with nearby high-rise housing built new at about the same time (1975): Central Grammar's 80 units cost about $18,500 each, roughly two-thirds the cost of the new units—and its units, while varying in area, are on the average half again as big.

At the Stephen Palmer Apartments (this page), the attic's ceilings were high enough to admit the addition of bedroom lofts overlooking living rooms (bottom left). And in the cater-cornered area formerly used as a front entrance, space was divided equally between high-ceilinged living and sleeping quarters by a tall plumbing core.

Of the several such projects Anderson Notter Finegold has already completed or is presently working on, all are intended as housing for the elderly. The Palmer Apartments are unique in the architects' experience because financing was conventional. That is not to say, however, that the project received no encouragement or assistance from the town. Abandoning its early intention to demolish the 63-year-old school, Needham leased the property to the developers for 50 years, with lease payments made in lieu of taxes.

CENTRAL GRAMMAR APARTMENTS, Gloucester, Massachusetts. Owner: *Gloucester Development Team and Associates*. Architects: *Anderson Notter Finegold Inc*. Engineers: *Arthur Choo Associates, Inc.* (structural); *Environmental Design Engineers, Inc.* (mechanical/electrical). Consultants: *Greater Boston Community Development, Inc.; Community Research Applications, Inc.; New England Non-Profit Housing Development, Inc.* Contractor: *Gloucester Construction Company, Inc.*

STEPHEN PALMER APARTMENTS, Needham, Massachusetts. Architects: *Anderson Notter Finegold Inc.* Developer: *Stephen Palmer Associates, a partnership of Anderson Notter Finegold.* Contractor: *Denehy Construction Company, Inc.*

One of the chief amenities offered to housing in recycled schools is space, not only floor space that can be turned to larger-then-normal apartments, but volume—high ceilings and the windows to go with them. Corridors are often of a width to accommodate casual lounge space. Beyond that, the old buildings have detailing not reproducible today and valuable to residents for its familiarity. At Gloucester (across page), the architects incorporated existing oak wainscoting and oak classroom closets in the new units, and preserved the rusticated granite entrance portals.

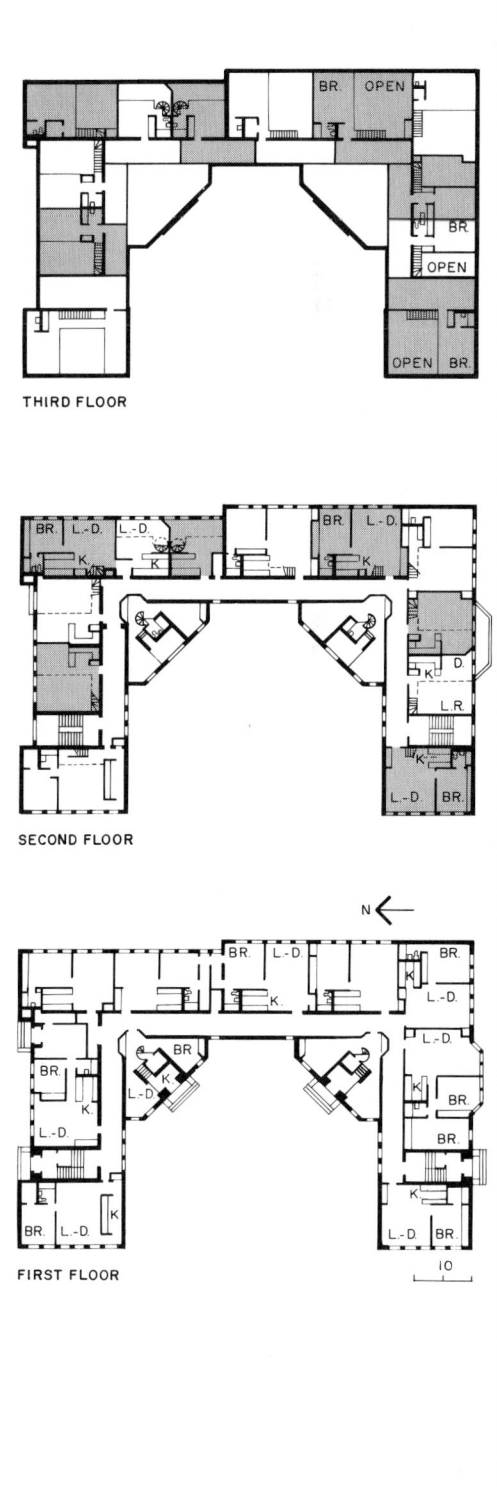

9

At the high tide of Victorian beach resorts toward the end of the last century, the Rockingham Hotel in Portsmouth, New Hampshire, was cited in nearly every travel guide. Rebuilt after a disastrous fire in 1885 by Portsmouth brewer Frank Jones after plans by Boston architect Jabez Sears, the Rockingham's sumptuous rooms served several generations of tourists and played an important and continuing role in the city's economic life. Gradually, as rail travel declined and as standards of amenity changed, the Rockingham's future seemed less and less secure. It was recently purchased by the North American Development Corporation which commissioned Boston architects Stahl/Bennett, Inc. to convert the venerable hotel into condominium apartments.

The architect's plans recycle the original 87-room hotel into 35 apartments—mostly one-bedroom, but with some 1100-square-foot duplex designs as well. Where possible, significant interior details and material—patterned ceilings, marble floors, mahogany paneling, leaded glass windows, and original lighting fixtures—are being preserved, but all apartments will be renovated to contemporary standards of comfort, convenience and safety. New kitchen and bathrooms will be installed throughout.

A new wing is being added at the rear, along with new retail space, a pool deck, a dining terrace and other amenities. The old dining room, however, will remain after refurbishing to serve inside and outside trade.

The Rockingham has been built and rebuilt several times. On each of these previous occasions, parts of the old were preserved and new parts were added. The present architects understood this, knew their work was part of the same historical process, and enjoyed laminating a new layer of experience to these century-old walls. The care with which they have gone about their task suggest that this history may well continue and that future architects may find a good deal worth saving in the work just completed.

THE ROCKINGHAM CONDOMINIUMS, Portsmouth, New Hampshire. Owner: *North American Development Corporation.* Architects: *Stahl/Bennett, Inc.*—Frederick A. Stahl, partner-in-charge: Allen Trousdale, project architect. Engineers: *Weidemann, Brown, Inc.* (structural), *AMC Engineers* (mechanical); *Metcalf Engineering* (electrical); *Tsoumas Associates* (plumbing). Graphics: *Corporate Design Systems.* Contractor: *Noram Construction Company.*

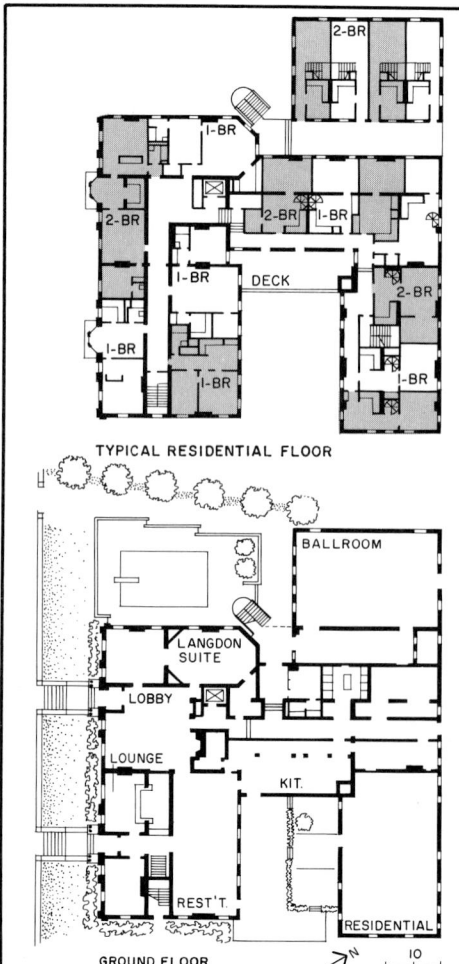

Steve Rosenthal photos

The street level includes a restaurant and lounge as well as an outdoor cafe open during the summer months in the landscaped court (see rendering above).

10

The renovation of a New York City office building into apartments has not only given a boost to inner-city housing but has done so in a luxurious manner, providing a quality of living space that can be an inducement for people to stay or move into the center city. Even though the building was not originally designed as an apartment complex, it can seriously compete with other luxury housing in the city because of its design amenities.

Constructed in 1929, this 24-story office building, located near the United Nations on Manhattan's East Side, was severely damaged by a gas explosion in 1974. The explosion funneled up the elevator shafts on the west side, blowing out a 50-foot-wide section of the brick facade from the street level to the top story, but structural damage was confined to the bank of elevators. The architects converted the service elevators to passenger use and cut away the demolished shafts and bent steel frame, leaving a V-shaped end wall (right). This provides a small street level courtyard and opens up the full 200-foot height of the west wall of apartments to natural light. This change also decreased the building's total volume, and zoning regulations permitted this "lost" space to be regained in the form of greenhouse-type windows installed on the exterior of most upper floors above the 17th level, where setbacks in the ziggurat building allow it visually and functionally, as can be seen in each of the photographs and drawings shown.

The interiors were designed to capitalize on views, light and spatial variety. A total of 341 apartments benefit from the commercial proportions of the building—12-foot-high ceilings, and 8-foot-high windows running the width of most apartments. Because setbacks occur on nearly every floor, and because of the

Bill Rothschild photos except as noted

The addition of greenhouses to the exterior is a major aspect of this conversion of office building to apartments. Each glass enclosure extends the apartment outward onto the terrace, and visually highlights the linear apartment design.

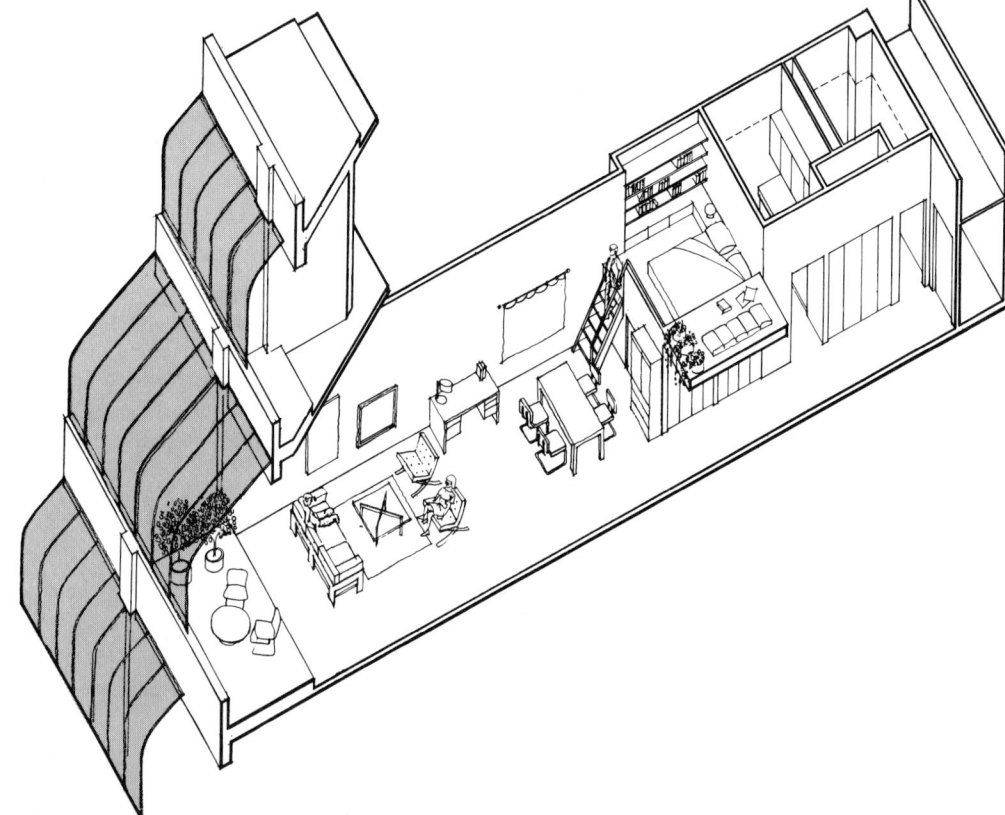

need to comply with regulations set by the city's J-51 tax abatement program (which made this conversion possible) regarding the ratio of bedroom apartments to studios, each floor posed a separate planning problem. This was solved by the design of linear apartments (some 80 feet in length), running from the elevator core to the perimeter; kitchen and bath facilities that did not exist in the original were positioned near the central elevator core to simplify utilities. All the units are spacious, however, with the smallest studio 850 square feet.

An example of the creative utilization of the structure's idiosyncrasies is the redesign of the service elevators for passenger use. Because the cab platforms were larger than permitted by building codes, a glass-enclosed terrarium was located in the rear of each, providing an unexpected, yet pleasing experience.

The building's entrance was formerly the truck loading dock. Now multi-leveled (with a barrier-free access ramp) connecting a 100-foot-long lobby with elevators and street level entrance, it has been designed in a modern idiom but reminiscent of the building's 1929 origin.

The project is the largest carried out so far under New York City's J-51 tax abatement program, which provides tax incentives for the conversion of commercial properties into residential use (explained in detail on page 111). It also has turned a disaster into a very successful asset.

TURTLE BAY TOWERS, New York, New York. Owner: *Rockrose Development Corporation*. Architects: *Bernard Rothzeid & Partners—Peter Thomson*, partner-in-charge; *Bernard Rothzeid and Carmi Bee*, project designers; *Vinod Devgan*, job captain. Engineers: *Harwood and Gould* (structural); *George Langer* (mechanical/electrical). Consultants: *Ranger Farrell Associates* (acoustical); *Nathan Silberman* (codes); *Soloman Sheer* (Board of Standard Appeals). Interior design: *Bernard Rothzeid & Partners—Marjorie Colt*. General contractor: *Rockrose Construction Corporation*.

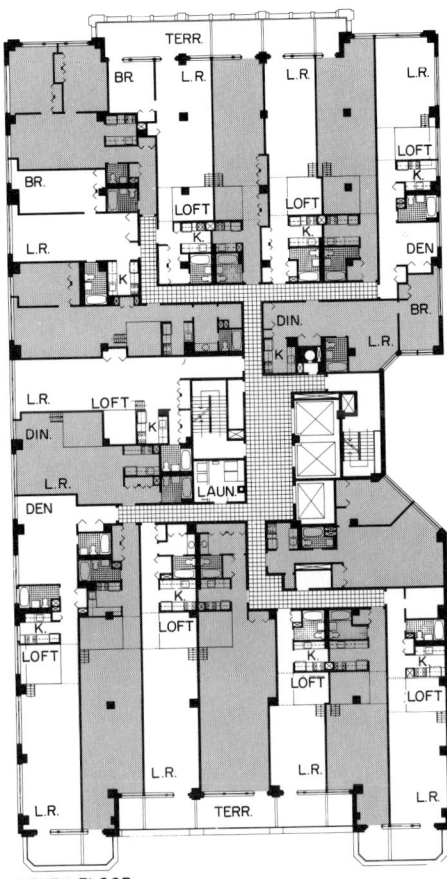

Lofts were included in the design of many apartments, especially studios, for they provide a spatial variety to the predominantly linear units. There are 341 apartments on the half-acre site, with configurations varying from studios to "townhouses" on the upper floors.

TENTH FLOOR

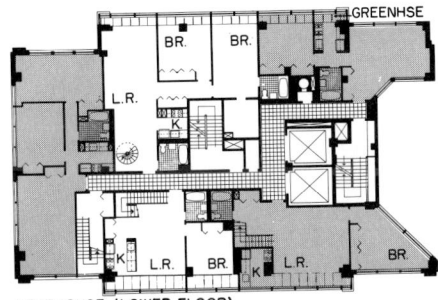

PENTHOUSE (LOWER FLOOR)

PENTHOUSE (UPPER FLOOR)

FOURTH FLOOR

Susan Schwartz

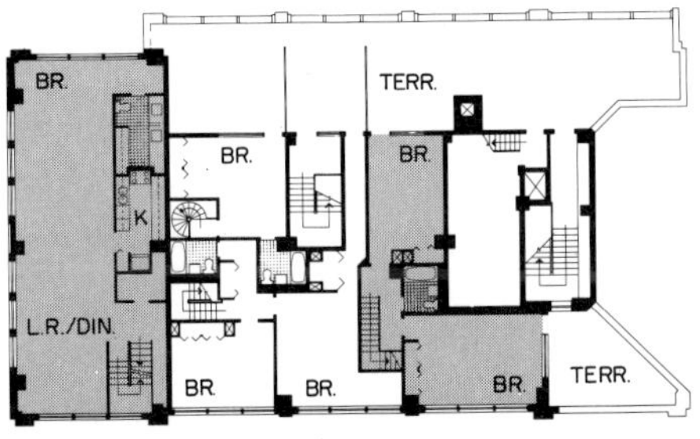

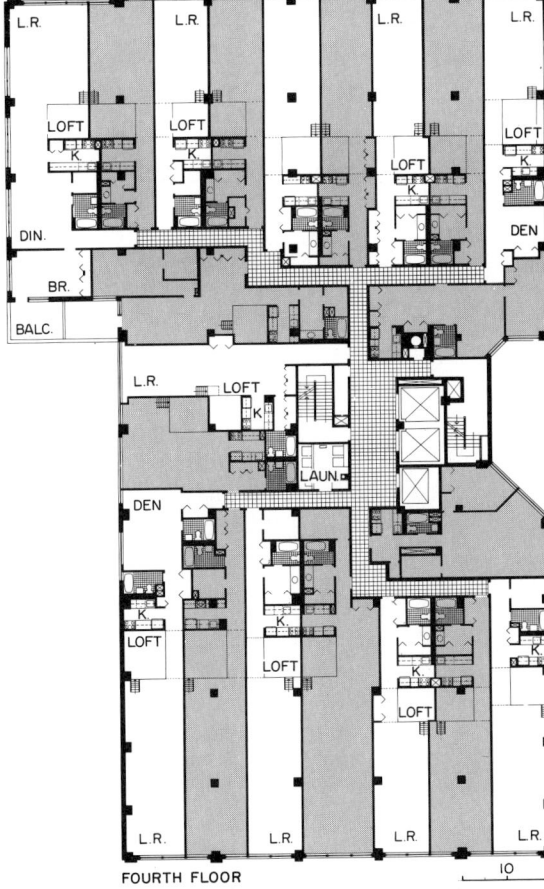

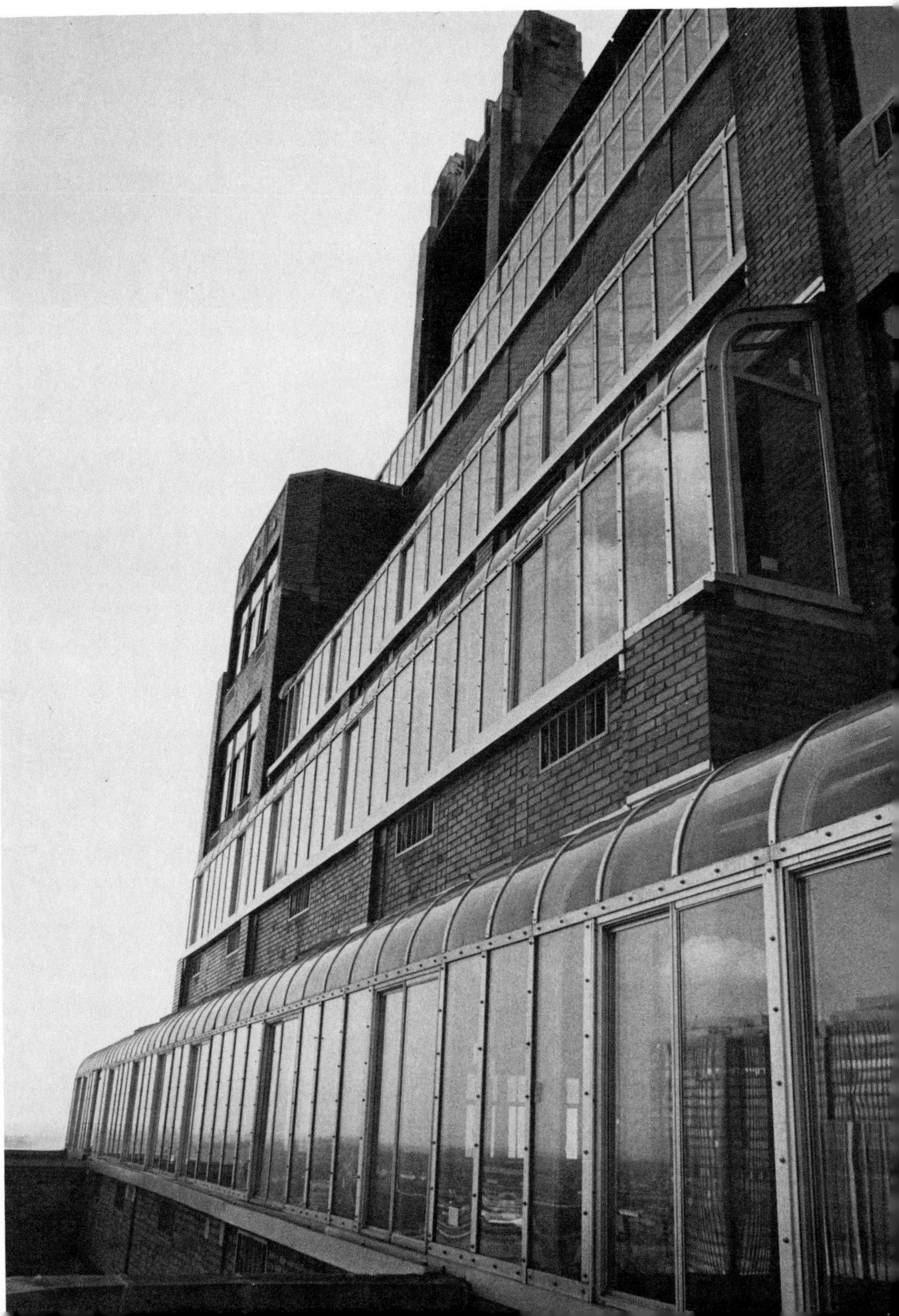

11

To redeem this Telegraph Hill house from physical dilapidation and put it back on a sound economic footing, San Francisco architects Peters & Clayberg undertook a major renovation that totally reorganized their interiors to create three apartments and one new commercial space—now a small boutique. All apartments are reached by a scissor stair set back in the recessed entrance—an entrance that cuts back to provide private outdoor sitting areas (see plan) at the rear of the lot.

In the taller, uphill section, the architects designed two floor-through apartments, each with two bedrooms, and in the smaller structure, a studio apartment plus laundry room and tenant storage area. Each apartment is graced with an outdoor patio and other amenities. In the upstairs apartments, the architects added large bay windows for view and light. Downstairs, the existing change in floor level was used effectively to separate dining and living areas. All apartments had new wiring and plumbing. New and old elements were fused throughout in ways that are mutually complementary.

New finishes in all the apartments included drywall for partitions and ceilings, carpet for most floors. The window frames are bronze-colored anodized aluminum with dark green trim.

The significance of this renovation is not in either its extent or in any surprising new use to which the buildings can be put. It is not flashy or assertive. But it is the kind of small-scale urban housing for which San Francisco is justly famous and the architects have successfully reminted—at modest expense—what too many others in the recent past have been willing to throw away.

UNION STREET APARTMENTS
Architects: Peters Clayberg & Caulfield
Owner: George E. L. Stewart
Project name: Union Street Apartments
Contractor: Frank Rosenmayr
Photographer: R. M. Clayberg

SECTION A-A

UPPER

LOWER

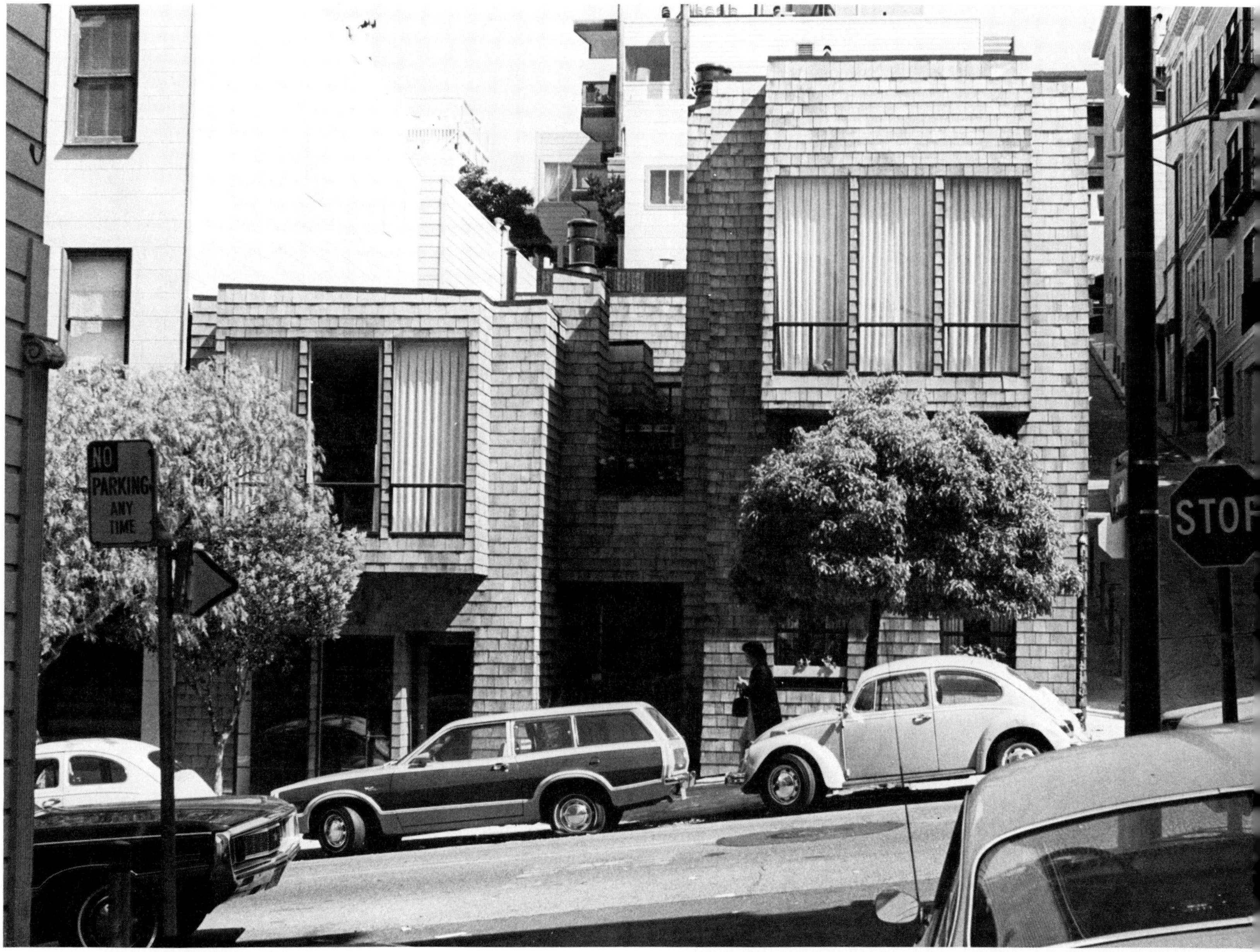

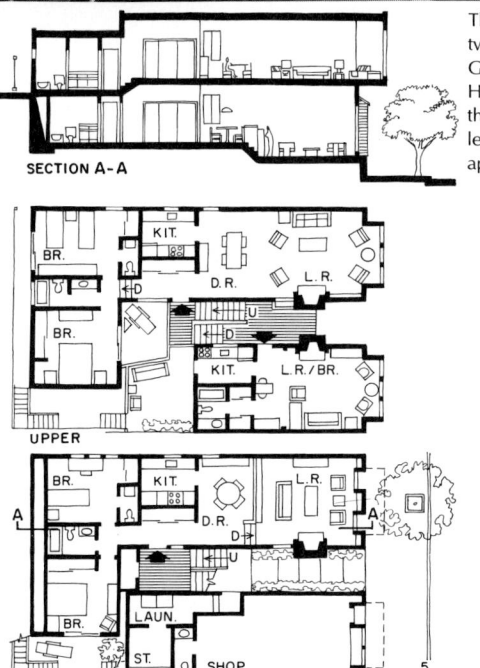

The site, which slopes sharply in two directions, is just a block from Grant Street on historic Telegraph Hill. Taking advantage of the slope, the architects employed changes of level to enrich and animate the apartment plans.

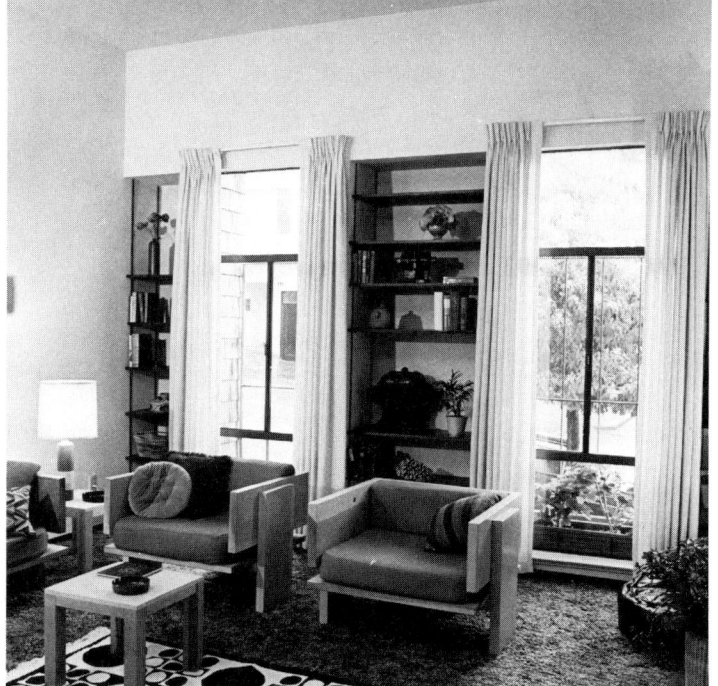

12

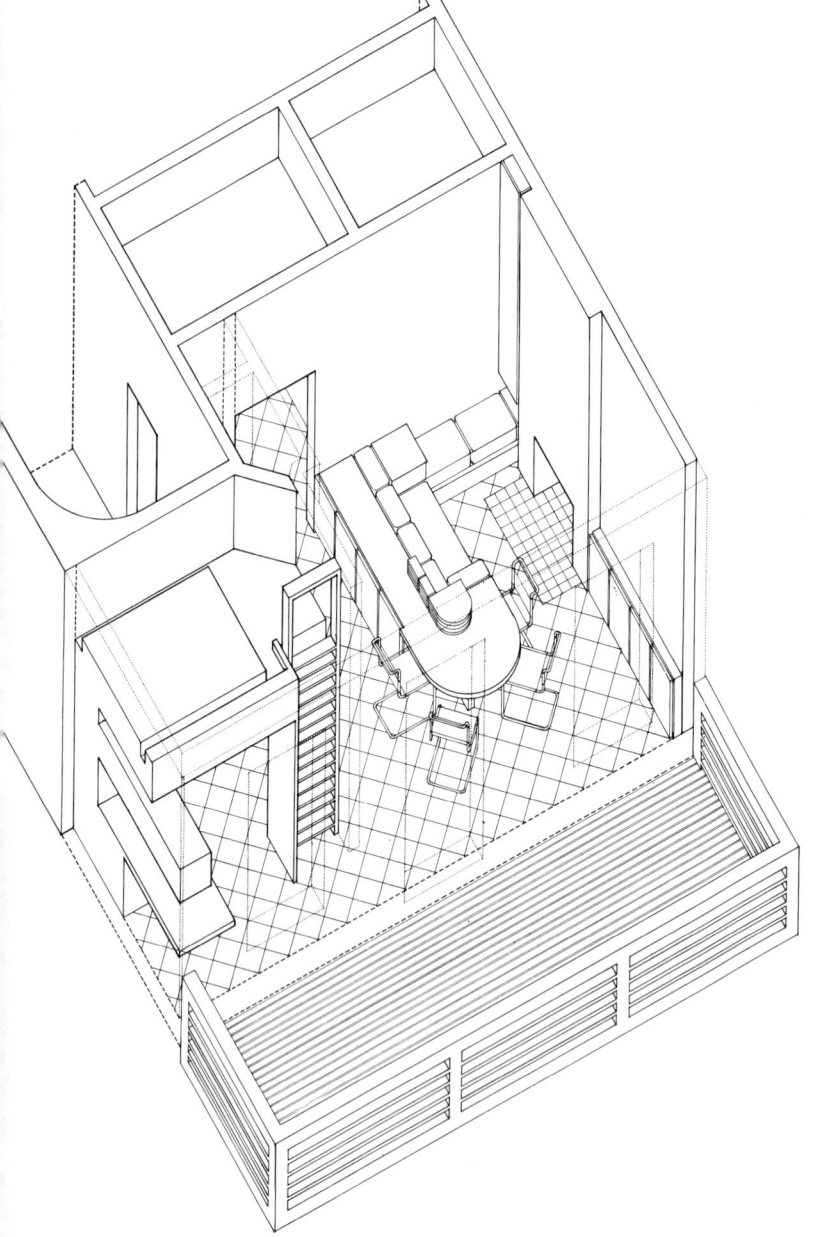

The original renovation of this 1850s brownstone established a one-bedroom apartment, but as the bedroom was only seven by eight feet—with an 11-foot ceiling, Rubin subdivided the space horizontally creating a sleeping loft above and a work space under. In the main space, he removed the massive marble mantle, rebuilt the fireplace wall and removed that portion of the bedroom wall that intersected the window wall.

In the space created by this series of adjustments, Rubin designed and installed a handsome seating area and table unit. The latter, which includes low cabinets, was covered in white plastic laminate. Other cabinets along the fireplace wall house hi-fi equipment and concealed lighting. To add space to his apartment, Rubin also decked the roof of the projecting sun porch below and thereby developed a narrow but welcome terrace.

The result is a tidy, contemporary and surprisingly comfortable living space fashioned with wit out of what was little more than remnants from the past.

PRIVATE APARTMENT, New York City. Architect: *Michael Rubin*. Cabinetry: *Gene Black (Materials Design Workshop)*.

13

This small apartment is one of the best interiors Paul Rudolph has yet done. His client is psychotherapist Joanna T. Steichen, whose distinguished art collection includes photographs by her late husband Edward Steichen. (Rudolph was the architect for the famous "The Family of Man" photographic exhibition created by Edward Steichen for the Museum of Modern Art in 1955.) Rudolph insists that his own contribution to the design of Mrs. Steichen's apartment was modest: "She is a friend, the remodeling was down the street from where I live. I just gave her practical advice, produced a few working drawings and dropped in from time to time to see how things were coming along." In other words, he helped her create a setting for herself, her work and her collection, but did not do it for her.

They started with a basement apartment with huge windows facing south and east. It has an 18 ft-6 in. high major space and a two-story area with heights of 8 ft-6 in. per story. Two new levels were added to the high space—a mezzanine which doubles as a sleeping loft for guests or a sitting area (opposite page, middle), and, a few steps above it, a bridge which serves as Mrs. Steichen's study and work area (opposite page, bottom left). The new levels are supported by light steel members bearing on existing masonry. Below the sleeping loft is a low-ceilinged, intimate seating alcove (opposite page, top and bottom right), ideal for parties or group therapy. The dining area is located under the work study bridge and the high-ceilinged space which remains is part of the living area. Wall finishes, lighting, cabinet work and shelving have been carefully detailed to enhance the art collection. The cove lighting above the seating area consists of 7-watt bulbs 1 ft on centers.

APARTMENT RENOVATION, New York, New York. Owner: *Joanna T. Steichen*. Architect: *Paul Rudolph—project architect: Peter Mullen*. General contractor: *The Ormar Building Corporation*.

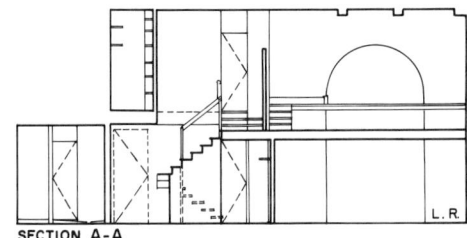

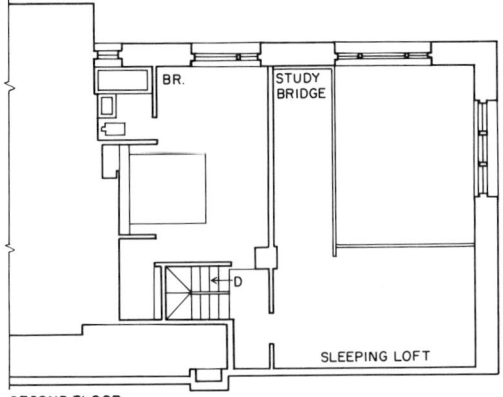

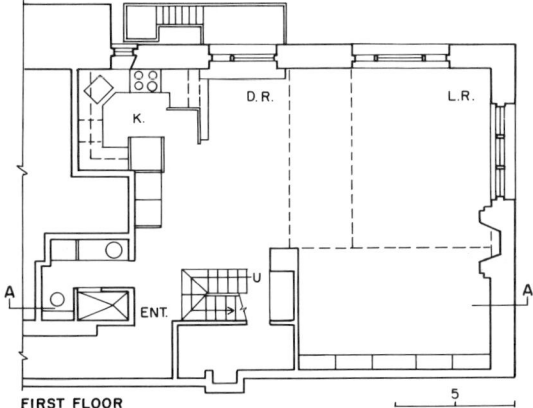

Mrs. Steichen's collection consists in part of small objects, for which Rudolph has designed appropriately scaled shelving. A few large objects occupy the high-ceilinged space. All the new walls are metal stud and drywall. To conceal the difference between the old walls and the new walls, a spray-on textured acoustic surface was applied to all the walls and painted with a flat oil base paint. The ceilings are white and so are most walls. Where Edward Steichen's photographs are assembled, however, a dark brown is quite effectively used as a background.

Cervin Robinson photos

14

In renovating this 50-year-old duplex apartment, architects Robert Stern and John Hagmann, had to overcome the insistent pattern of small rooms along narrow corridors that was the apartment's principal spatial feature both upstairs and down. They had also to liberate some space vertically without giving up living areas. They accomplished both of these requirements by a process of simplification—by subtracting unnecessary elements and allowing space to flow freely over, through or around the elements that were left. Two staircases were added: one (photo right) replaces an ornamental stair near the entrance and a second, at the rear of the apartment, connects the kitchen with the children's bedrooms. Two gently arched partitions along the corridors relieve the severity of the rectilinear plan and shorten the apartment's apparent length.

Along the north wall, an inner lining of cabinet work designed by the architects closes out openings to an airshaft. On the remaining exposures, the lining is modified to admit light while it conceals air conditioning, curtains in pockets, and lighting behind a valance.

The apartment's parquet floor was retained, and with it, a record of the location of original partitions fixed by interruptions in the parquet pattern—a faintly visible reminder of earlier days and occupants.

PRIVATE APARTMENT, New York City. Architects: Robert A. M. Stern & John S. Hagmann. Engineers: Soldos/Silman (structural); Langer/Polise (mechanical). Consultant: Carroll Cline (lighting). Contractor: Garson-Bergman, Inc.

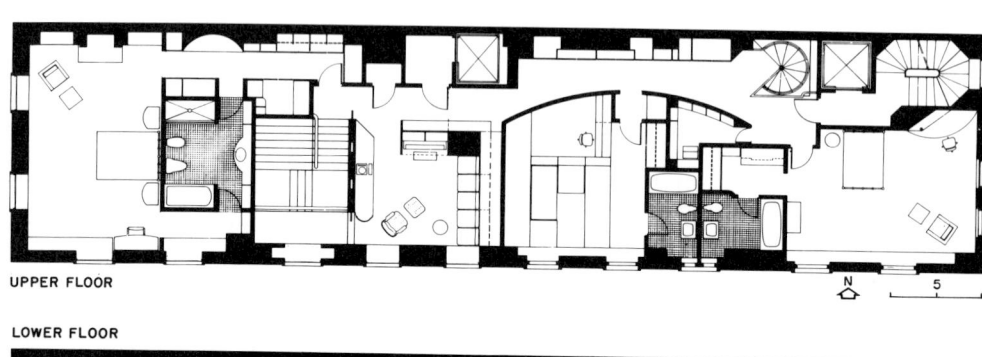

UPPER FLOOR

LOWER FLOOR

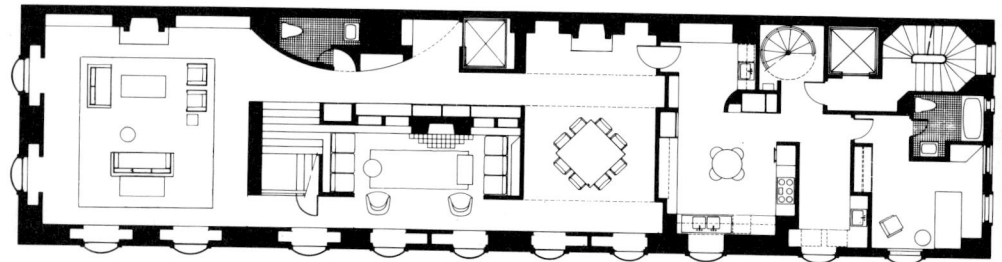

Norman McGrath photos

The whole design expression is relatively restrained and placid in deference to the owner's growing collection of sculpture and painting. Colors are rather muted and lighting is soft. Detailing throughout is elegant and expressive.

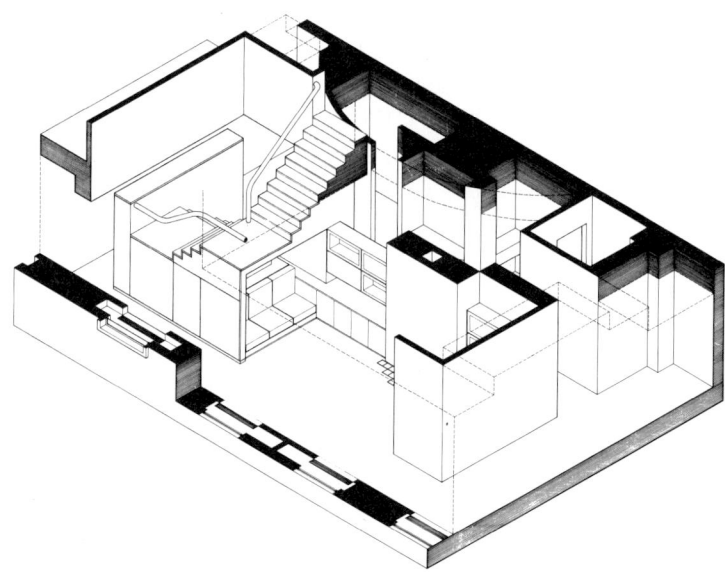

177

15

Fire destroyed one of a pair of Beacon Hill rowhouses in 1967, leaving a charred, gaping hole in the street facade until 1972 when architect James McNeely, in partnership with a local attorney, purchased the empty site and the undamaged bowfront next door.

The partners developed a plan to unite the two structures by serving both with a common elevator, stair and fire escape. Floor alignments could not be reconciled for the older structure had ceiling heights up to 14 feet. The new structure was designed with more standard eight foot ceilings (see section above). As a result, the elevator cab opens in both directions and stops within the shaft at different levels to serve either side.

In final form, the project includes 12 two bedroom apartments, two single-bedroom apartments and three studio apartments all sold as condominiums during construction or soon after. Those who purchased during construction had many choices in finish materials so the interiors vary considerably, reflecting a wide range of individual tastes. Common areas are kept to a minimum and maintenance charges, the architect reports, are among the lowest in Boston.

What is perhaps most important is that this well designed infill housing—the first of its kind in this Boston district—is housing of a type so many American cities desperately need. The new construction does not shoulder aside its older neighbors. It fits snugly into position respecting the scale, form and finish of adjoining buildings but keeps its own personality intact as it completes the street scene in a venerable but still handsome Boston neighborhood.

32 AND 34 HANCOCK STREET
Architect: James McNeely
  16 Joy Street
  Boston, Massachusetts
Owners:
  Phoenix House Partners
Engineers:
  Craig Barnes (structural)
  Leo Brissette (mechanical)
Contractor: for building shell:
  John R. Clark & Associates
Photographer: William Owens

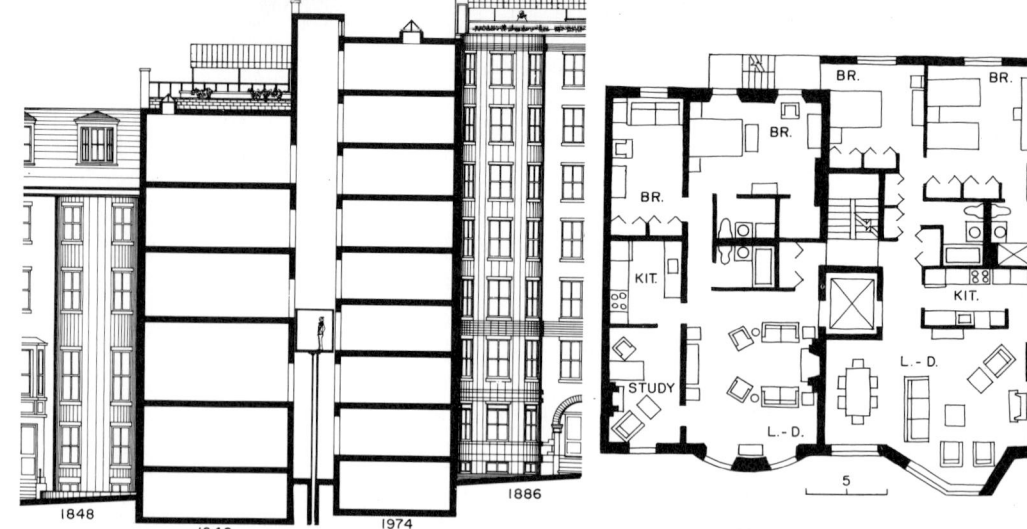

16

Two apartments and the architects' own offices share a Beaux Arts townhouse, a consistent design language, and a contemporary elegance that fits their context well. Although the first two floors of the turn-of-the-century building had been completely remodeled by McKim, Mead and White in 1917, a subsequent conversion to apartments left only isolated details from grander times. Accordingly, the architects—much of whose work is concerned with preservation—were able to extensively revise floor plans and to plan around existing elements in a thoroughly new manner, with a clear conscience.

In the ground floor apartment designed for Mr. and Mrs. Thomas Seaman (isometric and photos on this page), only the living room with its ceiling moldings and fireplace survived intact. And this became the focus around which spaces were altered not only for functional reasons, but to bring the living room into a better formal relationship with the rest. Two small spaces at the entrance (bottom of isometric) were combined into one large kitchen, dining and entry area with a tile floor. A Renaissance relief that belonged to the owners was mounted on the low division wall between living and entry area, and serves as an eye-diverting focus before entering the living room itself. The living room has been painted a strong terra cotta color to emphasize its importance. Elsewhere in the apartment, partitions have been removed to provide a study adjacent to the living room and a large bath.

Architect Randolph Croxton's own apartment (photos and isometric on the opposite page) has a plan similar to the Seaman apartment, although the divisions between kitchen (bottom photo) and entry and between living room and study have been purposely accentuated instead of reduced. The wall between the living room and the study (sometimes used as a dining room, as in the photo) was thickened by the addition of bookcases. Ceiling moldings and the marble surfaces around the fireplace were the only original elements left in the living room when Croxton moved in. According to Croxton: "It was not easy to detail the fireplace and surrounding cabinetry to look like it had always been there."

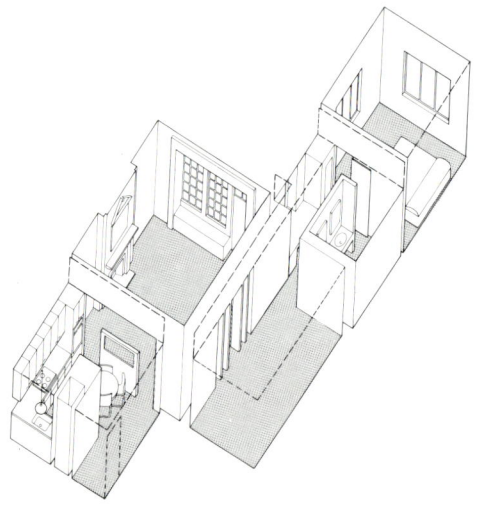

THE SEAMAN AND CROXTON RESIDENCES, New York, New York. Architects: *The Croxton Collaborative*—project architect: *Randolph R. Croxton;* associate-in-charge: *John T. Oblenus.* Lighting consultant: *Caroll Cline.*

Otto Baitz photos

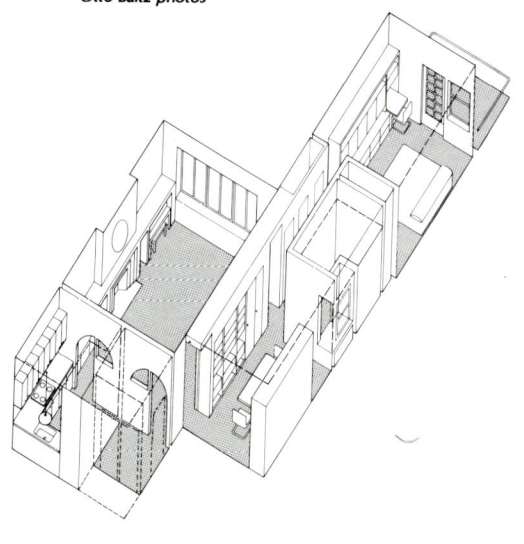

181

17

In this remapping scheme, a large assembly of rooms in a relatively unhierarchical pattern is rearranged to form three distinct realms, subtly connected. The key is the reconfiguration of the main entrance and, from that, the entrances to the public rooms, the bedrooms, and the kitchen. The new semicircular entrance hall is seen in the large color photograph below, and the entrance from it to the living room is shown in the photograph immediately on the right. This latter element takes an irregular bite out of the study (top photo, opposite page), which in turn loses its direct connection with the entrance, but gains a new relationship to the master bedroom.

PRIVATE APARTMENT, New York, New York. Architects: *R. M. Kliment and Frances Halsband*—project architect: *Jennie Young.* Engineer: *Charles Beers, Airaconda, Inc.* (mechanical). Consultants: *Howard Brandston Lighting Design* (lighting); *Philip Golden, Consultants Collaborative* (kitchen). Contractor: *Garson-Bergman, Inc.*

Laura Rosen photos

18

In a new speculatively built suburban apartment building, the client-couple (she is an antique dealer) purchased unpartitioned floor space, and asked the architects to design something more than the builder's suggested plan, a series of box-like rooms. The result is an enormous (2500-square-foot) and gracious space that defies the restrictions of "standard" ceiling heights and of the anticipated compartmented uses. The kitchen, normally on the outside wall, was located in the center of the apartment, and its curved solid-glass-block (epoxy jointed) wall was used to modulate the living space undulating around it—and to provide a sparkling transfer of light back and forth (see overleaf). The effect on the living room side is heightened by multiple small lights on the kitchen ceiling. The doors of the bedrooms can be opened to visually extend the main space during the day. Like many of the partitions, those in the entrance hall (photo, below) are built by cabinet-makers and lacquered. The small hall opposite the entrance leads to the coat closet. The floors are rough-cut, "thin-set" slate that had to be ground in place to make an even surface. Many antiques from the owner's collection blend well with the contemporary furniture recommended by the architects, and contributing to the spacious and luxurious ambiance.

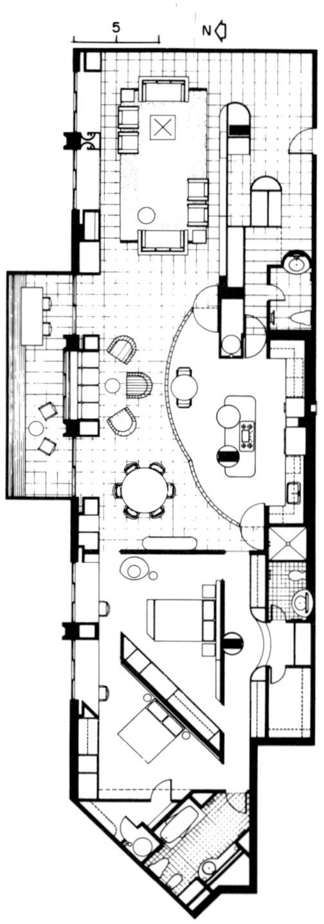

PRIVATE APARTMENT, Elkins Park, Pennsylvania. Architects: *Robert Stern & John Hagmann*—assistants: *Joan Won Yee Chan and Ronnie Fisher.* Engineers: *Robert Silman & Associates* (structural).

Functionally many small low rooms, the apartment's presence is that of spatial grandeur. Within the current standard of smaller over-all space this is achieved by immediate visual contact with every extremity of an above-average area (a 15-foot bay was added from the next apartment at the living-room end). Doors that reveal the full length of the window wall can close off the bedrooms at night (photos, right). Projecting air-handling units were covered by a new inside "wall" into which cabinets are recessed.

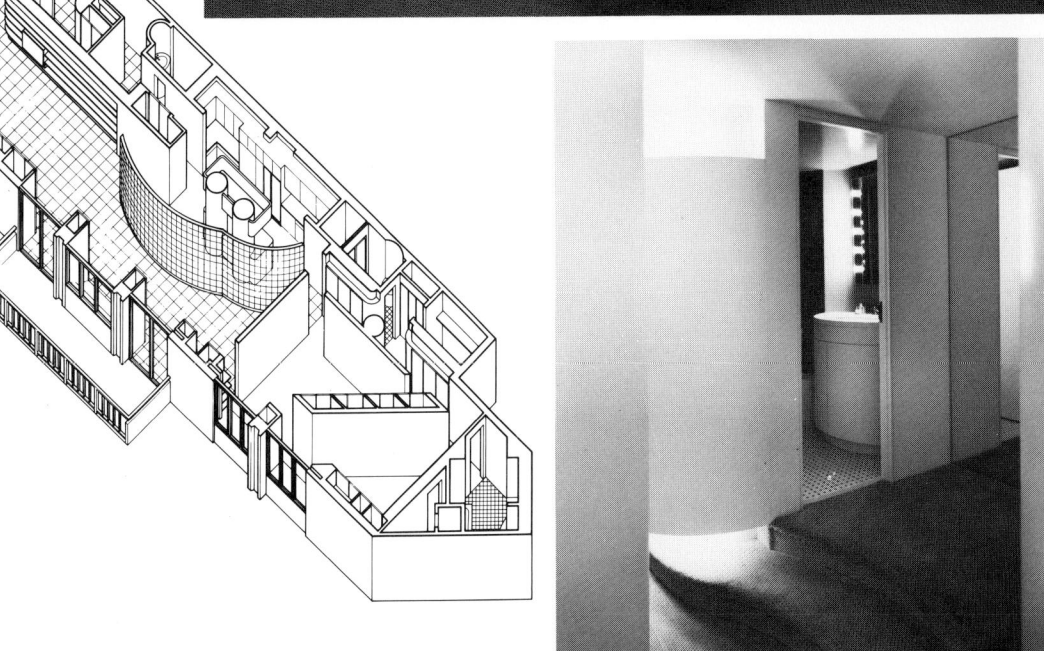

19

In this apartment renovation for designer Kay Unger, the architects had three givens: a stepped down living room, a northern exposure, and a regular grid of columns. Within these constraints, they were free to plan a series of interconnected spaces that pivot around cabinets, columns and a travertine-clad fireplace wall. The two-riser change of level and the sweeping arc of the sofa back define the living room but only as part of the larger entrance and gallery space. The private zones, in-

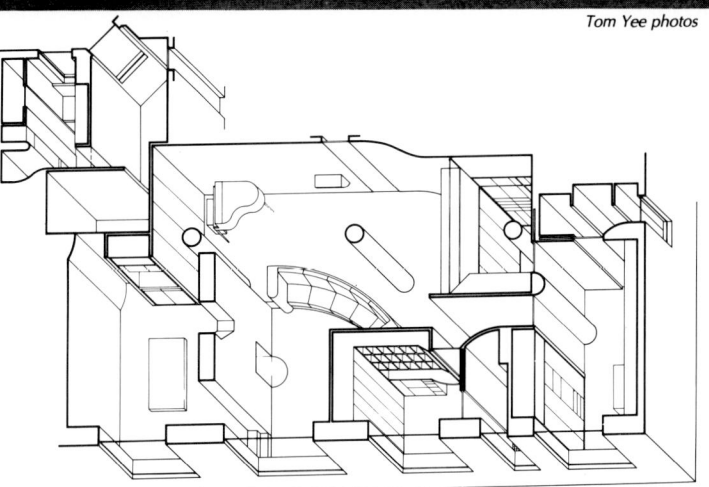

Tom Yee photos

cluding a den that doubles as a guestroom, are grouped at the apartment's west end. The existing kitchen, next to a small studio, was not renovated at the request of the owner.

The extensive cabinet work almost all of it designed by the architects, is finished in white oak and detailed with exquisite care. The walls are covered in white vinyl and the carpet is a soft gray-brown. The selective use of floor-to-ceiling mirrors on one wall of the living room is echoed in the choice of polished metal window blinds that, by reflection, turn the apartment inward on itself at night.

The 6-foot by 6-foot painting of an Old Law tenement, by Hugh Kepets, a curious and ironic contrast to its surroundings, is a very strong graphic element facing the entrance.

UNGER APARTMENT, New York City. Architects: *Gwathmey-Siegel—Peter Szilagyi, job captain.* Contractor: *All Building Construction Corporation.*

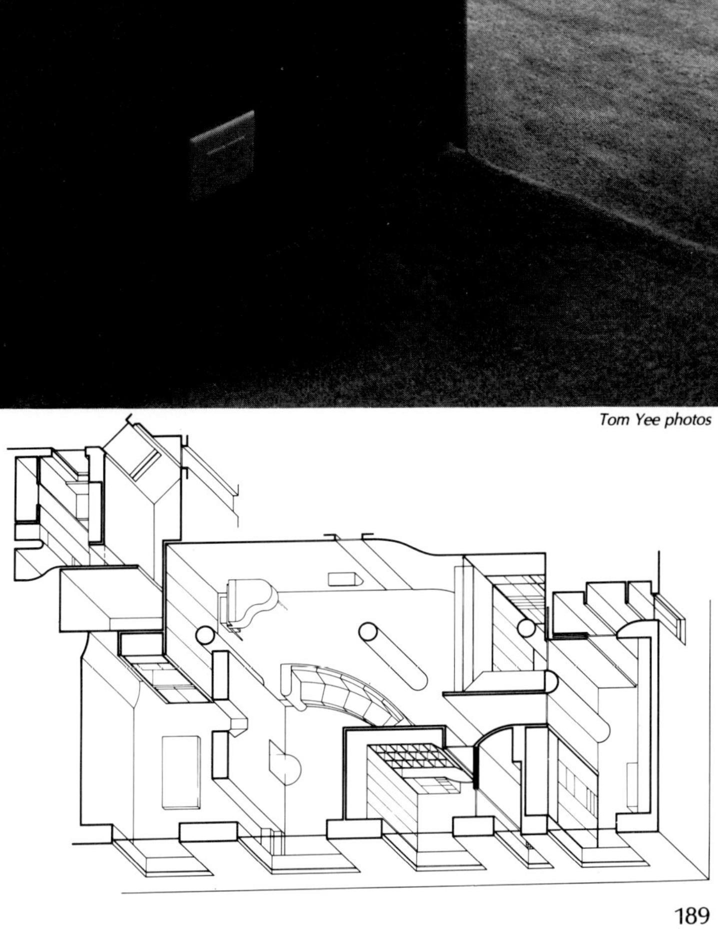

In the apartment's rather extensive private areas, skillfully designed and detailed cabinetwork is an integral part of the solution. Also important is the lighting, which is carefully balanced and flexible. Throughout the apartment, mirrors are used to expand the spaces in subtle—and sometimes surprising—ways.

20

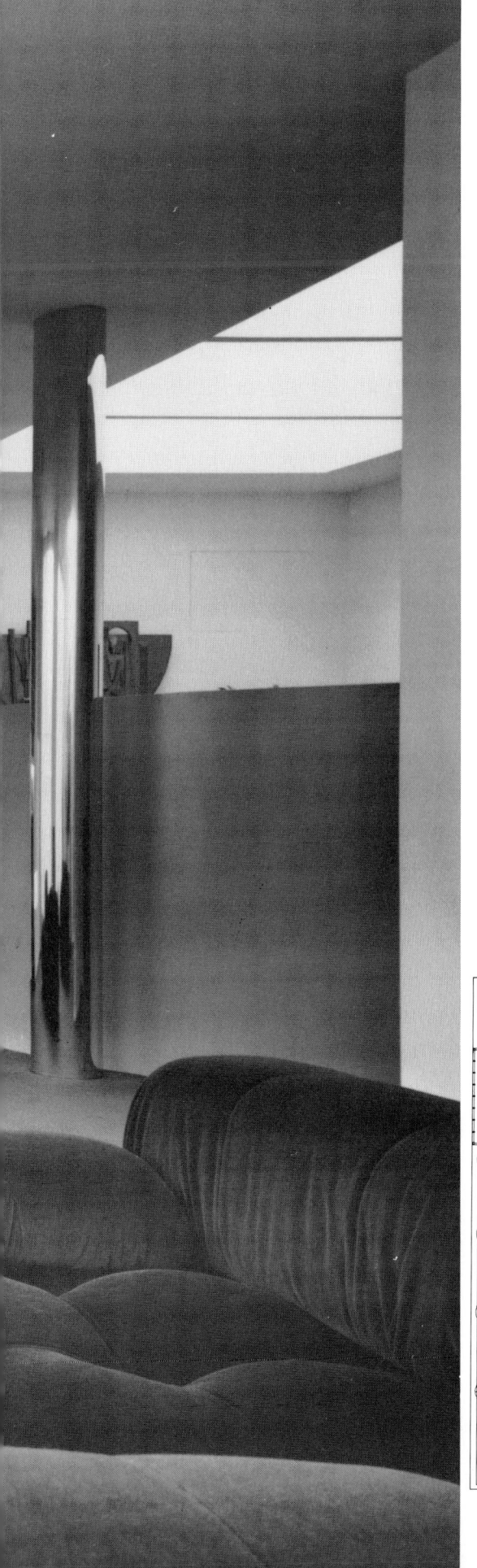

Once a dark "rabbit warren" of rooms that were a haunt of colorful Mayor Jimmy Walker, architect Ulrich Franzen's penthouse apartment is today spacious and filled with natural light. According to Franzen, the obvious advantage of a penthouse is that it can be designed almost independently from the rest of the building, like a "house in the sky." Accordingly, many of the original walls were replaced by low partitions. Overhead glazing, which admits the brightest south light, was introduced in the darkest room. Small exterior doors onto the north terrace were greatly widened to provide an eye-level view of a nearby church's dome, which becomes a strong decorative element. The raised library area is used for ordinary living-room functions, and overlooks what Franzen refers to as the "parlor" (foreground, photo at left) used for entertaining. But as opposed to parlors of the past, the room is furnished *less* conventionally than the rest of the apartment and most clearly satisfies friends' and clients' expectations of a noted designer's lifestyle. Chromed metal covers the one visible column.

FRANZEN APARTMENT, New York, New York. Architect: *Ulrich Franzen.* Engineers: *Andrew Eliot* (structural); *Aaron Zichman* (mechanical). General contractor: *Van Hyning Construction Company.*

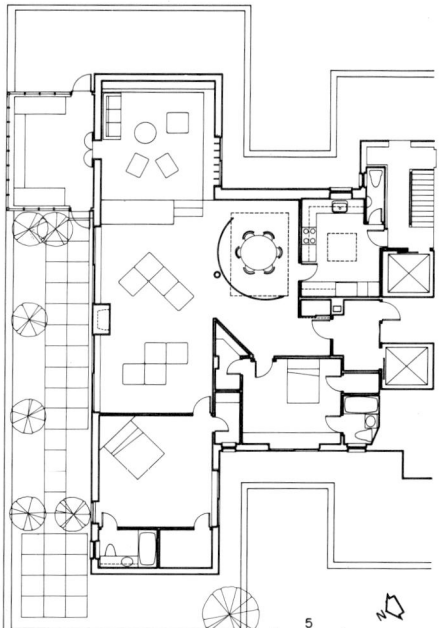

Norman McGrath photos

David Franzen & ESTO

Norman McGrath

The remaining element of the original apartment, a former north-facing greenhouse next to the library, is now Franzen's office for work at home. All of the rest of the rooftop structure was almost totally rebuilt within the existing structure. The surrounding higher buildings form an enormous room in which the "house on top of a building" gains a sense of containment that is unusual for a penthouse.

INDEX

Anderson Notter Associates, 148
Anderson Notter Finegold, 162, 163
Apartment Renovation, New York, New York, 174-175

Barber & McMurry Architects, 38
Barovetto, Ruscitto and Barovetto, 57
Boardwalk, Chicago, Illinois, 30, 37
Booth Nagle & Hartray, 111
British Columbia
    Vancouver, 63, 72
Buchsbaum, Alan, 154
Buchsbaum, Alan and Stephen Tilly, 157
Bull Field Volkmann Stockwell, 100, 131
Bull, Henrik, 125
Burdette Keeland and Associates, 59, 61
Butternut Hill Condominiums, Waitsfield, Vermont, 126-127

California
    Foster City, 64
    Malibu, 94
    Newport Beach, 96
    Placer County, 131
    San Francisco, 42, 57, 170
Callister Payne and Bischoff, 92
Campbell-Yost-Grube, 68
Central Grammar Apartments, Gloucester, Massachusetts, 162-163
Coastline Condominium, Malibu, California, 94-95
Coldspring, Baltimore, Maryland, 84-89
Colony Square, Atlanta, Georgia, 48-51
Concord Greene Apartments, 70-71
Conklin & Rossant, 104
Cooper Street Lofts, 142-143

Copland Finholm Hagman Yaw, 142
Croxton Collaborative, 180
Croxton, Randolph, 180

Davis, Brody & Associates, 29
Design Five, 126

Eastwood, Roosevelt Island, New York, 2-7
Elkhorn Valley, Sun Valley, Idaho, 132-137
Embarcadero Condominiums, Newport, Oregon, 68-69
Ethan's Glen, Houston, Texas, 82-83

Fairways, The, Vancouver, British Columbia, 72-75
False Creek Co-op Housing, Vancouver, British Columbia, 62-63
Fisher-Friedman Associates, 64, 82, 96
Five Speculative Townhouses, Houston, Texas, 60-61
Florida
    Jacksonville, 108
Florida Christian Home Apartments, Jacksonville, Florida, 108-110
Four Speculative Townhouses, Houston, Texas, 58-59
Franzen Apartment, New York, New York, 192-193
Franzen, Ulrich, 193
Freedman/Clements/Rumpel, 108

Galleria, New York, New York, 44-47
Gateview at Albany Hill, San Francisco, California, 40-43

Georgia
    Atlanta, 48
Goody, Clancy & Associates, 113, 116
Goody, Joan, 114
Grundy Tower, Bristol, Pennsylvania, 106-107
Gruzen & Partners, 118, 120
Gwathmey-Siegel, 189

Hallenbeck, Chamorro & Associates, 42
Haynes House, Smith House, Townhouses of Madison Park, Boston, Massachusetts, 10-11
Heaton Court Housing, Stockbridge, Massachusetts, 112-113
Henriquez Architects Urban Designers, 63
Heritage Gardens, Winthrop Housing for the Elderly, Winthrop, Massachusetts, 114-117
Highland Park Apartments, Chicago, Illinois, 111
Housing, low income
  Eastwood, Roosevelt Island, New York, 2-7
  Grundy Tower, Bristol, Pennsylvania, 106-107
  Haynes House, Smith House, Townhouses of Madison Park, Boston, Massachusetts, 10-11
  Mercantile Wharf Building, Boston, Massachusetts, 146-147
  Mission Park, Boston, Massachusetts, 12-16
  Tannery, The, Peabody, Massachusetts, 148-151
  Walnut Hill Apartments, Haverstraw, New York, 122-123
Housing, luxury
  Second Street Townhouses, Philadelphia, Pennsylvania, 90-91
  Victoria Mews, San Francisco, California, 54-57
Housing, mixed-income
  Villa Victoria, Boston, Massachusetts, 16-21
  Waterside, New York, New York, 24-29
Housing, moderate or middle income
  Eastwood, Roosevelt Island, New York, 2-7
  Gateview at Albany Hill, San Francisco, California, 40-43
  Mercantile Wharf Building, Boston, Massachusetts, 146-147
  Mission Park, Boston, Massachusetts, 12-15
  Riverview Housing Phases 1 and 2, Yonkers, New York, 8-9
  Walnut Hill Apartments, Haverstraw, New York, 122-123

Hudson on Memorial, Houston, Texas, 76-77
Hulbert, R.E. & Partners, 72
Huygens and Tappé, 70, 138

Idaho
    Sun Valley, 132
Illinois
    Chicago, 33, 37, 111
Islands, The, Foster City, California, 64-67

Jova Daniels Busby, 48

Kamnitzer, Marks, Cotton and Vreeland, 94
Kaplan/McLaughlin/Diaz, 76
Killingsworth, Brady & Associates, 134
Killingsworth, Edward, 134
Kliment, R.M. and Frances Halsband, 182

Lake Village East, Chicago, Illinois, 30-35
Landings, The, Grand Island, New York, 80-81
Littleton Quarter at Kingsmill, Kingsmill, Virginia, 92-93
Loft for Alan Buchsbaum, New York, New York, 154-157
Loft Restoration, New York, New York, 152-153

Maple Knoll Village, Springdale, Ohio, 118-121
Maryland
    Baltimore, 86, 104
Massachusetts
    Boston, 11, 13, 21, 147, 178
    Gloucester, 163
    Needham, 163
    Peabody, 148
    Stockbridge, 113
McNeely, James, 178
Meltzer, Marvin H. Architects, 158
Mercantile Wharf Building, Boston, Massachusetts, 146-147
Milne, Murray, 94
Mission Park, Boston, Massachusetts, 12-15
Monument East Apartments, Baltimore, Maryland, 104-105
Morgan, William Architects, 79
Morse & Harvey, 80

New Hampshire
    Portsmouth, 164
New York
    Grand Island, 80
    Haverstraw, 122
    New York, 29, 44, 153, 157, 158, 160, 168, 172, 174, 176, 180, 189, 193
    Roosevelt Island, 6
    Yonkers, 8
Northstar Village, Placer County, California, 131-132

Ohio
    Springdale, 120
Oregon
    Newport, 68

Pei, C.C., 160
Pennsylvania
    Bristol, 106
    Philadelphia, 90
Peters Clayberg & Caulfield, 170
Private Apartment, New York, New York, 172-173, 176-177, 182-187
Promontory Point, Newport Beach, California, 96-99

Riverview Housing Phases 1 and 2, Yonkers, New York, 8-9
Rinehart, Arley Associates, 128
Rockingham Condominiums, Portsmouth, New Hampshire, 164-165
Rokeby Condominium Apartments, Nashville, Tennessee, 38-39
Rooftop Apartment, New York, New York 160-161
Rothzeid, Bernard & Partners, 168
Rubin, Michael, 172
Rudolph, Paul, 174

Safdie, Moshe & Associates Architects, 86
Samton, Peter, 120
Sauer, Louis Associates, 90, 106
Sea Gardens, 78-79
Seaman and Croxton Residences, New York, New York, 180-181
Second Street Townhouses, Philadelphia, Pennsylvania, 90-91
Sert, Jackson and Associates, 6, 8

Sert, Josep Lluis, ix, 1, 3
Sharratt, John, 10-11, 12-13, 17-18, 147
Sharratt, John Associates, 11, 13, 21, 147
Smotrich & Platt, 122
Specter, David Kenneth, 44
Stahl/Bennett, 164
Stephen Palmer Apartments, Needham, Massachusetts, 163
Stern, Robert A.M. & John S. Hagmann, 176
Styles, architectural
    French Second Empire, 147
    Georgian, 57
    Victorian, 20, 55-57, 142

Tannery, The, Peabody, Massachusetts, 148-151
Tennessee
    Nashville, 38
Texas
    Houston, 59, 61, 76, 82
32 and 34 Hancock Street, Boston, Massachusetts, 178-179
Tigerman, Stanley, 30, 33, 35, 37
Turtle Bay Towers, New York, New York, 166-169
240 East 26th Street Apartments, New York, New York, 158-159

Unger Apartment, New York, New York, 188-191
Union Street Apartments, San Francisco, California, 170-171

Venetian Gardens, 100-101
Vermont
    Waitsfield, 126
Victoria Mews, San Francisco, California, 54-57
Villa Victoria, Boston, Massachusetts, 16-21
Village at Loon Mountain, 138-141
Village Point Condominiums, 128-129
Virginia
    Kingsmill, 92

Walnut Hill Apartments, Haverstraw, New York, 122-123
Waterside, New York, New York, 24-29
Weese, Ben, 30-31, 33-34, 37
Weese, Harry & Associates, 33

NA
7860
.A7
1981

474344

SEP 1 4 1999

WITHDRAWN